Keepers of Culture

KEEPERS OF CULTURE

*The Art-Thought of
Kenyon Cox, Royal Cortissoz,
and Frank Jewett Mather, Jr.*

H. WAYNE MORGAN

THE KENT STATE UNIVERSITY PRESS
Kent, Ohio, and London, England

© 1989 by The Kent State University Press, Kent, Ohio 44242
All rights reserved
Library of Congress Catalog Card Number 89-32669
ISBN 0-87338-390-7
Manufactured in the United States of America

Library of Congress Cataloging-in-Publication Data

Morgan, H. Wayne (Howard Wayne)
    Keepers of culture : the art-thought of Kenyon Cox, Royal
Cortissoz, and Frank Jewett Mather, Jr. / H. Wayne Morgan.
        p.   cm.
    Bibliography: p.
    Includes index.
    ISBN 0-87338-390-7 (alk. paper) ∞
    1. Art criticism—United States—History—19th century.   2. Art criti-
cism—United States—History—20th century.   3. Cox, Kenyon, 1856–
1919—Philosophy.   4. Cortissoz, Royal, 1869–1948—Philosophy.   5.
Mather, Frank Jewett, 1868–1953—Philosophy.   I. Title.
    N7475.M67   1989
701'.18'0973—dc20   89-32669
                                                                              CIP

British Library Cataloging-in-Publication data are available.

For

ANNE

Contents

Preface

The conflict between modern and traditional art at the beginning of this century is one of the best-known episodes in American cultural history. In the sense that their styles and attitudes of mind dominated the discussion and production of new art, the modernists won the war. But the traditionalists remained strong in the arenas of public opinion and taste. It is a testament to the importance of the ideas involved that the basic issues are not yet settled in the larger cultural world. Fortunately, it is not necessary or possible to choose between the two. No one doubts that modernism, whatever its forms, has been a great and logical addition to art. Yet those who dislike what they usually loosely label "modern art" or "abstraction" have retained an audience. Perhaps the issues involved recur cyclically because they represent varied emphases in cultural desires.

This book is an introduction to the traditionalist art-thought of the late nineteenth and early twentieth centuries. I use *traditional* throughout in a commonsense way, as the protagonists of the story did. It includes the beliefs that there are no sharp breaks in life, that any new idea must convince people of its familiar and workable antecedents before it can claim legitimacy, that cultural attributes are interdependent, and that ideas and taste change slowly for understandable reasons. The debate suggests that people naturally seek to retain the security of the well-known and familiar, while at the same time and without contradiction in their own minds desire the new and challenging.

This is a very personal book that has arisen out of my general research in the period. It is a purely introductory overview, couched as analytical biographies in order to make human what otherwise might be an abstract and artificial subject. The biographical details of these men's lives are interesting in themselves. I also hope to show that traditional art-thought in these, and presumably in other cases, was an organic part of each subject's life. It thus matched in personal ways the intellectual insistence on integration and organic development in society and culture among such observers.

In my view the three men whose ideas are presented here best represented American traditionalism. All commanded significant audiences during lifetimes of writing on both the current art scene and on the larger ideals and ambitions involved in art production and appreciation. Each was well grounded in cultural history and presented a thoughtful view of the role of art in modern life. Much of what they said remains valid. They shared central beliefs about art and its mission, and their ideas often overlapped. But traditionalism was no more a single, codified movement than was modernism. The work of these three men typified the differences as well as the similarities in the art-thought that confronted what seemed to them a destructive innovation.

Kenyon Cox, a painter as well as a critic, revealed a steadfast devotion to the ideals of a high art tradition, derived in his later years chiefly from admiration for the Italian Renaissance. Learned about western art history, he surveyed the current art scene in many reviews and analytical essays and wrote with care. His central attitudes did not change much, as opposition to modernism consumed him after about 1900. Because of his caustic tongue and sharp pen, he became the most notable foe of modernism. Yet he was far from the purely negative or irrational thinker that his enemies portrayed.

Royal Cortissoz, who was art editor of the *New York Tribune* for more than fifty years after 1891, was an appreciator or connoisseur. He lacked Cox's focus on art history as such and had a broader definition of acceptable art. His belief in beauty in a well-done and recognizable form left him open to more innovation than Cox. He prized individual gesture in the artist, so long as the resulting art work did not depart from recognizable reality or create an antagonistic response from the viewer. He sought the spirit of tradition, which rested on harmony and security, rather than any fixed appearance of art. Retaining catholic tastes, he based his views on a self-confessed ideal of common sense that left art appreciation open to any sensitive person. He was well suited to speak to and for the growing middle class of like mind in the Progressive era of his middle years. This viewpoint was equally adaptable, if more debatable intellectually, when modernism triumphed. The fact that he remained a significant figure in art circles long after his tastes ceased to be dominant, testified to the nature of the audience for whom and to whom he spoke for more than fifty years.

Frank Jewett Mather, Jr., was the most genial and realistic of these critics in estimating how art appealed in society. A trained scholar, versed in the history of language, philosophy, and the arts, he was learned but undogmatic and open to considerable change. Much of his mindset reflected Mather's personality and experience. He knew a lot about many things and was concerned to see that the arts remained integrated in public esteem and thought. Mather took comfort from the history of art, which revealed to him that great works and their creators survived the vicissitudes of time and criticism. This sense of historical process and his great need for the unifying power of the art experience let Mather escape the bitterness that so affected Cox, and to a lesser extent Cortissoz, as tastes changed.

For traditionalists, the individual art experience involved an expanded imagination, a sense of unity between artist and appreciator, and, above all, an enhanced feeling of harmony with life in general. A set of sociological tenets also informed the lives of these and other traditionalists. They believed in the power of the creative act to move others of like mind, thus creating bonds among people that radiated out into society to promote cohesion and order. They considered the artist to be a special person with a crucial mission to maintain and extend traditional values, as well as forms of art, that promoted order and integration in society and in individual personalities. They held that society in turn had to see the artist as a harbinger of an intensified emotional life, but one which accommodated changed perception in constructive ways. Their chief fear in the long debate with the modernists was that the new art, which seemed shocking in forms and disruptive in intent, would separate artist and public to the detriment of both. If art and responses to it were indeed community acts, traditionalists could not fail to respond sharply to the aims they perceived in modern art. They were realistic in believing that the individual personality and society were fragile constructs, with many conflicting tastes and ambitions, and that any cohesive force was fundamentally sound. But they were less interested in using art as a means of overt social control in the service of a narrow group than in seeing its effects multiply through individuals to sustain a social order that valued the arts.

The traditionalists lost the battle in art history, but the time has come to reexamine their views and aspirations within the context of their era. Their positions were logical and thoughtful and made sense in the context of the social and cultural changes at work in their lifetimes. Through the lives and works of these three important spokesmen I hope to focus some attention on interesting and important issues in the debate. Their approaches were typical of larger and widely held attitudes, yet each differed enough from the others to show the complexity and logic in the body of thought called traditionalism.

I wish to thank several people who helped me with encouragement and advice. I am especially grateful to Professor H. Barbara Weinberg of Queens College and the City University of New York for generously sharing with me her great knowledge of nineteenth-century art. Richard Murray, of the National Museum of American Art in Washington, was equally kind. Garnett McCoy of the Archives of American Art was very helpful. I profited from their advice, even though I did not always take it. They are in no way responsible for the final result. I must thank the staffs of all the manuscript depositories mentioned in the notes for their invaluable help. Thanks are due the following depositories for permission to use unpublished materials from the persons and collections noted: Scribner's and Macmillan Companies (Scribner Archives); the Albany Institute of History and Art (Will H. Low); the Collection of American Literature, Beinecke Rare Book and Manuscript Library, Yale University (Royal Cortissoz, James B. Carrington, Alfred Stieglitz); Avery Architectural and Fine Arts Library, Columbia University in the City of New York (Kenyon Cox); the New-York Historical Society (Stanford White and Edwin H. Blashfield); the Frick Art Reference Library (the diary of Theodore Robinson); the Archives of American Art, Smithsonian Institution (Allyn Cox, August Florian Jaccaci, and Henry Moser, the last owned by Mr. James M. Fetherolf, filmed by the Archives of American Art, Smithsonian Institution); Dartmouth College Library (Augustus Saint-Gaudens); the Princeton University Library (Frank Jewett Mather, Jr., Paul Elmer More, and the Scribner Archives); the Rare Books and Manuscripts Division, the New York Public Library, Astor, Lenox, and Tilden foundations (Century Company Records and Charles H. Towne); and the Berenson Archive, Villa i Tatti, Florence, Italy. I have cited a good deal of relevant literature at appropriate points in the notes and thus append only a selected bibliography. In the interest of brevity, I use the protagonists' initials, KC, RC, and FJM, in the notes.

Introduction: Traditional versus Modern

The generation that followed the Civil War was one of the most unusual in American history. The nation's economy moved rapidly from one based on agriculture and life in small towns to one focused on industrial cities. A changed emotional tone followed. Americans welcomed the possibilities of wealth and power inherent in the new industrial order yet suspected the shifts of authority from individuals and small social units to impersonal entities. As the country and its people changed their ways of making livings, so they unwillingly altered habits of mind, expectations, and aspirations. For traditionalist thinkers, this flux called for orderly change and reassuring institutions. Kenyon Cox intuitively understood the division in American thought between old and new. The typical person might welcome the latest thing that affected the surface of living but stubbornly defend older ways of acting that governed life itself. This was especially true in cultural matters, where people remained defensive and suspicious toward new ideas that seemed complex or mysterious. "We are, in all things, at bottom, a conservative people," Cox said in 1911, "but in nothing are we so much so as in all matters concerning art."[1]

The art world had never seemed more vital or interesting. The level of criticism, the number and variety of exhibitions, the comment on artistic matters in major newspapers and periodicals were all on an ever-rising curve. Knowledge of world art affairs increased through reporting from overseas, traveling shows, reproductions, and books, all of which were available to interested patrons, especially in major cities. In the midst of unprecedented material growth and social change, art seemed to attract more practitioners and a broader base of public support than ever before.[2] Ironically enough, this sense of cultural progress may have let the traditionalists overestimate the value of art to American society, as well as the roles it could play in modern life.

Traditionalists did perceive that this rate and kind of art development needed rationalization. Many conflicting aims and ambitions animated the art world. Artists, critics, and connoisseurs wanted to examine and appreciate innovations yet reluctantly abandoned familiar tastes and ideals. All periods are transitional, and there is always a currently modern art; but this era had a greater sense of accelerated change than its predecessors, which reinforced the common human tendency to retain or modify the old while accepting the new. American life was also simply diverse, with many conflicting aims.

Changes of form and taste had altered every art form by the end of the nineteenth century. Poetry, the novel, music, painting, sculpture, and architecture all changed their forms and purposes under pressures for expression that matched developments in society and signalled the advent of a new generation. The art world always focused on and believed in the individual creator yet increasingly recognized interactions with larger social processes.

Like the fall of a governmental system in a revolution, the end of cultural styles and tastes seemed more sudden than was the case. The existing order in painting had yielded for some time to various innovations styled *modern.* The late nineteenth-century art world had seen a procession of new art. The romanticism of the 1830s and 1840s had no broad impact on Americans, though there was some interest in the unusual artistic personality and in the colorful and action-laden works of the best such painters. The next generation of modernists, the Barbizon school, had a powerful influence in America. Their landscape work was especially influential and opened up fresh vistas of new interpretation as well as technique. The works of Camille Corot, Charles-François Daubigny, and Henri Rousseau linked artists and viewers in a poetic mood that enhanced art's ability to enrich the imagination and expand the emotions. In the 1870s, the Munich school reminded critics and patrons of the appeals of rich painting in a bravura manner that emphasized texture and motion within an old-master-like tradition. Many people accepted the general thrusts of these changes. Such new art remained in the inheritance of fine painting, with familiar interpreted subject matter that was accessible to the art public. Such innovative artists were also seeking cultural authority and did not repudiate their potential publics.

Attention naturally focused on the appearance of painting. As the century progressed, advanced artists steadily emphasized loosened form, rich surfaces, higher colors, and light. Sound drawing and substance remained, but innovative painters began to seek a sense of motion, a major quality of the new industrial culture. There was a shift away from the familiar anecdotal or rhetorical subjects to those taken from daily life, which a new broadly based art community liked and understood. These changes reflected alterations in taste and expectations that flowed from industrialism's new order. The art audience valued the grand tradition and its old masters but expected different approaches in depicting its own times. A demand grew to express a fresh sense of motion and human vitality in the arts, for recognizable subject matter treated in an exciting and imaginative way. This audience was primarily urban—which heightened its sense of change and motion—newly middle-class, affluent if not rich, and wanted art to be decorative and pleasing as well as challenging.

At the same time, parallel concerns that art not yield too rapidly to change or accept chaotic individualism among artists developed. In this view, all that changed, or proclaimed itself new, was not necessarily valid or useful. As in the economic and social spheres, the art world seemed to want to retain a cohesive sense of purpose based on familiar forms and ideas without preventing acceptable innovation. This became increasingly difficult, given the era's sense of rapid change and the ready availability of information about the examples of everything new. On the whole, it seemed possible to cope with these changes. There was no sense that inherited forms and attitudes were being overwhelmed until the new century dawned. But traditionalist painters steadily reemphasized their views and met the new twentieth-century modernism with a coherent and logical set of answers. Most such painters were well trained in European or American academies. They hoped to produce art that had ideas as well as interesting appearances, that was conceptual as well as perceptual.[3] There was a somewhat specious division between people who preferred an art for its own sake, a view that rested on some kind of concern for autonomous design, and those who believed that painting, however well or unusually done, had to transmit ideas through evoking mood and reflection. Traditionalists realized that the inherited styles and intentions in painting faced some kind of major change, but they were less certain of how to direct or revitalize them.

These thinkers were knowledgeable about current philosophical and esthetic issues, but were not formal logicians or intellectuals. They were more likely to note contemporary writers such as Matthew Arnold, Walter Pater, or John Addington Symonds than earlier basic thinkers like Immanuel Kant or Arthur Schopenhauer. They found attractive in such general thought the idea that the art experience expanded consciousness, was important to the world, and made both artist and appreciator significant in the scheme of things. They welcomed any efforts to make art a vital factor in ordering and clarifying their rapidly developing society.

They were equally prone to cite the history of the western art on which they had matured in place of formal ideas. The term *classicism* or some variant came to summarize their intellectual stance, which focused on the great body of art created since the Renaissance. Their reverence for the achievements of centuries of painting made them appeal to this work as a kind of second form of nature on which artists drew for inspiration and against which their performance was measured. Any sharp departure from this tradition was suspect, both as art and as social statement.

The traditionalists also represented those in the art community who sought large, elevating expressions beyond the factual study of nature. They hoped to create emotional connections to the past, perhaps flavored with glimpses of the future; this intensified the importance of their daily lives and the world around them. All of this seemed doubly important, given the era's increasing emphasis on the isolated fact and the momentary sensation.

Classical ideals aimed to overcome disorder in life and to ensure a balance between individual expression and the needs of the larger human order. "Classicism and romanticism are tempers of mind which equally affect the form and the substance of art," Kenyon Cox explained in 1894, "classicism being reasonable, logical, and constructive, while romanticism is emotional and sensuous. In classicism the intellect dominates the feelings, while in romanticism the feelings dominate the intellect."[4] The painter John La Farge stated this ideal well in 1893: "The contradictions of the world of existence; its overprofusion; its suggesting the opposite; its constantly taking in our eyes the appearance of a world of chance," he noted, "makes us realize in art another world, which has some rules, some order made to our size, to our reason."[5] Such a view, stated formally in rules governing design, composition, and subject matter, aimed to satisfy the needs of the sensitive person for purpose and order. Its adherents did not see this as mere escapism but as a way of intensifying and expanding thought and perception and thus of extending mental and emotional boundaries with suitable caution. Traditionalist art-thought rested on varying definitions of the desire for harmony and cohesion, thus placing emotion at the service of reason. Intensity of feeling and expansion of taste were vital but should not proceed beyond defined bounds lest these threaten the stability of the person and of society.

This classicism recognized duality in human nature and ambitions and hoped through art to modify demands for self-expression and innovation until they fitted into acceptable canons of taste and action. To the traditionalist, this classicism could become a universal language that unified disparate peoples and tastes in a society that needed direction and some easily recognizable standards of certitude. In the larger social sense, traditionalists such as Cox saw the art urge and its products as stabilizers in societies, both ancient and modern, a kind of glue that held groups together so that individuals could function. Art in all societies was based on "rhythm, harmony, proportion—some form of order, in a word. . . ." In the end, such art was "the great binder together and social organizer as well as the great educator."[6] For Cox and other traditionalists, the artist was always an exceptional personality, with important precepts for society concerning unification, integrated and thoughtful emotion, and sheer beauty. But to be understandable, those messages must be orderly. "Art is a human activity consisting in this, that one man consciously, by means of certain *ordered* external signs, hands on to others feelings that he has lived through, etc.," Cox insisted in 1898. "Or, in briefer form: Art is the *harmonic* expression of human emotion."[7]

Traditionalists believed that the sensitive individual expressed the deepest feelings in reacting to art. The creative artist was rewarded in the acts of production, but the intelligent viewer shared in the moment of creativity and in the sense of exalted harmony that followed appreciating it. Such persons "become for an instant the man who made it and who is at his best very often; and they feel that they are better than themselves. . . . During these moments we, the spectators, live a serene and complete existence," La Farge said.[8] Such reactions followed the creation of an elevated mood through association with greatness. The process involved memory, a thoughtful desire for harmony, and knowledge of the intellectual ambitions behind art. This all made the viewer part of the task of moving tradition forward without risking discontinuity. "And we can think of these as a bridge over which our spirit passes," La Farge continued, speaking of drawing, "beyond these things implied, to reach still further, to newer sights, or to some meaning more or less recognized by us, according to the intensity of our desire, according to memories suggested to our view of our relations with the universe, or what the universe itself may mean."⁹ Such nineteenth-century thinkers held that in the interchange between art and viewer, one gift spoke to another. A later, more psychologically oriented age would hold that one need spoke to another. For the traditionalist the result was the same. This expanded experience enriched the individual but also reminded people that society was interconnected and that social cohesion and progress rested on caution in the face of change.

Traditionalists did not usually believe that a work of art was important or moving for any specific moral content or reference to facts, but for conveying a sense of harmony, reverie, and thoughtful references to ideas beyond individualism. They disliked the painted anecdote but understood that people required recognizable subjects before they could reflect on art's broad intentions. Will H. Low, a minor painter but an interesting thinker, answered the objection to subject matter candidly. Art must always be technically well done, but this was no more its purpose than was some easily read subject. The point was to produce art with recognizable content that transcended mere realism. "A picture is a painted thought, the better its execution the clearer its expression," he insisted in 1899, "and a part, and a most important part, of an artist's education should be to differentiate between those thoughts fitted to be pictorially expressed and those where words are the only medium of expression. A painted anecdote is, of course, the negation of art."¹⁰

Kenyon Cox agreed that painting had its own conventions and rules and could be expressed only through appropriate media. In this view, it could not be like poetry or music. At the same time, he accorded plastic art special roles in thought and emotion. The subject of a painting was not the same as its theme or emotional goal. He held that "art in general has a place apart from science and morality while it yet cannot escape quite from either, and must, as an expression of man's spirit, say something to man's intellectual and moral nature as well as to his senses."¹¹ Traditionalists sought to combine idealism and realism, to present large ideas and eternal verities in recognizable forms. This effort reached its height for them in painting the figure, which was a metaphor for much of human life, and in using allegorical figures and symbols in mural paintings.

These aspirations gained added importance in the context of the times, when innovations in technology and corresponding changes in public thought challenged inherited ideals. Traditionalist art-thinkers were usually skeptical about science, as they perceived it, because it focused on facts and often seemed trivial. Such science was to thought what mere realism was to painting. They also saw the scientific temper as atomizing, in breaking up the parts of nature for study, and in seeing people and their works as aspects of a broader scheme. Traditionalists clearly wished to counteract this trend with an emphasis on a certain kind of elevating and cohesive art experience that made people important in the cultural context.

Traditionalists adapted to evolutionary doctrine. They tended to deemphasize the theory's focus on struggle in favor of its insistence on continuity in nature and society. Evolutionary doctrine at least resembled classicism in holding that there were no sharp breaks in history and that the new had to prove itself with relationships to the old and through fulfilling familiar functions in changed ways. They also generally accepted the views of Hippolyte Taine, who held that art, like anything else, was the product of a particular moment, place, and people. But they insisted that the artist had something unique to say to persons of like mind, however much the age and culture shaped the artist's work.[12] They also held that art creation and appreciation were above all individual acts that had general consequences. From Herbert Spencer, the English popularizer of Darwin's theories in the social realm, they accepted the broad belief in some ability to shape society in the midst of ongoing evolution. Kenyon Cox expressed this in a widely noted essay, "The Illusion of Progress," in 1913. He agreed that evolution was a fact of life and thought but believed that eternal verities, needs, and expressions had changed little over time. The "progress" that the public saw in medicine or machinery was not exactly the same in art. The new was not necessarily more efficient, striking, or valid than what it replaced.[13]

Traditionalists did not oppose change but asked that any new art be recognizable, be based on great precedents, and be suited to broad cultural needs. It should appeal to both the senses and the mind and evoke intelligent responses from an audience which it had the ability to expand. It should above all stress emotional unity rather than a potentially disordering eccentricity. It must not threaten the artist's role as a purveyor of unifying and elevating emotions. Painting had natural rules and conventions yet was not exclusively concerned with itself but with the world around it. The artist was indeed a special personality with unusual insights but could not be eccentric or bizarre for fear of social rejection. It was possible to lead successfully toward innovation only if someone followed. Traditionalists suspected the claims of any volatile genius, agreeing with the critic W. J. Stillman's succinct observation: "In the best art individuality is merged with the type."[14] Kenyon Cox rejected the notion of the isolated artist, ahead of the times, almost revelling in an unpopularity that would prove the artist's merit. "After all, why should not art be popular?" Cox asked in 1911. "The greatest art always has been so." Reasonable innovation in recognizable forms could retain audiences. "Under proper conditions art would always be popular, for the artist would be one of the people, having the same ideals and thoughts and feelings as the public he served, and would, quite naturally, express the mind of his public as his public would have it expressed."[15] This fear of a division between artist and public was especially strong among established painters who believed that their expanded ability to express ideas with first-rate training had brought America into world culture. Any change in the public's positive perception of the artist threatened that progress.

For all its sense of achievement, the art world faced a crisis at the end of the century. For reasons rooted deeply in social tensions and individual psychology, a major alteration in perception and expectations of art filled the air. Dissatisfaction with reigning styles was strong among artists and critics, both in the United States and abroad. Theodore Robinson, trained in the best academic tradition of Jean-Léon Gérôme, but practicing now a modified impressionism, caught this mood after visiting an academic watercolor show in 1894. He was certainly no modernist but understood that reigning tastes were coming to an end. "The w.c. show not very inspiring," he wrote in his diary. "It is melancholy to see most everybody settling down and doing his little game—uninteresting, tiresome. 'Woe to them that are at east in Zion,' and our only safety is in constant research."[16]

The problem, as people like Robinson well knew, was how to change without abandoning art's cultural roles. Impressionism had summarized the generation's broad acceptance of change in dealing with mundane life, heightening color and light, deemphasizing formal drawing, and using random composition. The next logical step involved a dual departure from tradition, an emphasis on the individual artist's perceptions at the expense of communicating with the world and some kind of summary, abstracted style. By the beginning of the new century, European artists were moving toward new and unusual subject matter and bold, often outrageous ways of painting.[17]

Traditionalists had accepted a good deal of change but believed that the new wave of modernism involved more than a desire to alter the appearance of painting. With their sociological view of art as part of general culture, they perceived that this was a movement with larger ramifications than earlier modernisms. It rested on a set of ideas and ambitions that seemed to be the antithesis of their ideals. There was in it a sense of fragmented time, of ambiguity and flux, which was pervaded with a threatening air of uncertainty. This attitude fueled the idea that the perceptive artist was now entitled to speak in a special, even unknown, voice, since there was in this way of thinking no longer any accepted or unified viewpoint of life and the world.[18] Increasingly for the moderns, the artist's gestures and concerns were the messages an individual could give. The unknown rather than the known, nuance rather than certainty, and the random instead of the familiar and recognizable were the hallmarks of modernism in all the arts.[19]

There was no single modernism, of course; but whatever their approaches, the new artists seemed to share several fundamental attitudes. For them, changes in communication and technology had created a new era that required fresh means of expression. The traditionalists, for whom all generations were linked, with no sharp breaks in history, could not accept such a notion. The modernists believed that formal treatments of observable and agreed-upon reality were at a dead end. The artist must move on to some new style that involved condensed forms, unusual drawing and design, and striking colors to intensify expression. The traditionalist equally could not accept what seemed a shocking departure from nature, the book of life upon which both creator and patron drew for inspiration. New interpretation, yes; repudiation, no. The modernist believed that the creative individual could bring a kind of order, or at least an expressed understanding, to these changed perceptions through artistic gesture. The modernist's work was thus a way of capturing chaotic experience or startling insights and of comprehending unsettling views of nature. The traditionalists often called this mere egotism, seeing it as an attitude that was contemptuous of society and would make art seem strange and reduce its authority.[20] Traditionalists never understood the driving power behind modernism but realized that it possessed a vitality they could not explain except through an appeal to some idea of decadence.

The often-rancorous debate between traditionalists and modernists rose steadily in volume until the advent of World War I. The fervor of the argument testified to the importance each side attached to views that transcended any mere change of styles. The traditionalists disliked modernist use of distortion, especially of the human form, which played a strong role in their art ideals. This deviation seemed irrational, a willful rejection of thought, composition, and reflection. They believed that all the talk about basic forms and shapes, strong outlines, and noncomplementary colors was a cover for falsifying nature for egotistical purposes, to shock or to gain notoriety. They saw modernism as another cyclical outbreak of romanticism, but this time with a cutting edge that threatened inherited thought in general.[21] Traditionalists agreed with modernists on the artist's special nature and role in society. But they insisted more strongly than ever that these must be logical and understandable to the world at large. The artist could be in advance of what most sensitive people thought they wanted from art, but not so unusual that patrons could not catch up. The artist spoke a special language, but it *was* a language. The artist's creations had to have meanings for others, or they merely represented whims. The traditionalists who surveyed the art scene around 1912 saw an emerging personalism registered in distorted reality, that rested on some kind of rejection of centuries of cultural authority, and that frankly sought to replace long-standing canons of painting. Above all, this modernism was apparently committed to provoking reactions in viewers that seemed disruptive, shocking, or morbidly personal, all of which flew in the face of traditional ideals.

The modernists dismissed their foes as conservatives or reactionaries, out of touch with the times, mired in an academicism that had nothing more to say. But in the retrospect of calmer times, similarities, as well as differences, between the opponents emerged. The modernists hoped to attain grandeur and idealism in much of their work. They did not see their approaches as confused or merely destructive, but as efforts to find intense feeling and to make large statements in new ways. They also hoped to restore vitality and meaning to more mundane subjects. Both groups faced formidable obstacles in seeking either to extend or renovate their art heritages. The traditionalists could not infuse their subject matter or technique with the added intensities and dynamics of modern technological life. Nor could they educate any large public to the level of knowledge necessary to appreciate their more elaborate compositions. By the same token, the moderns seldom spoke to any large public, and modernism quickly became the province of an even smaller community than prior generations of artists had commanded.

Whether the artist disavowed society, as the traditionalists contended, or the society abandoned the artist, as the modernists broadly held, the result was the same. For a great variety of reasons, art steadily came to seem an adjunct, however significant, to the main business of living for most people. The continuing stream of modernism naturally will always command an influential but not likely a mass audience. The diverse forms of a more traditional art will be popular in other quarters. Those who can benefit from each will do so. Perhaps that is enough.

KENYON COX

Traditionalist Painter and Critic

When Kenyon Cox was a small boy, he read in a newspaper that two stores advertised "the best" of a certain product with different brand names. The story puzzled and upset the youngster. Since there could be only one "best" of anything, someone was either misinformed or lying.[1] This concern for the truth as he saw it shaped the youth and then the man who became a well-known painter and traditionalist critic of the arts. Such seriousness reflected Cox's heritage and upbringing. He was born in Warren, Ohio, on 27 October 1856, into a family that became prominent in both state and national affairs. His father, Jacob Dolson Cox, was a major general on the Union side in the Civil War and then served as governor of Ohio from 1866 to 1868. He was secretary of the interior for President Grant in 1869–70. He held one term in the national House of Representatives from 1877 to 1879. An able lawyer, the elder Cox was dean of the Cincinnati Law School from 1880 until his retirement in 1897, while also serving as president of the University of Cincinnati between 1885 and 1889. Kenyon's mother, Helen Finney Cox, was a daughter of the famous evangelist Charles Grandison Finney. Both parents were closely connected to Oberlin College and its tradition of social work and humanitarian concerns.

Ill health dominated young Cox's life. He was underweight, prone to colds, and given to bouts of mild depression when his physical stamina did not equal his demands for success. At adolescence he also suffered from a dangerous tumor in the left cheek near the parotid gland, that often bled profusely and threatened the major blood vessels of the neck and the brain. Doctors hoped to avoid the major operation that could as easily kill as cure the boy, but the condition worsened. In 1869 the family agreed to two operations. Though weak and bedridden for a long time, Cox survived and finally matured into a tall, somewhat gangly, dark-haired young man who developed the necessary physical and emotional resilience for the arduous career that lay ahead.[2]

Cox was clearly different from other young people, both in terms of health and personality. Illness kept him out of school, and he learned to read, write, and draw under his mother's patient supervision. The reading regimen, which included novels, history, and art studies, gave him a breadth of understanding, if not always a depth of knowledge, that set him apart from peers. He often revealed a wry sense of humor and was capable of the usual high jinks as an art student. But Cox early adopted a serious demeanor that was based on the belief that art was a great calling and should be the center of the sensitive person's life. This sense of being special intellectually, as well as removed from the life that seemed to satisfy most people around him, contributed to Cox's sometimes abrupt but defensive manner.

Cox could barely remember a time when art was not his special interest. As a small child he drew with crayons and pencil and sent a sample of his work to his father at the wartime front.[3] In Warren he became familiar with a local painter and found the idea of an artistic career fascinating. In short order "he announced his firm intention to become a painter. His family received this declaration, as well-regulated families usually do, with deprecating smiles."[4] But Cox was determined and had already begun to see the world in pictorial terms. So serious a young man was bound to keep a journal, and he did. In it, in 1876 he analyzed a pretty young lady in church as if she were sitting for a portrait, noting her demeanor, the curves of her body, the folds of her clothing, and the effect of her jewelry.[5]

Whatever his ambition to become an artist, the level of Cox's talent was less certain. The Ohio of his youth was provincial and boasted few opportunities either to see much art or to compare his own efforts with work of genuine quality. He knew that he needed training and an environment that emphasized the arts if he was to become a painter. And from the first he insisted on seeking the best and testing himself to his limit.

He began formal studies at the McMicken School of Design, attached to the University of Cincinnati, between ages thirteen and eighteen. The school, which emphasized the industrial arts, was at best a beginning. No one with Cox's ambitions could have become either adequately trained or accepted in the art world with an education from it. His willfulness dominated, and in short order he cut classes to sketch from nature, read, or see the local sights.

Cox's parents did not quite know what to do with their independent-minded son. They were not wealthy but could afford some kind of special schooling for him and agreed that he needed an excellent education. He also understood that he could not succeed in the highly competitive art world without European training. His reading revealed to him that the arts were in a major transition of styles and subject matter. Students could understand this process only in places where culture was central. By the mid-seventies, enough young Americans had studied in Munich, Dresden, London, and Paris to make the point that art was international.

The family was not ready to send him abroad but allowed him to attend the prestigious Pennsylvania Academy of Fine Arts in Philadelphia for the 1876–77 term. That fall Cox established a studio in Elbow Lane with his friends, Robert Blum, who became a well-known painter, and Alfred Brennan, later a successful illustrator. But he was soon behaving as he had at the McMicken School, reporting that the curriculum was dull and the instructors old-fashioned. He cut classes to sketch and visited the galleries of the Centennial Exposition, which offered a cross section of world art and made him feel even more the need for foreign study. His heart was set on Paris because its schools offered the most exacting training, and its collections encompassed the world's heritage. Some time that spring or summer, Cox's parents relented and agreed to finance two years of study in Paris.[6]

Cox began his apprenticeship with eclectic tastes. He was much enamored of the work of the Spanish artist Mariano Fortuny, who worked in a colorful realistic style and with a nervous line that made his canvases seem astonishingly dynamic to younger painters. He appeared to bridge the gap between traditionalists and moderns in depicting genre scenes set in fashionable circumstances or exotic locales, all done with a vigor and lushness that matched the modern temperament's demand for rich effects. Fortuny also showed how a painter could lead an exotic and important life in an era that seemed to glorify the sober businessman or empty politician. The young Cox had a strong interest in the exotic places that had fascinated painters since the beginning of the century and wanted to visit North Africa and the Near East, and developed a taste for Japanese culture.[7] He was interested in the ancient Peruvians, which also betrayed an emotional need for imagination and large ideas in art.

Cox arrived in Paris in late October.[8] The government-sponsored Ecole des Beaux-Arts was full, and it seemed unlikely that a foreigner could enter any time soon. Somewhat unexpectedly, he turned to one of the city's most famous and controversial painters, Emile Carolus-

Duran. Cox knew little about him but liked the facilities, models, and students at his teaching atelier. Cox had a strong need to identify with a teacher who commanded broad intellectual ideals, emphasized technical skills, and had personal character befitting an important artist. This was part of his belief that art was a high calling and the artist a special personality. He had failed to apply himself elsewhere precisely because he did not admire the teachers or the curriculum. At first Carolus-Duran seemed to satisfy these needs. He was individualistic, to say the least. His work was modern in emphasizing spontaneity, yet traditional in relying on technical study and emotional attitudes derived from past masters. Carolus-Duran was a deliberate showman, partly to irritate established types who had ignored him when he was a struggling young man but also because he wanted the art life to be exotic and exciting.

His teaching methods and ideas seemed strange to academicians. Academic theory held that painters must choose and compose subjects worthy of the ideas they wished to express, should paint and draw to control and idealize expression, and should emphasize concepts. Careful drawing, harmonious tones, and controlled arrangement were the hallmarks of academic training. Carolus-Duran violated these precepts. He appreciated the need to train the eye and hand in order to create truthful form with emotional power. But he also knew that the academic routine too often thwarted individualism and spontaneity. To promote these, he insisted that his students paint directly on the canvas, using a loaded brush, with a minimum of preparatory drawing. He also allowed them to paint from daily life or the imagination, a welcome complement to the subjects that dominated academic training. For students this was a change of psychology as well as technique. The famous academician William-Adolphe Bouguereau once asked a student: "Does M. Duran ever make you draw?" The student might have answered yes, but not so much in line or shading as in forms, colors, and effects. Carolus-Duran himself said: "Draw? Of course! But why not draw with the brush? Anathema to the conventional, delight to the students!"[9]

His critics saw an undisciplined individualism in methods that overemphasized expression and looseness of form at the expense of formal ideals. But they were wrong, for Carolus-Duran seldom departed from interpreted nature and always counseled students to draw on the inspiration of great masters such as Rubens and Velázquez. He simply believed that modern times required new approaches in painting and that expression, rich effects, and light were in order.

Cox appreciated this approach, but there was a streak of self-advertisement in Carolus-Duran that did not fit his ideal of a mentor. More to the point, he soon realized that Carolus-Duran's methods were successful only for one who, like himself, thoroughly understood design, composition, and the rendering of form. Cox was moving steadily toward the French academic ideal of disciplined expression founded on rigorous draftsmanship. By early 1878 he concluded that he needed more formal training, but he always saw his first teacher as a significant figure in the modern approach that emphasized light, color, and motion.[10]

Cox looked to the Ecole des Beaux-Arts, whose emphasis on drawing and figure painting seemed appropriate to his needs. The school's approach rested on the assumptions that technical training focused talent and that individuality was well expressed only when disciplined. The most facile pupil, in this view, had no future outside the mainstream of art. Students inevitably wearied of drawing from casts, or even live models, and much of Carolus-Duran's appeal lay in the prospect of shortening this process. But the academic approach was designed to train the eye and hand to compose and interpret nature as well as to depict it. This method also made the student feel a part of the great tradition. The academic pupil and teacher understood that tastes changed. The nineteenth century differed from earlier times because of scientific, technological, and democratic forces. But these changes could become part of the ongoing culture only if enfolded into the traditional framework. The great question was how to alter the appearance of painting without losing its seriousness and without repudiating the slowly accumulated inherited ideals in the name of chaotic individualism.[11]

Cox entered the teaching atelier of Alexandre Cabanel in April 1878 and matriculated as his student in the Ecole proper in August of that year. Cox seemed happy with this choice and worked steadily to improve his drawing. He and his good friend Theodore Robinson, later famous for a modified impressionist style, toured northern Italy in the fall of 1878, a trip that gave Cox a sense of the great Italian tradition.

On his return from Italy in October 1878 Cox found the Ecole in an uproar; Cabanal and other instructors had dropped many students, including Cox, who had to start over or go elsewhere.[12] Cox spent most of the winter working at the Académie Julian, a famous private atelier, then enrolled with Jean-Léon Gérôme at the Ecole des Beaux Arts in February 1879. Cox did not especially admire Gérôme's art, done with sound realism and evenly applied color. Moments from Roman history, such as the death of Caesar, or from gladiatorial combats, were among his famous subjects. They allowed Gérôme to display an extraordinary skill in depicting details and to capture a certain grandeur in such scenes. He was equally noted for elegant genre studies drawn from the life of northern Africa and the Near East. His approach did not seem especially modern, but there were good reasons for Gérôme's fame. He offered order in a period of rapid change and was precise without being literal. He depicted the exotic and historical in a manner that most art lovers could understand and valued and demanded accuracy while others too often accepted haste. His work clearly reflected an understanding of the great masters. The themes of human relationships and actions in his best art were timeless, whatever their trappings, and his technique was impressive.[13]

Gérôme was a justly famous teacher and was especially influential among Americans. He had a formidable demeanor but spoke carefully and to the point in making criticisms. He tolerated a reasonable individuality but allowed no shortcuts in training either the hand or eye. Cox appreciated Gérôme's approach to art and his dignified manner, which combined in a way that seemed appropriate to the high calling of art.[14] Cox's maturity as a painter dated from his enrollment in Gérôme's studio. He studied with Gérôme until he left Paris in the fall of 1882, yet he was in the odd position of having found a mentor but not necessarily an example. At this point Cox preferred a looser composition, a more fluid line, and higher color than Gérôme espoused. Cox's student work that survived or was described in his correspondence or reviews combined the academic and modern. He drew in a sound academic manner, but his informal sketches were often fluid and charming. He painted in rather broad masses of complementary colors and worked outdoors as well as in the studio. Though he did not use the term, Cox was something of an academic modern. He believed in academic craftsmanship and composition but also sought spontaneity and a sense of contemporary life. The influence of Fortuny and Carolus-Duran remained.

Cox took from his new master what was suitable at this point in his career: the careful and accurate rendering of nature, a concern for form and volume, and attention to appropriate detail. In short, the search for a kind of truth that involved the mind and eye, the here and now, but that reverberated with associations from the past and from controlled imagination. Above all, Cox appreciated Gérôme's disdain for "all *chic* and cleverness."[15] Cox did not follow his master's example in painting but benefited greatly from his larger legacy.

Like most students, Cox spent his time drawing and painting. But a strong curiosity and concern about historical and theoretical issues set him apart from peers. He remained interested in Peruvian and Japanese culture. His attraction to Fortuny and his followers steadily declined as he embraced the academic ideal, but their energetic line was appealing. He admired much Gothic architecture, which he studied on several trips in the region around Paris.

At the same time, he wished to understand the modern temper and its need for new artistic expressions. The French art scene offered a wide array of styles and subject matter outside the official tradition. Public and critical attention often focused on the latest challenge to orthodoxy, a new broad trend labelled *realism,* which demanded fidelity to nature. The most discussed of these realists was Jules Bastien-Lepage, who carried the demand for exactitude to its limits, in almost photographic effects. He and other such realists also elevated contemporary subject matter. This approach gained a great deal of attention because it seemed to be an acceptable and vital step beyond academicism that did not sacrifice artistic skill or put the painter outside the mainstream of life. It seemed instead to redefine the range of life suitable for painting and to demand an ever-intensifying ability in the artist. This particular kind of realism aroused skepticism as well as admiration. To critics it merely reproduced appearance rather than interpreting life or expanding experience.[16]

Cox admired the technical skill in most of these canvases and accepted the desire of realists such as Bastien-Lepage to move beyond academicism. He appreciated the skill and truthfulness involved yet remained skeptical of the emotional satisfaction in this method. Its practitioners were naive in believing that they could actually reproduce the appearance of nature or that this was art if they could. In his view, no artist or anyone else ever lived in the moment. Memory and the human urge to order, select, and intensify experiences always ruled both artist and appreciator. The technical skill of such realists was often amazing, but their painting was simply not grand or intense enough to suit him. The greatest fault was "the lack of intelligent and artistic selection of subject, and the feeling that it makes no difference what one paints so long as he paints it truly," he said in 1879.[17] A hundred exact studies of peasant life, for instance, would not delineate the historic human relationship to nature and the soil. Bastien-Lepage could never equal Jean-François Millet, whose peasant studies became icons for a whole generation precisely because they recalled epic themes in a grand manner that made the artist an interpreter as well as recorder. Because it focused on particular moments, this realism seemed parochial and transitory. It resembled photography, and Cox never considered the photograph to be art.[18] Cox later thought that those realists' extraordinary technical skill had exaggerated their appeal, especially to students like himself; but he did appreciate their insistence on fidelity to nature and desire to communicate with an audience.[19]

The youthful Cox had settled on a different ideal of painting, which steadily developed with his career as an artist and thinker and which combined realism and idealism. Technical skill was vital for any artist who would render either nature or ideas, but art was basically a method of communication between a creator and an audience of like mind and need. The artist thus selected from experience and perception and intensified with skill and personality those aspects of life that could enrich others with a new or intensified experience. The artist was "not to invent something not in nature, but to choose from nature those truths which come home to the individual mind, so making you *see,* not nature, but the artist's view of nature," he wrote his father from Paris in 1878. "And he is the noblest artist who succeeds in reproducing the greatest and truest feelings and conveying to the beholder the noblest emotions, and in this, I think, is [the] true morality of art, which has no business to instruct but only to move."[20] There was no departure from reality in emphasizing pictorial qualities or using dramatic line or enriched tones, if doing so intensified experience. But painting must rest on recognizable form and represent creative and unifying ideas: order, harmony, and beauty were its main goals. This aspect of the classical, or academic, ideal became a major factor in Cox's development as a painter and critic.

Cox thought that the subject in every painting should evoke memory, imagination, and possibilities. He believed when young and old in the responsibility of the artist to enrich individual and collective life.

"The business of the painter as imitator is to give us, temporarily, the benefit of his power of vision, of his training and knowledge, of his perception of the significance of things, and by so doing to give us an unwonted sense of physical and mental efficiency which is in the highest degree pleasurable," he wrote in 1916. "We feel ourselves, for the moment, possessed of clearer senses, of more lively emotions, of greater intellectual powers, than we had imagined; we live more intensely and rejoice in our perceptions of this intensity of life."[21] These were the views of an experienced thinker, but they grew logically from the ideals of the young art student.

Cox returned home in late 1882, still somewhat uncertain about how to develop a career. His credentials were as good as those of most beginners. He had superb training with a world-renowned mentor. He had exhibited at every salon between 1879 and 1882 and had even sold a few paintings. He was an excellent draftsman, especially in detailing the figure. His point of view and literary skills also fitted him for criticism. Cox realized that he could not fulfill his ambitions in Cincinnati but dreaded entering the competitive and uncertain New York art world. He wrote Theodore Robinson, who was making a haphazard living from illustration and decorating. His friend urged Cox to take the plunge, come to New York, seek illustration work, try to exhibit, and somehow get started on his own. In the fall of 1883 the family supported his move.[22]

New York artists often made a living drawing for the daily press, designing material for manufacturers of commercial and household products, and making illustrations for magazines and books. Both the number and variety of magazines grew enormously in the late nineteenth century. In the era before the easy and cheap reproduction of photographs, these publications required a great quantity of covers, illustrations, and allied decorative work, such as headbands, titles, and colophons.[23]

Cox was soon well known among younger people in the New York art world. Though a meticulous worker, he met deadlines and produced a steady flow of work for such publications as *Century* and *Scribner's*. A great coup came in 1886, when he illustrated a deluxe edition of Dante Gabriel Rossetti's *The Blessed Damozel*. The substantial fee of $1,500 was most welcome, as were the prestige and attention that came with such a commission. This was also a chance to draw the figure in various moods and poses. The resulting work was a noted effort in illustration.

Each figure, done in sepia tone, accompanied a stanza or two of the poem and was suitable for framing. Cox drew the figures nude or in draperies reminiscent of historical models. They had a strong sense of volume, with a somewhat modern appearance.[24]

Cox was never affluent and often lived on the edge of want like most other artists, but such commercial work was a major source of income until his last years. He often complained of the grind, the more so because it kept him from painting, but there was no alternative.[25] He also produced a steady flow of other kinds of designs throughout his life. He drew elegant seals for the Art Students League, the University Club in New York, and the Boston Public Library. He made bookplates for friends and collectors, designed diplomas for colleges and notices of awards and special honors for businesses and societies, sketched out stained glass projects, and even planned tombstones, which sculptors completed.[26]

His most unusual special commission was a design for the back of a proposed small-sized one-hundred-dollar bill in 1912. Cox produced for it one of the most elegant designs in the history of American currency, a group of allegorical figures that denoted peace, labor, and plenty. They were done with simplicity and a strong presence, in a kind of small mural.[27] Cox's illustrational work retained a high quality; and he believed that each such effort, however small, could remind viewers of traditional ideals and the importance of careful artwork.

Teaching was another source of income. He must have smiled at his friend Robinson's observation in 1883 that teaching was "that great resource of the impecunious painter in America."[28] He privately instructed a few pupils soon after arriving in New York. In 1884 he joined the staff of the Art Students League and taught drawing there until retiring in 1909. He was a rigorous taskmaster, much like his mentor Gérôme, but generally remained patient in the face of student performances.[29] He attended closely to teaching in order to provide new artists with technical skill and traditional ideals.

Despite modest success, Cox was frustrated at not developing a career purely as a painter. His ever-practical father objected to the son's dogged insistence on painting the nude, which he thought blocked Kenyon's advancement. The father believed that his son should do landscapes and portraits, for which there was at least a modest market. Kenyon demurred, in the belief that he was not a good landscape painter, though he had done several creditable such works as

The mature Kenyon Cox, probably in the mid-1890s. (Archives of American Art, Smithsonian Institution.)

a student and did in fact paint some impressive landscapes in mid-career. The real problem was his almost consuming interest in figure painting. "But oh! how I long for a chance to try what I can do at painting on a large scale subject with nude figures," he wrote Will Low in 1886. "I shall do it yet, if I live ten or twenty years."[30]

Cox had not come to this position lightly or recently. He had always seen the figure as the basis of all art, since it required realism in depicting form and idealism in depicting actions and personality. He understood the technical fascinations of anatomy to painters who were intent on rendering the tones, lines, and textures of flesh. But he saw something larger in such studies. The figure was a metaphor for much of the human condition, encompassing as it did personality, purposeful motion, elegance, and timeless principles of harmonious action. Anatomy was a fascinating process as well as a set of facts.

True to his academic training and classical ideals, he believed that the ability to suggest the functions as well as the appearance of the human form underlay all successful art. The draftsman set the standards of proportion, balance, and truthfulness to nature for painting. But above all, because of a great body of painting and sculpture accumulated since antiquity and from all cultures, the figure embodied ideas. This love of the figure dominated Cox's thinking throughout his life. The mature man refined the ideas he had developed as a student. In 1917 he summarized the idea that the great figure painter depicted energy and desire and linked the viewer to grand ideals. "We become the imitators of the imitation, and feel inspired to put ourselves in the attitude so clearly realized for us," he wrote, "we feel in our own bodies the stresses and relaxations we have been made to observe, and through feeling these are put into the mental state that caused them. By painting bodies the artist has forced us to paint souls. By the representation of the forms and movements of the human figure Michelangelo has made us feel the languid rousing into consciousness of the new-made Adam and the creative energy of the outstretched arm of the Almighty from whose finger flows the vivifying spark."[31]

This was all very well for the artist or critic but found little favor among a prudish public. Cox's mother well represented respectable opinion when she worried that he would attract ridicule or worse for studies that involved nudes, however allegorical or ideal. "It is just such feeling that makes great art almost hopeless in this country," he responded to her in 1885. "I insist that there is nothing immodest whatever about the nude when treated from a high artistic point of view, and that it is impossible for it to be as suggestive and lascivious as a figure partially draped and knowingly uncovered. The nude is pure. It is the *undressed* that is impure."[32] Artists' models were more likely to be bored than erotically interested or interesting. They had "no more to do with the feeling of the artist than so many paint brushes."[33]

The American art public's unwillingness to purchase many nude studies doubtless affected Cox's career. He complained at least once about the arbitrary removal of illustrations of nude figures from one of his articles, especially since this made the text senseless.[34] He did sell a few such studies, usually to fellow painters and decorators such as Stanford White.[35] By 1900, when public resistance to the nude seemed as strong as ever despite great progress in elevating the country's taste, Cox found the situation somewhat amusing. It was certainly ironic that so sober and upright a man as Kenyon Cox seemed immoral because he painted nudes. "Exactly why people will persist in finding impropriety in my work I find it difficult to imagine, but they always have," he wrote fellow muralist Edwin H. Blashfield, "and I am sure if I painted a figure not only draped but [with] the face covered as well, there are people who would find it immodest and vote to 'relegate it to the tenderloin.' "[36]

In due course Cox stopped struggling against unchanging opinion. He continued to study, teach from the nude, and make preparatory drawings of nude figures for murals. But he later cautioned his son Allyn, who became a distinguished muralist, about depicting the nude. "As art, you are right," he admonished gently in showing how to cover the male genitalia with a bit of drapery in one sketch, "but you are likely to get into trouble with the prudish, and I know by experience how difficult it is to get it out of people's heads that you are indecent if you once get it in."[37] Of course, snobbery played its part. The occasional collector bought a nude, provided it had the certification of European origin. Perhaps Cox agreed with his acquaintance Frank J. Mather, Jr., who later said that "the connoisseurs of our by no means naughty nineties may have felt that a conscientious nude, like a cask of sherry, needs a sea voyage to make it desirable."[38]

Fate and developments in American taste somewhat unexpectedly gave Cox the opportunity to paint the figure in elevated modes when, starting in the 1890s, he became a muralist. The widely supported effort to decorate commercial and public buildings reflected the nation's material and artistic coming of age. The new generation of painters trained abroad had both the skills and the desire to work in large scales and for public purposes. The art public had developed sufficiently to welcome civic adornment, which carried with it a sense of being a part of world culture. A generation-long building boom that followed recovery from the depression of the 1890s allowed both artists and patrons to develop large decorative projects aimed at celebrating American civilization as part of world culture.

Muralists drew on an ancient tradition in aspiring to make buildings into elevated experiences, as well as places in which to work, live, or visit. Decorating a bank with murals did not celebrate money-making but reminded people that they were engaged in activities with symbolic, as well as material, meanings. The railroads that built grand stations hoped to give travelers a sense of purpose, to elevate journeys into experiences. The lavish new hotels and apartment houses that boasted lobbies filled with statuary and ceilings covered with murals gave visitors and dwellers a feeling of importance in a large civic tradition. New buildings with decorations were intended to increase the sense of significance in office work. Government at all levels sought to enhance its authority with classical architecture and allegorical murals that emphasized the lasting content in processes such as Justice, Legislation, or Government.

Muralists thought that the ideas behind such works were crucial at this particular stage of national development when the country seemed to lack focus and certitude amid economic expansion and social change. Murals could foster something beyond the individual and enrich a civic tradition. They could help unify the diverse population. Works with historical themes spoke of the powerful emotional appeals in the nation's shared past. Others that used abstract means reminded everyone of the nation's role in an ongoing cultural tradition. In more personal ways, murals also expressed yearnings for mystery and large emotions, as well as splendid effects. In many ways, the great murals were the abstract art of their generation. But they remained realistic in employing the figure or historical associations which the public could understand.[39]

Cox embraced mural painting for both artistic and cultural reasons. It afforded the painter a chance to develop large ideas in dramatic forms, a very different challenge from easel painting. The successful decoration linked the artist to the greatest masters of the past and made the work significant in social life. The best projects integrated painting, sculpture, decoration, and architecture into a unified whole in a visual and emotional experience that was intense yet controlled and harmonious, always major aims of traditionalist thinkers. The experience of working on and placing murals often gave artists the sense of unity and importance they longed for; they were preparing enduring works for the polity at large. Mural painting offered the chance to broaden public art appreciation and to remind viewers that their civilization was linked to the grand past. Cox thought this crucial for a generation that worshiped the fact and superficial imitation in the arts. He saw muralism as a way of channeling or at least complementing a general modern thrust toward mere realism that contained no ideas.

Cox later said that he had always wanted to paint decorations, and his first opportunity to do a mural came in 1892, when the managers of the World's Columbian Exposition asked leading painters to decorate its lavish temporary structures. Most of these buildings derived from Greco-Roman and Renaissance models, with interior spaces suitable for murals. Cox's *Ceramic Painting,* for the dome of the east portal of the Manufactures Building, was an elegantly drawn female figure holding a ceramic jug. The strong outline drawing and modeling, easy treatment of drapery, and solid form testified to his training and potential as a muralist.[40] Cox was also well acquainted with many examples of European murals. The Paris of his youthful student years was full of such works, which provided employment for outstanding contemporary artists. He had also seen examples of the Italian mural tradition during his trip of 1878. In 1889 he visited the Low Countries and France, where he saw many other such works, and in 1893 refreshed himself with another Italian tour.

Cox hoped to place the United States in the forefront of this revitalized mural tradition and thought a great deal about how to make such decorations suitable to modern life. Among contemporaries he admired the murals of Paul Baudry, who had decorated the Paris Opéra. But he also gave high praise to Pierre Puvis de Chavannes. "Of the men of today it is Puvis first and the rest [are] nowhere," he wrote his mother in 1893 after seeing some of the works in place in Amiens.[41]

At first glance, this attraction seemed odd. Puvis's work was stylized and abstract, a contrast to those works that led to the modern taste for realism and familiar classicism. But in many ways his approach was a viable answer to the problem of combining traditional motifs and modern techniques. Beginning in the 1860s, Puvis developed an approach that appealed to those seeking condensed form and intense meaning without formalistic classicism and to traditionalists trying to retain ideas in painting. His mature mural employed figures, often in antique settings, that lay flat on the canvas without much modeling or detail. He emphasized clear lines and masses. A typical work was in low-keyed colors, and the total effect was one of detachment, calm, and stoical nobility. Cox found this striking. "A desire for Greek simplicity and grandeur, a desire for Gothic sentiment and directness of expression—these two desires have pushed him forward to new and ever new suppressions of the useless, the insignificant, the cumbrous," he wrote in 1896. "He has come to leave out not only every detail that may interfere with the effect of the whole, but every detail that is not absolutely necessary to the expression of the whole. He has eliminated now for the sake of perfect clarity, and now for the sake of quaint simplicity."[42]

Cox was also drawn to Puvis for reasons other than an arresting technique. Puvis dealt with ideas in capital letters, whether in depicting an ancient grove where the muses met, in suggesting the impact of poverty on a poor fisherman's family, or in extolling austerity and piety in religious works. His gift for evoking memory and suggestion through condensation brought these ideas forward in the minds of sympathetic viewers. The actual techniques emphasized but did not override the message, and the two seemed a harmonious whole. Traditional ideas from history and the human condition rather than particular painters or periods were Puvis's antecedents. His style matched an interest in the enduring, the harmonious, the stoical views that had shaped humanity's relations to nature, art, and grand ideas.

Puvis fascinated Cox but did not in the end form his style as a mural painter. In a few works, Cox included a certain flatness and emphasis on outlined forms that were reminiscent of the French master but developed reservations about Puvis's color scheme. He came to believe that most of the spaces available to American muralists required a richer color and more emphasis on figures and action than Puvis's technique allowed. If anything, Americans overreacted and produced highly colored murals that spoke too loudly in their bid for attention. But Cox abandoned Puvis's "harmonization by paleness" and said frankly that "if I had my two lunettes in the Library of Congress to paint again the result, whether better or worse, would be something very different from the ghosts of paintings I actually placed there."[43] The mature Cox found the Italian Renaissance tradition more appealing, with its rich color, realized figures, and complex accessories.

Muralists engaged in much discussion on how to influence a mass democratic society. The decorator of a home for a wealthy client usually opted for some scheme that was part of a general decor and that had little if any intellectual content. The muralist for a public building often faced the challenge of dealing with a many-faceted constituency that wanted to celebrate the area's history or alleged unique qualities at the expense of general ideas.

The painter often compromised and employed a historical subject that neutralized local differences, afforded the chance to paint sumptuously, and had at least the hope of echoing large ideas. This produced a great array of sometimes impressive but more often hackneyed decorations. A typical mural in a courthouse, for example, might show an allegorical figure leading modern pioneers in covered wagons over such a title as *The Spirit of Progress Leading Settlers West.* Likely as not, prominent local persons or their ancestors would figure in the scene. A variant of this approach might involve a locally famous event accurately rendered to illustrate a larger process such as settlement or economic development.

Cox understood the appeals of historicism as a way of reconciling realistic treatment and classical idealism. He also knew that the burgeoning mural movement drew on no large American tradition of public decoration that emphasized abstraction or allegory. He thought that in the hands of a master decorator such as his friend Edwin H. Blashfield, the mixture of allegory and fact could be successful. He praised Blashfield's elaborate decoration for the Baltimore Court House, *Washington Laying Down His Commission* (1902). In this work a central female figure sat enthroned above the legend *Patriae,* with figures on each side holding various symbols of war and peace, power and responsibility. Washington, realistically dressed in a Continental army uniform, surrendered his wartime command. The figures were beautifully drawn, and the scene sumptuously painted. The major theme was the wisdom of Washington's refusing to turn military command into personal power.

This particular mixture of the antique and the recent past, the allegorical, and the realistic did not offend Cox because it was well done and internally logical. "So swiftly is time foreshortened as it recedes into the past that Washington, in blue and buff, seems naturally enough placed amid the half-medieval, half-ancient costumes of the symbolical figures about him," he wrote. "They are all removed from the present, which is, for us, the only real, and seem equally to belong to an ideal world. The effect of the whole is sumptuously decorative, while the larger implications of the story to be told are much more clearly expressed than they could be by a realistic representation of the scene that occurred in Annapolis in 1783." He thought the same was true of Augustus Saint-Gaudens's famous equestrian statue of General William T. Sherman, which an idealized female Victory led. In a few instances such as these real people and events filled such important and familiar roles in national life that they were allegorical.[44]

Cox thought this was seldom the case in using history for murals. America's past was not as lengthy or dramatic as that of Europe, which had produced such effective murals. The religious dimension was missing. Modern costumes and accoutrements were unattractive to the painter and inhibited tendencies toward large effects that were appropriate to grand ideas. As he bluntly said, "The painter who cares greatly for the expressiveness of the body will feel little attraction to belt buckles and brass buttons."[45] Above all, the historical story too easily became parochial. History as incident was different from history as ideal within the western art tradition.

These considerations, combined with his natural bent toward figure painting and a strong predilection for Renaissance models, made Cox one of the chief spokesmen for the use of allegorical figures and designs in murals. The figure expressed ideas, and formal compositions were in order for most buildings. This tradition best emphasized continuity and timelessness, which Cox thought appropriate in a democratic society too accustomed to accept change without much discussion. "Again, mural painting is especially an art of formal and symmetrical composition, of monumental arrangements and balanced lines and masses," he held in 1911, "and such composition necessarily destroys all illusion of veracity in the depiction of historical incident." In the end, "we must admit the symbolical or we must give up monumental and decorative painting altogether."[46]

Cox put these and other ideas to the test in a long series of murals. In the mid-1890s the architects of the new Library of Congress in Washington hoped to make the building a showcase of American artistic skill and a symbol of the government's and nation's interest in civic art. They invited the country's best-known painters and sculptors to contribute to the building's lavish decorations. Cox had the chance to paint two large lunettes, each 34 feet long and 9.5 feet high, for the ends of the Southwest Gallery. The decorations were to symbolize both the building's cultural functions and the nation's entry into world cultural affairs.

Cox was flattered but hesitated for financial reasons, a major consideration for decorators. The fees for murals were often substantial, but the work involved considerable costs for materials and assistants. Such commissions also required lengthy attention, thus keeping an artist from doing other works. Cox finally agreed because "the opportunity to do a fine thing for a public building is so tempting."[47]

He worked for about a year on the two lunettes, entitled *The Arts* and *The Sciences*. In each case he depicted various aspects of the subjects in idealized female figures drawn from Renaissance models. The compositions were pyramidal and symmetrical, with attention focused on allegorical figures grouped in the center of a classical balustrade, amid attendants symbolizing various branches and purposes of the arts and sciences. There were rich touches, such as a peacock in *The Sciences,* flaming braziers in both compositions, and various symbolic objects. The backgrounds suggested bucolic classical views. As usual, Cox painted the figures and their draperies with great skill, and with a hint of the flattening that informed Puvis's work. The French painter's influence was most noticeable in the light coloration. Cox supervised their installation and was especially satisfied that the workmen liked them. He was unabashedly enthusiastic himself. "They're *both* daisies," he wrote his wife, Louise, in New York. "Really, I think it is time I got away from them or I shall grow too conceited to live. At any rate, they absolutely and entirely belong to the place."[48]

Cox's reputation as a muralist grew with the new century, and he soon received regular inquiries about such commissions. The demand for murals was cumulative, as each widely discussed project made such decorations seem not only attractive but necessary to architects and building commissions. This was especially true in the design of several lavish state capitols in the Midwest, including those in St. Paul, Des Moines, and Madison, for which Cox furnished works.

The Iowa project was especially challenging. Cox wanted to present a thematic scheme in lunettes at the bottom of the dome. He decided that they must deal with a universal rather than a local topic and that, while allegorical, they should be understandable to the varied public that used the building. He chose a striking idea, a series of eight pictures, each with a central figure and appropriate accoutrements rep-

Kenyon Cox. *The Arts*, 1896. (Oil on canvas, 9.5 x 34 feet. Library of Congress.) This was one of two complex lunettes Cox did for a large room in the new Library of Congress building. The work manages to be serious in tone and content, but rather informal and pleasant in effect.

resenting a major stage of human development in the progress of civilization. The series went from *Hunting,* the first social stage, to *Art,* the last and highest state, a sequence that said volumes about the traditionalists' idea of progress. *Art* was laden with symbols of people's needs to relax, enjoy, and imagine after struggling for security. In this panel a violoncello represented music, a palette and brush symbolized painting, and a classical building decorated with statuary spoke for architecture and sculpture. The central female figure of *Art* wore gold and crimson robes and a wreath of gold. Cox painted the scene in brilliant colors to contrast with his more sober treatment of *Science* in the series.[49]

Cox thoroughly enjoyed painting these decorations. They almost effortlessly allowed him to develop his idea of change and were sumptuous figure paintings, the thing he did best. "I really think I've scored ten—which is most satisfactory," he wrote his wife while installing the paintings in the spring of 1906.[50] "They seem to me, at present, the only *real* things I ever did," he wrote Augustus Saint-Gaudens, "the only things that I can conceive of as really counting with serious works of art."[51] He was correct, and these works remain instructive and impressive.

The commission for the state capitol in Madison was much more challenging, involving different kinds of work in two places. For the wall behind the president's platform in the senate chamber, Cox designed a traditional work entitled *The Marriage of the Atlantic and the Pacific* (1914–15). Elaborate marble Corinthian columns separated it into three parts, each about eleven feet high and seven feet wide. One side offered female figures representing Europe and her ideals, while on the other side similar figures represented Asia and hers. In the middle panel an enthroned America presided over the union of East and West through the Panama Canal. Cox painted the figures and their draperies with a sure touch. His was a story of the transmission of culture and achievements and of the similarity of enduring ideas behind different civilizations.

The same large idea was behind the second set of works, four great figures, *Government, Legislation, Liberty,* and *Justice,* in the pendentives at the bottom of the dome (1912–14). These spaces were twenty-four feet wide and twelve feet high, ample for a truly monumental statement. Each figure sat in a circular space surrounded with fasces and crossed ribbons, with a gold background and oak foliage. A gold and purple guilloche border framed each ensemble. The figures were armed with the classical regalia and symbols of their missions and authority. *Legislation* was understandable through its clear resemblance to accepted images of Moses, the greatest lawgiver. *Government* was an equally familiar soldier and statesman. *Justice* balanced her scales, while *Liberty* guarded the ballot box. Each was in a different primary color and had a sense of grace that did not detract from its monumental qualities. The decorations were composed of 400,000 pieces of mosaic glass that imparted a rich surface effect to each singly and to the entire group in the relatively defined rotunda space. The figures recalled the history and ideals behind them without any great need for explanation. The group spoke for what people thought their representatives should be doing. In their dignity and appropriateness, as well as their artistic beauty, these remain among the most effective public decorations in America.[52]

Cox's mature style naturally reflected the man behind the brush. Little if anything in his painting was impulsive or solely expressive. The energetic, nervous touch of his friend John Singer Sargent was not for him. Nor were the richly textured surface effects of another friend, William Merritt Chase. Cox found such canvases often beautiful, but lacking in ideas and elevating mood. He always wanted an emotional, indeed a sensual, reaction to painting, but it had to be integrative and produce a sense of harmony and exaltation rather than mere passing sensation. His expressiveness lay in creating a total effect of thoughtfulness, reflection, and symbolism that placed the viewer in a broad cultural context. Murals especially required careful delineation of figures, attention to large masses, monumentality, and the reflective mood that he thought necessary to convey any lasting message. Cox took art and its mission seriously and found it most moving and meaningful in a grand style that made artist and viewer feel part of the great tradition. There was much truth in a newspaper reviewer's observation in 1914 that "Mr. Cox's work is essentially formal rather than spontaneous."[53]

Cox often criticized his own work and constantly struggled for appropriate effects. He was disappointed in his lunette for the entrance to the supreme court chamber in the Minnesota state capitol, *The Contemplative Spirit of the East* (1904). In an effort to induce a reflective mood, he had made the colors too dark, and poor lighting only worsened this flaw. The outlines of the winged figures involved were not strong enough, and the composition was too crowded to create a spacious effect.[54] And in some of his most ambitious works he made a mistake common to muralists, that of including too much symbolic information.

But Cox meant for his murals to be colorful, emotional, and pleasing to the eye as well as instructive to the mind. His initial sketches for such designs were often fluid and informal. He then steadily modeled the figures until they took on almost three-dimensional qualities. In due course he clothed them in elegant draperies and painted the final canvas in modulated but rich colors. He never altered his careful draftsmanship, and the style naturally became formalistic, given the conventions of mural painting. His marriage of academic drawing and careful finish did not produce the sumptuously textured surfaces or sense of energy in the works of some other muralists, such as Edwin H. Blashfield. But where it was appropriate, Cox tried to develop a sense of the modern concern for action and drama with floating allegorical figures, flowing drapery, and smooth lines.

In some ways he best attained his ideal of mural painting in works that were little known because of their locations. In *The Light of Learning* (1910), a memorial lunette for the public library in Winona, Minnesota, a group of female figures representing Romance, Art, Philosophy, History, Science, and Poetry flanked the central enthroned figure of Learning. All spoke for the mission of a public library in conserving and distributing knowledge and culture. The pyramidal, symmetrical composition retained considerable sense of action and was richly colored.

Cox's brother, Dolson, funded an administration building at Oberlin College in 1914 as a memorial to their parents and commissioned Kenyon to decorate a small foyer with murals to honor them. He chose a suitable theme for his father's career and for traditionalist ideals—two figures representing the man of action, or warrior, and the man of thought or learning. For his mother he employed a winged figure symbolizing the spirits of self-sacrifice and of love. Both works were small, placed just above eye level, and were painted in rich colors such as maroon, red, blue, and green that created striking effects of both energy and repose.[55] These were among Cox's best works, combining a sense of individual human aspirations and achievements with symbolic meaning.

Cox exhibited figure studies, portraits, and other easel works in his

Kenyon Cox. *Nude Study for the Figure of Law,* Minnesota State Capitol, 1904. (Graphite on laid tracing paper mounted on board, 19⅜ x 15⅜ in. Carnegie Museum of Art, Pittsburgh, Andrew Carnegie Fund, 1906.) This is a good example of Cox's meticulous academic figure drawing.

middle years but spent the last period of his life as a muralist and critic. This not only suited his ideals and talents but was also financially necessary, since the commissions afforded at least a precarious living. He thought that mural painting became a major part of the renaissance in

American art and believed that it had at least modified the heedless rush toward materialism and the mundane. Muralism also helped retain the best traditional values and allowed painters to enlarge their skills.

Cox's idealism about the importance of art to the public was strong as he began his career in mural painting. He believed with others in the power of murals to remind people of enduring demands made upon individuals and their societies and of the need for cohesive emotional and institutional bonds in society. Whether in the familiar terms of history or incident or in the larger abstractions he preferred, murals could uplift people and emphasize the grand ideals and feelings he thought more necessary than ever in a materialistic age. "I, for one, believe that the day of mere fact and of mere research is nearly ended, and the day of the isolated easel-picture, too," he wrote in an 1896 essay on Puvis de Chavannes. "We are already taking the first steps even here in America; and before long we shall have come back to the old true notion that the highest aim of art is to make some useful thing beautiful." This in turn would expand both the artist's role and the public's consciousness. "Art will again enter that service which is for it the most perfect freedom, and as the highest aim of the painter will be to beautify the walls of the temples and palaces of the people, so the highest name he will give himself will be that of 'decorator.' "[56]

Cox developed his ideas in print as well as paint. By the 1890s he was a well-known reviewer of exhibitions and art books for the New York newspapers and for the magazines that influenced the middle class. His development as a critic had its ups and downs. It began while he was a student in Paris, when he wrote a three-part review of the Salon of 1879 for his hometown newspaper in Cincinnati. The words did not come as easily as he had expected, and he immediately saw both the rewards and the pitfalls of art criticism. The critic could hope to educate an audience but could seldom divine how much it understood of either the technical or cultural aspects of art. He was also acutely conscious of the danger of offending fellow painters, who might return the favor with interest.

But criticism came naturally for Cox, given his knowledge of art history and his belief in propagating a body of ideas about art. Once he moved to New York in 1883, he was steadily drawn into writing. He needed the income but basically hoped to spread traditionalist ideas and to encourage the new generation of artists who were determined to raise the nation's level of taste. By the fall of 1885 he was writing unsigned exhibition reviews for the *Nation* and the *New York Evening Post*. The secret inevitably became public, and he had several unpleasant confrontations with people whose works he had criticized. "Artists are certainly the *irritable genus*," he wrote a friend in 1886, "and can't bear anything less than unlimited soft soap apparently. . . . It seems that painters resent the apparent attitude of superiority criticism necessarily gives much more in a brother painter than in one whom they can laugh at as really knowing nothing."[57] As his friend Edwin H. Blashfield said later, "Poor Cox used to grieve to me, 'If I find their work unsympathetic and say it in print, so and so, and so and so find it very unkind in me, because as they say, I am a competing comrade.' "[58] Cox also wearied of making the exhibition rounds that become every critic's lot.

Cox came to criticism at an important moment in its evolution. The old days of haphazard reviewing, which often was either uncritical or completely biased, yielded to a new sophistication. The audience for cultural matters expanded as the nation's cities and wealth grew. Beginning in the 1870s, an increasing number of professional journals devoted to art and other magazines served the literate and affluent middle class. Cables brought European art news daily, along with the details of wars and revolutions. An increased flow of photographs, books, and magazines concerned with current and historical art circulated through the nation. More and more accurate scholarly studies of past masters were available, and these helped sharpen debates over trends, schools, and individual styles. Criticism steadily became more exact in its approach and less likely to accept marginal work. Behind this stood the idea that the late nineteenth century, which intelligent persons must try to understand, if not always accept, was a major period in cultural development.

These critical wars were as heated as political campaigns. Cox favored careful analysis of both the technical and intellectual content of painting, and he displayed great erudition about the purely technical aspects of painting. But he found the Olympian tone in some criticism irritating, especially where it involved lowering the estimation of some of the giants who shaped his tastes. He once suggested wryly that if Michelangelo's Sistine frescoes appeared in 1886, the critics would savage them as either too symbolic or too naturalistic.[59]

Nor was he overly impressed with the contextual analysis that used internal similarities of style and subject matter to date and verify works for which there was little documentation. On the whole, Cox thought that this increased the number of schools in art history, especially for Italy, and tended to reduce the proper reputations of great masters. He was wary of any scientific claims to do more than help date works or detect forgeries. Science certainly could not determine the nature of great art or explain why it appealed. In the end, only the sympathetic viewer who loved art and understood its associations and demands could attest to its greatness. "The more important the question to be solved, the less aid 'Method' gives in its solution," he wrote in 1902, "and the more we fall back on that personal artistic sense which existed before 'Method' was heard of."[60]

Cox tended to focus on artistic skills in reviewing exhibitions and was harsh with those who failed to meet his demands for sound drawing and design. He required that subject matter involve some kind of important idea, however expressed. He saw the works of specific artists as expressions of their personalities and eras. He wrote clearly and integrated illustrative pictures with the text. His approach to broader topics, such as trends or schools of painting, was equally rooted in a sociological conception of art as the expression of a given time and place, though he always emphasized themes of long standing. He tried not to condescend to any audience and aimed "to interest 'the school-teacher at Oshkosh,' who may see, or hope to see, the pictures by the artists spoken of," as well as those who were already knowledgeable.[61]

The steady stream of written work bearing his name was somewhat ironic. "I hate writing," he frankly told the editor of *Century Magazine* in 1897. It interrupted his painting and, given his insistence on accuracy and breadth, required a great deal of background reading. Sometimes the results did not seem impressive enough, considering his tendency toward brevity. "I *never* write as long a thing as I set out to do. I am an invincible writer-down."[62]

As time went on and Cox became embroiled in the bitter controversies over modernism, he was noted for a sharp pen and cutting bon mots. This demeanor, which often seemed arrogant or insensitive to others, testified to his concern that modernism imperiled the entire art tradition. Cox was one of those people who usually did not know when he seemed harsh to others because he was simply speaking deeply held convictions. Friends sometimes chided him for this truculent tone. "Then too, I am temperamentally never as *sure* of *anything* as you are certain of *everything*," Will Low wrote him in 1911. In his late years, Cox sometimes felt ostracized and grasped at straws of approval. Once on the lecture circuit he overheard a group at the next dinner table, who did not know who he was, praise his books and style, as he duly reported to his wife.[63]

In both his painting and writing Cox espoused a coherent interpretation of art that he called the classic point of view.[64] This body of thought offered an alternative to the modernism based on individuality that Cox disliked. It was also a formula for codifying skills and viewpoints that expressed traditional ideals.

Cox never modified his belief in careful drawing and the other technical abilities he learned as a student; these prepared the painter to express ideals. Even as a student he had believed that no personal expression or insight, however deeply felt, survived if poorly executed. Technical merit basically fixed an artist's place. This insistence on formal, rigorous training in rendering nature, especially the figure, brought Cox up against the bogeyman of academicism. It was ironic that as the nation's cultural sense broadened and an increasing number of institutions devoted to the teaching of art appeared, critics attacked the academic approach. By *academic* they generally meant an attention to the details of appearance rather than to the content of a subject, reliance on subjects unsuitable to modern life, slavishness to mere discipline that sacrificed valid individuality, and opposition to innovation.[65]

Cox adopted a rule of reason in this debate. As a thinker and painter he was an academic, but he did not believe that his training or ideals denied individualism or growth. He simply insisted that any new idea be expressed well, be recognizable as part of the ongoing tradition, that it stir the eye and mind to a new level of positive experience. He did not think that true academic training thwarted any of these goals, and none of them was attainable without disciplined talent.

Cox believed that such teaching, which he did at the Art Students League, must retain the intellectual ambitions of traditional training. The result was, inevitably, the academic label. The characteristics of this kind of teaching were clear, as he wrote in 1917: "a certain elevation of subject and of treatment . . . faultless composition according to traditional standards . . . correct drawing of the human figure in which a thorough acquaintance with natural forms is controlled by an idealism founded upon classical sculpture" and knowledge of anatomy and perspective. The use of color, light, and shade was more personal but had to reflect seriousness and harmony. In general, good academics "have maintained a certain standard of propriety and of sound workmanship and have discouraged all extravagance or eccentricity." Individuality or genius were all very well; but they flowered only under such discipline, which focused and intensified talent. The true academic prized discipline only to express ideas in coherent and effective ways. Any general attack on academic training, especially in an America that was just attaining a high level of art appreciation and technical skill, was unwarranted.[66]

Design and the choice of subject were equally important in expressing ideas. Cox saw painting as an effort to balance realism, the depiction of natural appearances, with idealism, the effort to communicate large ideals that moved and enriched the personality. Pure imitation of appearances was probably impossible but was best left to photographers in any event. Pure idealism was equally impossible, since it tended to an abstraction or mere decorativeness that viewers could not understand. The artist interpreted, organized, and presented in understandable and moving ways an idealism that spoke in some familiar form. Though the artist was unique, those who spoke within a tradition that people comprehended, would have their effect. This expression always involved memory, mood, reflection, and a conscious effort to order and make understandable the art involved.[67]

Although Cox focused on figure painting as the greatest vehicle for expressing classical ideals, he did not limit his approach to any form or subject matter. Landscape, genre, portraiture, still life could as easily express his ideas. The point was simply that the successful artist created a reflective mood and an expanded imaginative experience, whatever the subject.

Design was the basis of such expression and was a conscious effort to achieve clarity and unity in order to impose wholeness on an otherwise disparate collection of forms and ideas. Cox disliked the word *composition,* which had become fashionable, because it was indefinite. "The word design conveys the finer and truer idea of an original guiding thought, a principle of unity, out of which the parts and details of a picture are developed by a natural and organic growth. You compose a pudding or a black draught—you design a work of art."[68] This led him to define painting with concern for form and function:

The art of painting is the selective representation on a plane surface of objects or actions, real or imagined, by means of spaces, lines, colors, and variations of light and dark, all of which elements, as well as the materials employed, have been subjected to some principle of order for their attainment of unity.[69]

Similar principles held for the choice of subject matter. The artist's overriding concern to communicate required a familiar vehicle. Every great painting had a subject. Some of the greatest masters, such as Rembrandt, communicated via biblical stories. The Italian masters relied on religious or historical events. Cox saw allegory and symbolism, personified in the human form, as proper vehicles for great ideas. Art was imitative, and subject matter was necessary, provided that it went beyond mere realism or sentiment to express large emotions and ideals. But it was one of Cox's cardinal tenets that art must be representational and familiar in some way in order to reach an audience. "The truth seems to be that the art impulse—the love of harmony—has moulded the material of art into various and strange shapes," he wrote in 1898, "but that material has always been the representation of observed natural facts."[70]

Within Cox's historical and developmental scheme of culture, painting was derived from the human needs to express oneself, to explain the mysteries in living, and to enliven life with decoration and play. In these ways people had always given order and some sense of ongoing purpose to an otherwise uncertain and sometimes dangerous existence.[71] The artist was a personality who could intensify experiences, clarify the unclear, and express the unusual. "The business of the painter as imitator is to give us, temporarily, the benefit of his power of vision, of his training and knowledge, of his perception of the significance of things, and by so doing to give us an unwonted sense of physical and mental efficiency which is in the highest degree pleasurable. We feel ourselves, for the moment, possessed of clearer senses, of more lively emotions, of greater intellectual powers, than we had imagined; we live more intensely, and rejoice in our perception of this intensity of life." Such a reaction rested on a sense of harmony as well as intensity; it was "life-communicating and life-enhancing, and may therefore give us that highest of pleasures, the sense of superiority to our ordinary selves."[72]

This classicism was often depicted as cool and detached, but Cox disagreed. For the sensitive and receptive person, the art-moment offered an unsurpassable elevation and unity of the mind and senses, as he remembered from seeing Michelangelo's great sculptures for the Medici Chapel. "Nothing in the whole range of art is so overwhelming, so 'intolerable.' Its enormous melancholy catches one by the throat and chokes one with the poignancy of sensation. One gazes with a hushed intensity, one cannot tear oneself away, and yet one breathes a long sigh of relief when one gets out at last into the sunlit air of Florence."[73]

Practice and appreciation of this classicism required knowledge of great works and artists. The Italian Renaissance painters, especially the Venetians, were most important to Cox personally. Several trips to northern Italy to see their works in place reminded him that great art survived politics, wars, and revolutions. It represented human experiences, emotions, and ambitions that seemed eternal, though they might be reexpressed in cycles of taste. Any knowledge of this art prompted caution about sudden changes in human affairs and about the validity of new styles. That art also became part of the memory and shared ideals which held societies together. "The great traditions of the world are not here by accident," he insisted at the height of the fiery debate over modernism in 1913. "They exist because humanity found them to be for its own good. Art has a social function. In all the great periods of art it has spoken to the people in a language that they understood and expressed what they would have it express."[74]

While this classicism emphasized continuity, Cox understood that art and its audience changed. In a technical sense he knew that art was an effort to render motion or change, both visually and psychologically. Visually, the painter tried to depict action and purpose; emotionally, he tried to expand or intensify consciousness. But in the traditional ideal this effort had to show motion and change as expressions of important purposes rather than for their own sake. Classicism also tended to deal with motion and change after the fact, as composed acts dependent upon analysis, reflection, and thought. But the classical ideal was an effort to change within limits, to act with exalted purpose, to unify rather than disturb. It shunned the conflagration, however spectacular, in favor of a well-laid fire. In cultural terms, this classicism hoped to manage change without threatening social cohesion. "It does not deny originality and individuality—they are as welcome as inevitable. It does not consider tradition as immutable or set rigid bounds to invention," he insisted in a famous definition in 1911. "But it desires that each new presentation of truth and beauty shall show us the old truth and the old beauty, seen only from a different angle and colored by a different medium. It wishes to add link by link to the chain of tradition, but it does not wish to break the chain."[75] This need for tradition gained added force for Cox because of the unusual rate of change in every aspect of contemporary life. The wise person chose from this welter of innovation and newness only those ideas, tastes, or improvements that promised to endure through logical attachments to the great needs and ideals that had always moved humanity. The rest was noise in the marketplace.

The art wars of Cox's lifetime involved differing ideas of how to be contemporary, democratic, and interesting without sacrificing importance. Realism seemed trivial; allegory was often remote. Efforts to combine the two produced many solutions. Cox found most art work of his time ephemeral but praised several contemporaries who he thought upheld the classical ideal. In sculpture he liked the work of Paul Dubois and of his friend Augustus Saint-Gaudens. Their works seemed to harmonize the modern yearning for energetic appearances and symbolic importance. In architecture he appreciated the revival of Renaissance ideals associated with the firm of McKim, Mead and White. Among painters he praised many Americans who retained a thoughtful formalism in their work while using some modern techniques. In many ways, he reserved his highest praise for Jean-François Millet, who offered a major solution to the dilemma of being modern in appearance and traditional in tone and purpose. Millet avoided the details so dear to realists but painted with a sense of design and broad gesture that made the actions of the subjects in his pictures almost palpable. While gleaning, sowing, or tending flocks, they idealized human deeds and patterns of action that were as old as civilization and that would outlast all current events. "It is the permanent, the essential, the eternally significant that he paints," Cox noted in 1908. "The apparent localization of his subjects in time and space is an illusion. He is not concerned with the nineteenth century or with Barbizon, but with mankind."[76] Millet's greatest works involved people who managed to be both real and noble.

These views naturally developed over time but basically were always part of Cox's thinking. He was bound to dislike new styles that emphasized individual gesture over intellectual order or those that dissolved recognizable form. The first of these major changes was impressionism, just appearing when Cox was a student in the late 1870s. He referred to it in a three-part article he wrote for his hometown newspaper on the Salon of 1879, mainly to criticize its apparent form-lessness and lack of thought. Like most other observers, Cox never expected impressionism to triumph with either the critics or the art public. But by the 1890s, when he was a well-known spokesman for the traditionalist viewpoint, it dominated the debate in the art world. Though it first seemed to be only another eccentric way of painting, impressionism quickly registered a major shift in taste and perception.

Cox disliked impressionism's emphasis on light and changing sur-face effects. Various kinds of realistic painting had drawn attention to these in his youth and middle years. Bastien-Lepage and his followers had meticulously depicted the envelope of air between the viewer and the subject, as well as the effect of light on subject matter. Many other realistic painters had opened their canvases to light and higher colors. The impressionists now seemed to take this process a large step further and concentrated on light and its effects on color and surface motion at the expense of ideas, interpreted form, and reflection.

Painting outdoors as such never offended Cox; he and fellow aca-demic students did so in the art colonies around Paris during their summer breaks. But he did not focus on light or transitory effects for their own sake. He composed outdoor scenes, painted them in com-plementary colors, and used light to interpret form and to create mood. In this he resembled the Barbizon painters, such as Camille Corot, who had a powerful impact on Americans. Their landscapes in particular fostered a mood that let the viewer relate to the painting with memory, reflection, and a sense of integrated and emotionally elevating effect. They employed colors such as gray, green, and blue with subdued light effects, and painted in feathery brush strokes that created blurred, ambiguous, but recognizable forms.

As a youth of twenty in 1876, Cox noted his appreciation of Corot, likening a sunrise to one of his paintings. But he was concerned about depth and substance. "There is, however, one thing he misses; the sharpness and precision of edge in everything, at such times, and in such lights, as he paints. Whether the two things are compatible, or, together, possible in painting is a great question. Certainly a combina-tion of delicacy of tone with precision of edge is the thing to try for."[77] This attitude continued in varying degrees throughout his early career and kept him from embracing impressionist techniques. "I do not like the effect of sunlight much anyhow," he wrote his father from the summer colony of Grez in 1879 where he was working outdoors, "preferring much [more] gray days when there is full color and everything is not eaten up with light."[78]

Like most academicians, Cox saw light as a way of creating tone and mood, a view he stated well in a lengthy essay on Rembrandt in 1894. He praised the Dutch master's great sense of humanity and ability to delineate character and individuality, whatever the subject's worldly role. He attributed much of this to Rembrandt's extraordinary use of light and shadow: "It is mystery and sentiment—a means of expressing the inexpressible and of realizing the supernatural—the only means known to art of saying what no one but Rembrandt has said."[79] As he put it in 1911: "In its fully developed form, light and shadow becomes mystery, absorbs substance as well as line, and becomes the one means for the expression of the otherwise inexpressible."[80] Light was meant to delineate or suggest ideas and moods, to help interpret substance and form, not just to please the eye momentarily with a passing bit of nature that had only a transitory effect on the viewer.

The impressionists' use of color was as controversial as their treatment of light. They juxtaposed complementary tones with small brush strokes that the eye blended. They also employed new colors, such as violet, and used familiar ones in unusual ways. Cox had little quarrel with the desire for more intense color in painting. But as with his view of light, he saw color as a way of emphasizing subject matter, not as an end in itself. Mere color divorced from ideas and mental associations was pleasing but did not evoke the unified emotion or contemplative mood he associated with high art. In letting in the light, impressionists risked creating a false world of exaggerated tones.[81] Cox also cautioned against fascination with color for its own sake, which would soon replace ideas with surface effects and reduce the artist to a mere recorder rather than an interpreter. Impressionism's "great defect was its neglect of art," he noted in 1911 of the mature movement, "for color, even more than drawing, requires that art shall control the study of nature, and that things shall be done for the purpose of expression, not merely for the love of imitation."[82] Impressionist works seemed to be a collection of brush strokes rather than thoughtful compositions. He held that "insofar as they have neglected design they have forgotten to be artists and contented themselves with being investigators. For without design there may be representation, but there can be no art."[83]

Cox disliked these tendencies especially in treating the human form. Too often impressionist figures lacked any anatomical presence and simply lay on the canvas as a collection of brush strokes, used as another means of depicting light or color effects. These figures might be interesting, even dynamic, but they had no presence or symbolism. "In the treatment of landscape, impressionism may still be tolerable, because light naturally plays a great role in landscape painting," he wrote in 1911, "but no painter who cares for the anatomy of earth or the growth and life of trees will ever be quite satisfied with it." Even this limited success was not true in impressionist treatment of human forms. "In figure painting it is intolerable. In its hands the human figure, the most beautiful and the most interesting thing in all the world, is merged into the landscape, as the landscape itself is lost in the light that falls upon it, and man himself becomes no more than an accident among other accidents."[84] Cox insisted that the figure paint-er depict character, idealism, and enduring truths, making humanity central in life.

Just how to do this in modern times puzzled many painters. Cox tried to fulfill his ideal in *An Eclogue* (1890), which showed four alle-gorical female figures in various stages of nudity in a bucolic setting, with a herdsman and dog in the background. As usual, the figures were elegantly drawn and well realized, with richly colored clothing. Two even boasted flaming red hair. They managed to seem both real and allegorical. Cox depicted the rustic setting in rich natural colors, includ-ing an almost dazzling yellow field where the dog and herdsman stood. The entire effect was sumptuous yet subdued, with deliberate echoes of Claude Lorrain and Nicolas Poussin, and the painting embodied classi-cal ideals as well as some rich modernistic effects.

Cox's views of impressionism evolved, and he remained more skep-tical than hostile toward it. It was not surprising that he first disliked it; he had good company among artists, critics, and patrons. Interestingly enough, like many other critics, he first saw impressionism as "scien-tific" in its investigations of light effects. This connection with science made the approach seem a studied effort to analyze nature's effects without the indefinable emotional qualities of artistic expression, as stated in carefully interpreted form, which underlay his own approach to art. Gradually he recognized that it was another effort to adapt painting to modern democratic demands for action, color, and informal subject matter. He appreciated the fresh emphasis on color to evoke delight or admiration but disliked the overuse of light that dissolved basic interpreted form. By the time of his mature years impressionism

Kenyon Cox. *An Eclogue,* 1890. (Oil on canvas, 48 x 60½ in. National Museum of American Art, Smithsonian Institution. Gift of Allyn Cox.) This handsome work was at least partially an effort on Cox's part to combine traditional ideals with modern methods.

had become almost academic, and he began to see the merits of its greatest practitioners, including Claude Monet, though he continued to dislike the work of lesser people. Cox praised those who took from impressionism a welcome informality and vigor without abandoning form or contemplation. He admired the subdued, poetic impressionism of J. Alden Weir and that of his friend Theodore Robinson. By the turn of the century, he thought that the excesses of impressionism were past. He praised those artists who used the approach yet retained a sense of substance and interpreted nature in their work. He would have agreed with his friend Robinson's private musings in 1894: "Altogether, the possibilities are very great for the moderns, but they must draw without ceasing or they will get left, and with the brilliancy and light of real outdoors, combine the austerity, the sobriety, that has always characterized good painting."[85]

50

Cox understood that impressionism was more than a way of paint-ing. It represented a growing tendency in democratic, industrialized societies to emphasize transitory effects over the inherited ideals of cohesion and controlled emotion. Given his sociological view of art, he found much of what impressionism represented unsettling.

The world of art was never at rest, any more than were those of economics or politics. By the beginning of the new century, Cox had seen numerous fresh approaches to painting come and go. But the 1890s saw the beginning of a series of linked and apparently forceful changes emanating from Europe that began to dominate painting, with similar impacts in literature, the drama, and other expressive media. Cox realized that there were many varieties of this modernism but, with his usual effort to organize and find cohesion, focused on the basic forces that were changing art. An emphasis on individual expres-sion at the expense of communicating with the public through familiar forms and methods was clearly growing. Equally strong was the ten-dency to dissolve or alter nature into basic forms or images, which the artist exaggerated for effect. And that effort to intensify momentary effect countered classicism's emphasis on harmony and unity.

Cox probably underestimated the impact of this modernism, ab-sorbed as he was in teaching and mural painting. But he soon devel-oped strong reasons for opposing it. Like most academic painters trained in the 1870s, he had a strong sense of having participated in and helped shape a crucial generation in American cultural history. The nation's painters now compared in technical skill with those of any other country. They had depicted a wide range of subject matter, and their efforts had helped bring America into world culture. By 1900 a strong supporting art world included regular and widely reported exhibitions, specialized journals and books, schools, museums, and col-lectors. These gains came with struggle and persistence. The fear of losing them if the public now concluded that the new experimentalists were either dangerous or irrelevant to society was a powerful aspect of Cox's opposition to modernism.

He thus spent a good deal of time and energy delineating the posi-tive developments he saw in American art. The elegant and effective appearance of the nation's painting after a generation of training and familiarity with historical models was praiseworthy. Cox did not see this as derivative of European art but as part of embracing world tradi-tion. American painting also retained some particular characteristics, including a concern for interpreted form, fidelity to observed nature and a certain sobriety that reflected interest in moods and ideas. He hoped that this sense of accomplishment would keep American art from succumbing to fads.[86] This generation of American painters also had reached the point of reproducing themselves through example, which gave the art world some depth as well as breadth. Work on murals for the capitols of Wisconsin, Minnesota, and Iowa impressed on him the growing art consciousness of the West. During his stay in Chicago for the Scammon Lectures in the spring of 1911, he noted the caliber of local painters. "I found a good deal that interested me," he wrote Blashfield, "and I thought we in New York might learn something from Chicago's spirit."[87]

Yet the lure of foreign ideas and examples was potent, and more and more modernist works appeared in exhibitions. By 1911, Cox recognized the gathering momentum behind this modernism and welcomed the chance to analyze and refute it. In the spring of that year he offered a series of public lectures and special classes at the Art Institute of Chicago. These Scammon Lectures constituted his "definitive credo—a detailed and explicit confession of artistic faith,"[88] and appeared as a book, *The Classic Point of View.* In them Cox displayed his customary ability to blend discussions of formal artistic matters, such as design and drawing, with historical examples and analysis. The work gained a good deal of public attention and helped make him the most noted opponent of modernism just as the debate peaked.

Never reticent about airing his views, Cox began to speak with a cutting tone that revealed his belief that art was threatened. He admitted privately that he was being extreme, yet he spoke for a great many silent but approving people and did not think he was a hidebound reactionary. "Of course, I am not without doubt, at times, whether I am merely growing old and stiff and unable to take in new things," he wrote Will Low in 1911. "I might believe this if my ideas were now what they were at 20 or 30. But they are not. I have changed very greatly and cannot but believe myself in progress, though the movement is in the opposite direction from that of many others. And again, I doubted for long, but the latest developments—Matisse and his unspeakable followers—leave me *no* doubts. This *cannot* be healthy art."[89]

Cox focused on several major cultural themes in attacking modernism. He believed that only art with traditional technical skill endured or affected the public. No new talent could survive or function apart from the tradition that produced it. Every change must be a reasonable extension of the cultural inheritance, and true innovation lay in saying something new in understandable ways. Above all, Cox feared the separation of artist and society. Outbreaks of romanticism emphasizing the individual as apart from society were common in history but left behind a mixed legacy. Such art was usually overly dramatic and self-conscious, however forcefully expressed. More to the point, the culture usually saw the rebel or romantic as bizarre rather than creative. More than anything else, Cox feared that the artist would cease to seem a significant personality and become to the public a marginal or negative figure. "There has been too much personality too; too much individual whim, due to lack of really complete education, and, in general, to lack of discipline," he told an interviewer in 1911."[90] Art was always properly individualistic, but exalting mere expression would make it a divisive rather than unifying force in human affairs. He cautioned young painters to avoid the powerful but destructive engine of modern publicity with its emphasis on self-advertisement and shortcuts to fame. The unwary painter might end up projecting in egocentric art only an introspection that spoke to no one else.

Cox liked some primitive or folk art and thought that a human need for self-expression through design was present in every society. But he disliked the new modernist view that this primitive art expressed emotions or basic principles that society had suppressed. He saw this argument as atavistic because it appeared to reject reason, composition, and fidelity to nature. To him and to many other critics, it represented an earlier stage of human history that had been left behind only with great effort. This progress was the theme of his murals for the Iowa state capitol. The infant might have more intense feelings than the adult but was not better for it. And like most other aspects of modernism, primitivism reduced communication between artist and public, which had a different view of art as a special effort.[91]

Cox inevitably disliked modernism's tendency to dissolve or distort form and to embrace abstraction. This reduced the artist's role as interpreter and said nothing lasting to the viewer. Cox admired abstract designs in Persian tiles or Turkish rugs, but these contained nothing for the mind, evoked no integrative and creative mood, however interesting to the eye.

Cox had noted this tendency toward abstraction in the work of James

McNeill Whistler. He admired many of this artist's qualities but found his development puzzling. While obviously interested in nature and a master colorist, Whistler produced little that Cox thought was truly moving or enduring. As the retrospective memorial exhibition of 1904 showed, Whistler's chief concern was for nuance, tone, and evanescence, qualities that seemed more appropriate to poetry and music than to painting. Cox always sought edifying and expanding reverie and reflection in painting, but Whistler's work appeared to lack great ideas. He seemed bent on painting the unpaintable, a tendency Cox had deplored years before in J. M. W. Turner. This had seemed a dead end then, and it remained so now. The great challenge to Cox was to give form and meaning to the attainable and to suggest great emotion beyond it. Whistler remained for him "a talent of nice discriminations and fastidious choice, of elegance rather than of strength."[92] These qualities were often pleasing, and Cox admired Whistler's ability to evoke certain moods through tonalism, but the implications were disturbing. "It would seem that painting can go no further in the direction of Whistler's later work without ceasing altogether to be the art we have now by that name."[93]

The discussion of modernism peaked at the so-called Armory Show, the International Exhibition of Modern Art in New York between 17 February and 15 March 1913. The show followed years of debate about modernism. It did not initiate America's interest in the new painting but did focus the debate because of its range of examples of both European and American art. It had great impact on the public as a controversial and widely reported event. Cox visited the exhibition and wrote a famous review for the 15 March *Harper's Weekly*. Terse, biting, and wide-ranging, it became a bible for opponents of modernism and made him a target for painters and critics who favored the moderns.

Cox emphasized cultural as well as technical qualities in discussing each major figure. He found Cézanne puzzling: "He seems always to have aimed at the great things." But the much-discussed emphasis on basic geometric forms and Cézanne's adoption of a new kind of perspective and design simply covered a lack of skill: "He could not learn to paint as others did, and he spent his life in the hopeless attempt to create a new art of painting for himself. Fumblingly and partially he can express himself to the few—he will never have anything for the many."

The work of others was even less satisfying. Van Gogh appeared to be in the grip of a fantastic need to express pure emotion without the artistic ability to refine or control it. The result was lurid paint. Gauguin was an effective decorator but hardly one to express important ideas to any public. His primitivism was an added burden. "His color is sometimes beautiful, but it is always unnecessarily false and often unpleasantly morbid." Henri Rousseau seemed merely amusing. He was the sort of amateur familiar from Cox's student days who hoped to exhibit but never did and who now appealed because he was bizarre. Cox saved his sharpest criticism for Henri Matisse, who offended many critics. His pictures seemed to lack composition, his figures were distorted or ugly, and his paint was random and garish. Cox thought most of the works expressed mere egotism and were calculated to shock or gain notoriety. On the whole, Cox found the show's display of individualism chaotic and destructive. He did praise many American works, which seemed positively sane alongside those of the Europeans.[94]

The *New York Times* published a lengthy interview with Cox in the Sunday edition of 16 March 1913, the day after the show closed. The reporter treated Cox with great deference, seeing him as a major spokesman for major art, with widely read books and murals that graced many public buildings. Cox himself seemed the essence of respectability and calm, wearing easy slippers and holding a corncob pipe, speaking carefully about a subject that aroused intense emotions.

Cox explained modernism in sociological terms. He thought that its most bizarre exponents drew on the symbolist movement of the 1890s, which had so influenced literature and poetry in seeking to intensify momentary experience without much reference to daily life or nature. But deeper forces were at work. "This is not a sudden disruption or eruption in the history of art," he noted. "It is the inevitable result of a tendency which has grown steadily stronger and stronger during the last fifty years. It is a tendency to abandon all discipline, all respect for tradition, and to insist that art shall be nothing but the expression of the individual." He blamed fellow critics for being hypnotized or for being "so frightened by what are thought to be the critical blunders of the last few generations that they dare not say any eccentric is bad for fear the eccentricity should turn out to be genius." He ended with the usual plea for an integrative rather than divisive art that spoke to society in familiar ways. He would not predict the outcome of the struggle, but artists and their public would either turn to a revitalized tradition, "or art will cease to exist."[95]

Cox elaborated these ideas in a major essay entitled "The Illusion of Progress." He saw modernism as another aspect of the frantic pace of contemporary living that piled fad upon whim in the name of progress. Advertising and communication fed on sensation; every season must be a newborn world. The inherited ideal of steady, continuing change that embraced innovation after thoughtful analysis was gone. "And as the pace of progress in science and in material things has become more and more rapid, we have come to expect a similar pace in art and letters," he noted, "to imagine that the art of the future must be far finer than the art of the present or than that of the past, and that the art of one decade, or even of one year, must supersede that of the preceding decade or the preceding year, as the 1913 model in automobiles supersedes the model of 1912."[96]

The debate had become a shouting match, with each side berating the other for views it did not necessarily hold while ignoring any validity in the other's views. Traditionalists especially disliked the modernists' reliance on sensationalism and shock, though this feeling may have resulted from shallow newspaper publicity rather than any intention of the exhibition's organizers. The same shrillness raged around other questions, such as women's rights or temperance, that pitted traditionalists against moderns. The moderns seemed to hold that to oppose their views was to be stupid and reactionary. They behaved as if none of their works would attain the oblivion that had hitherto been the fate of most innovation. Cox wrote Frank Jewett Mather, Jr., in 1915 that "one would think they might see that even if what they admire is as good as they think it, it does not follow that everything else is bad." He thought the moderns enjoyed an advantage from the publicity engine, which justified his bluntness. "I dare say you may be right as to my 'prosecuting attorney' attitude toward the eccentrics," he wrote Mather again in 1915. "It seemed to me that there were plenty of people proclaiming their merits and finding beauties in their work and I undertook to *faire leur procès* and demonstrate the essential falseness of their position. A prosecuting attorney is a rather necessary person at times, and if he be convinced of the guilt of the defendant, should do his best to secure conviction."[97]

In the years that followed, Cox continued to call for a return to traditional ideals. He welcomed any sign that modernism was receding. His essay, "Artist and Public," of 1914 reiterated the fear that the painter would abandon art's audience and cease to be important. He could not believe that people would reject thousands of years of art that involved ideas and understandable appearance in favor of abstraction.[98]

As Europe descended into the most destructive war in history, he hoped at least that the strangest of the new art would be a casualty. "The world will be too seriously occupied to puzzle itself with any sort of art that is not serious and comprehensive," he wrote Mather in 1915.[99] He wrote his son Allyn, studying in Rome, that the postwar world must of necessity return to discipline and coherent thinking in art.[100]

The intense debate over traditional versus modern art climaxed with the Armory Show and World War I. In the heat of the discussion it was easier to see the differences than the similarities among the partisans. The traditionalists represented an ancient and honorable view that rested on the need for order, analysis, and controlled change in society. The moderns represented a new, or at least recurrent, demand for intense, personal, and idiosyncratic experiences, which they thought matched the general tenor of modern society and which expanded individual personality. They also believed in a new dispensation for the current era, while traditionalists thought that contemporary society needed to control the rate of change to avoid breaking with the past. Art had been moving for some time toward new forms of representation and intellectual ambitions. But the pace of change seemed to quicken with the new century, giving all concerned a sense of either impending disaster for the established or of open possibilities for the new.

Cox typified the personality that found classicism natural and organic. Formal training that emphasized controlled but creative expression complemented his emotional and intellectual needs. But his larger view was sociological. Classicism represented a belief that society was balanced between harmonizing and disordering tendencies. It did not trust the individual's unfettered emotions. Since Cox thought that art represented the strongest human urges, any sudden changes in its forms or purposes would affect society at large. In this view, culture was not repressive or negative. It regulated, shaped, and directed new ideas that had social as well as esthetic consequences. It asked of them only the passwords of familiarity and usefulness. The moderns' talk of individual expression thus marked a path away from the integrated personality and stable society. Cox recognized the energy behind modernism, but this power required control and definition to be constructive.

Cox and the classicists envisioned a society in which art was central, not just as a thing to be observed and honored, but because it spoke clearly of past greatness and future prospects and represented mankind's ongoing efforts to express cohesive ideals. Cox was often a pessimist about people but not about art and its power to expand life's emotional possibilities. The moderns, of course, had similar aims. They thought that representational art had had its day and could not be refurbished. But they too accorded art a central role in society, demanding that it express basic motives and emotions through the intense individual act. They increasingly saw themselves as separated from many aspects of modern life but believed that a new public would respond to this intensity. They believed that they were part of the grand tradition of provoking thought, stirring imagination, expanding consciousness. But they also held that the formal qualities of art had changed and did not depend on realism, either for merit or effect. Both sides faced a dilemma. The moderns sought to bring viewers to fresh and often strange methods and perceptions which they insisted depicted a new reality. The traditionalists hoped to change without abandoning familiarity.

In Cox's case lay an added irony. In a curious way he was a modern. His allegorical works, especially the murals, represented ideas in abstracted forms. But of course he thought that allegorical paintings produced their unifying and advancing effects through condensing messages in the viewer's mind with familiar forms. The basic difference between traditional and modern always involved familiarity of subject matter and artistic language. The traditionalist simply did not believe that modernism could communicate with the public and feared that the artist's divisive, self-centered gesture had replaced the content of the work.

Fate had drawn Cox to the center of the debate over modernism, but he continued to write about other subjects and to paint. He completed a series of murals during these years, often receiving public acclaim. And the public that saw him as a learned critic, absorbed merely in abstruse intellectual discussions of art's meanings, knew little of his other side. In 1892, he had married one of his pupils at the Art Students League,

Louise H. King, who had a modest career as a painter, especially of children's portraits. Cox tended not to discuss his private life, but the couple had a happy and successful marriage. They had three children. The eldest, Leonard, born in 1894, emerged from World War I as a decorated hero and became an architect and city planner. The second son, Allyn, born in 1896, followed in his parents' footsteps to become an artist. He studied with his father and at the American Academy in Rome, then became a muralist. His best-known works were decorations in the U.S. Capitol, including a frieze under the dome, and elaborate murals on the corridor ceilings at the House of Representatives side of the building. The last child, a daughter named Caroline, was born in 1898. She too painted but did not develop a public career. She married a well-known archeologist, Ambrose Lansing. Despite his formidable public demeanor, Cox was a loving husband and father with a warm family life. His wife was often the recipient of deeply felt poems on holidays and anniversaries. Cox composed and illustrated for his children a collection of whimsical poems with accompanying mythical animals entitled *Mixed Beasts* (1904). He worked hard during the art season from October to April, then relaxed in the well-known art colonies of Cornish, New Hampshire, and Windsor, Vermont.[101]

At the same time, a sense of melancholy flavored Cox's life. Never financially secure, he lived uncertainly from a few sales, illustrations, writing, and mural commissions. His brother, Dolson, a wealthy industrialist, paid many of the family's bills, but the strain of making a living was constant and insoluble, given the artistic life.[102] He was also always conscious that his easel paintings did not command a large audience. "The people who really like my work for its own sake seem to be very few," he wrote his mother in 1901. "It's respected, not liked."[103] He privately doubted that his broad cultural emphasis would find much fertile soil. Friends often quoted a variation of his remark: "The majority of Americans still feel that they can be 'fairly comfortable' without art."[104] He became realistic about art's appeal to others. "We can hardly expect others to share our conviction that art is the only thing that really matters, the only expression of the human experience which endures."[105] But he meant to persevere. "One can only be one's self," he wrote Will Low in 1916, "and try to get the best out of one's own ideas and feelings—it is useless to try to do things as others see them."[106]

The struggle over modernism took a great toll from Cox's declining energy, and the uncertainty of the outcome was a source of pessimism.

Cox was the true believer who had glimpsed oblivion for his generation of artists, and at the hands of a modernism whose appeals he could not understand or accept. As he wrote to Blashfield: "Our doctrine is very hard to drive into modern heads—whether because the doctrine is weak or the heads of too hard wood!"[107] The war years were an added burden, as he worried over the fate of his eldest son, Leonard, in the American Expeditionary Force. Cox also devoted a good deal of energy to raising funds and support for the Allies. He aged prematurely and slowly ceased to paint. His last significant work was *Tradition* (1916), which showed an allegorical figure of tradition handing on the lamp of sound ideals to a new generation. He lived to see the war ended but died of pneumonia on 17 March 1919 in New York City.

The contest over modernism cooled, and the art public accepted some of the new wave of painting. At the same time, many people continued to appreciate and support traditional styles of painting and to appreciate revivals of recognized artists from the past. Many of the kinds of painting that Cox favored have lost their appeal, but the ideas he championed endure in several forms. A concern for properly interpreted reality persists. His insistence on careful formal training and on the artist's grounding in the large tradition are well worth remembering. The same is true of his caution against personal expression that does not communicate to an audience. He believed above all in the power of the art experience to enrich and expand the individual's life and, when repeated enough, to affect civic culture. He tried to fulfill this grand ideal, as his finest murals show.

ROYAL CORTISSOZ

Traditionalist for Everyman

There *was a time* when everyone in the New York art world, and many people elsewhere, immediately recognized the name Royal Cortissoz.[1] As the art critic of the prestigious *New York Tribune* for more than fifty years he commanded a large audience. Whether they agreed or not, painters, dealers, other critics, and the interested public read his judgments on several generations of painting in regular newspaper columns, books, and articles. He was a familiar figure at art openings and exhibitions, likely as not smoking a cigar while casting a practiced eye on the work of both established artists and novices. An avowed traditionalist, he was endowed with a catholic taste and wide-ranging interests. He ultimately became the voice of the intelligent but nonexpert Everyman who cared about art and the culture it symbolized.

This destiny was not predictable from his beginnings. Cortissoz was born in Brooklyn on 10 February 1869. His father was Francisco Emanuel, an Englishman of Spanish descent who emigrated to the United States in 1855. His mother, Julia da Costa Mauri, was from Martinique.[2] Cortissoz was apparently self-educated and was a voracious reader as a youth, with a particular interest in music, literature, drama, and painting. At sixteen he became an apprentice office boy in the great firm of McKim, Mead and White, where his lifelong interest in architecture began. He furnished modest articles and reviews of musical performances to a Kansas City paper, betraying an interest in journalism. In 1889 he joined the staff of the *New York Commercial Advertiser.* On 1 October 1891 he went to work for the *New York Tribune,* one of the country's great newspapers. Like any new reporter, Cortissoz covered a variety of subjects, though most were on the cultural beat. He wrote numerous reviews of musical and theatrical performances, and from 1897 to 1913 was also the paper's literary editor.[3] Capable of writing rapidly and accurately, Cortissoz enjoyed journalism and had a strong sense of working in an important medium among intelligent colleagues in a period when the press was a major factor in American life.

The city in which he lived and worked was nothing if not interesting.

As the nation's cultural capital, New York had outstanding private and public art collections and exciting theater and musical seasons. Its leading citizens were rich and sought varying kinds of cultural expression. Yet the city, like the nation, had expanded suddenly, without any plan, and exhibited enormous gaps between aspirations and achievements. The saying went that there was a lot of taste, most of it bad. But whatever its political and social conflicts, New York revealed an extraordinary cultural ferment. Dealers sold a wide variety of European art. American painters were organizing societies and special shows to promote their own work. The city's art life was rich and varied, often eccentric, but filled with a strong sense of developing accomplishment. Many specialized magazines and journals reported on the arts. The major newspapers, such as the *Tribune,* made every effort to cover all significant cultural events. The audience of educated people interested in art was expanding. Excitement was in the air. American art had the chance to enter the world's affairs, and Cortissoz wanted to be part of the process.[4]

The *Tribune* steadily expanded its art coverage, and by the mid-nineties Cortissoz was its principal critic. The work solved some emotional and intellectual problems for him. He had some talent at drawing but refused to study or practice art. "Perhaps I can draw," he once said, "but not in the manner to which the masters have accustomed me." He had the gift of appreciation and analysis but distrusted his own ability to attain high standards. He thus became a critic, as he put it, "by spontaneous combustion."[5] The materials, or needs, were there, and art appreciation lit the fire.

Cortissoz relished the role of art critic and the interesting life that followed, despite periods of anxiety and routine. "I suppose the luckless art critic comes in for a good deal of wrath in this world, but just the same, he has a joy in the work he is called upon to talk about which is past all computation," he wrote the sculptor Augustus Saint-Gaudens in 1897. "Perhaps it is the constant preoccupation with artistic things that helps him; at any rate, he lives as truly among works like yours as though he were in the studio where they are produced."[6]

He saw his role as that of link between artist and public; appreciation was creative and could be developed. In later years he answered a common charge with good humor. "There is the familiar hypothesis that the critic is an artist who has failed, but I need not dwell on this," he noted in 1923. "It is refuted by the testimony of uncounted exhibitions that, along with his betters, the artist who has failed goes right on painting."[7]

The *Tribune* had been a major newspaper and voice of moderate Republicanism since the days of Horace Greeley. In Cortissoz's time the chief editor and part-owner was Whitelaw Reid, a brilliant organizer and businessman as well as an important politician. He ran as Benjamin Harrison's vice presidential candidate in 1892, served President William McKinley in various diplomatic capacities, and was ambassador to the Court of St. James's from 1905 to 1912. Reid was a cultivated and socially prominent figure who made the paper speak as well for art as it did for politics. Cortissoz shared his general Republicanism but retained many independent views. He was never an apologist for the unlettered businessman, no matter how rich, who merely used art for social prestige or who denied social duties.[8] He was hardly a reformer but, like other traditionalists, hoped to make art central to American life and to let it ameliorate the nation's generalized materialism.

Cortissoz found newspaper work exciting and fulfilling but inevitably hectic, especially for one who also tried to keep abreast of the art literature and who traveled abroad in the summers to visit shows and museums. The daily writing obligations stood at his office doorway like demanding creditors. The mid-nineties were especially stressful as he worked to establish a reputation and to enhance the *Tribune*'s cultural leadership.[9] In due course, he fell victim to what the era called neurasthenia, or a nervous breakdown. The treatment was a lengthy trip around Cape Horn, during which he read Gibbon's *Decline and Fall of the Roman Empire* three times. Whether because of this great text, mere rest, or a change of scenery, he recovered; but he endured recurring bouts of anxiety and psychosomatic digestive ailments all his life.[10] In 1911 his friend Henry Adams, a fellow sufferer from depression, counseled him against overwork and too much reflection.[11] Reid was later sufficiently concerned to suggest that Cortissoz lighten his burdens. "I have often thought that his work would be somewhat improved by his doing less of it," he wrote a manager at the paper.[12] Cortissoz married Ellen McKay Hutchinson, a literary editor and reviewer for the *Tribune,* in 1897; and his marriage helped balance his life, though his wife also suffered from nervousness. Like Kenyon Cox, Cortissoz found in the art experience a sense of importance and wholeness that fulfilled basic emotional needs. As he said in midcareer,

"Our immortal longings are imperious and in the long run they are satisfied. Beauty is an element, and we must breathe it, like air, else we perish."[13]

Anyone who wrote as much and as long as Cortissoz did was bound both to alter some opinions and to retain certain fundamental views. Cortissoz changed, and his taste remained catholic, but his criticism rested on certain lasting ideals. He took as a guide Matthew Arnold, whose call for a careful and formal criticism in literature and the arts had a powerful impact on many late nineteenth-century thinkers. Cortissoz agreed with Arnold's basic observation that criticism was *"a disinterested endeavour to learn and propagate the best that is known and thought in the world."* By *best,* Arnold meant ideas derived from the ancients which had proved through endurance and adaptability their capacity to expand consciousness, explain living, and promote creativity. Arnold preached in a rather muscular style that culture could be learned and applied in daily life to counteract what he saw as the dangerous tendencies toward atomization, excessive individualism, and anarchy in modern life.[14]

Arnold also held that criticism and appreciation were basic in the creative process. The critic was not the equal of the artist but could be a second in the duel against ignorance and narrowness. Culture was a necessary part of life, and the artist was not set apart from social trends or obligations. Criticism needed rules and guidelines that gave it authority based on perception, analysis, and suggestion, all of which established defensible standards of judging good from bad. Arnold, like Cortissoz, held that "to have the sense of creative activity is the great happiness and the great proof of being alive, and it is not denied to criticism to have it; but then criticism must be sincere, simple, flexible, ardent, ever-widening in its knowledge." This goal suited Cortissoz's needs. "Then it may have, in no contemptible measure, a joyful sense of creative activity; a sense which a man of insight and conscience will prefer to what he might derive from a poor, starved, fragmentary, inadequate creation."[15] The critic could thus be an agent for excellence. Arnold, and Cortissoz, disliked the leveling tendencies in modern democratic societies that too often settled for fact rather than larger truth and for sensation instead of insight. But both believed that anyone with sufficient curiosity and intelligence could appreciate the arts. Cortissoz also liked the natural manner in which Arnold wore his role as critic. In 1930 he remarked to a friend that *Essays in Criticism*

(1865) remained the "Hope diamond" among his books for its emphasis on discipline, clarity, and excellence.[16]

In his own criticism, Cortissoz demanded three united qualities in a work of art, "an idea, beauty, and an indication of sound craftsmanship."[17] By *idea,* he did not mean anecdote or incident, elements he hated in painting, but some force that viewer and creator both recognized as part of a large ongoing tradition and that provoked reflection on meaning in life. By *beauty,* he meant a surface and design that pleased the eye, intrigued the mind, and produced harmony and order, the sense of a thing well and completely done. *Sound craftsmanship* meant evidence that the artist's abilities and intentions matched within a recognizable style that moved others.

He spelled out this viewpoint early in his career. In 1894 he distinguished between pictures and art. The modern public too often assumed that reproduced reality was art. "Any case of temporarily arrested motion will make a picture of this sort, as the kodak has proved," he thought. But this was not art, since it lacked the artist's individual expression. "The picture that is also a work of art, however, is one in which a quivering consciousness of the value of each line and shadow has so operated as to make each line form part of an indissoluble unit." Art transmitted a kind of dynamism rather than pure retrospective thought:

> Every work of art fulfills its purpose in striking a chord of intellectual, imaginative, sensuous, or emotional significance. The perfection of this chord is conditional upon the subtle correspondence in degree of exciting power between its component parts, upon the flawless harmony of its forces working to a common end. The secret of creation is nothing if not the secret of construction.

This "constructional idea" involved restrained expression that achieved harmony. It was "an idea which makes for the lucid symmetry of an exquisitely adjusted organic unit. It makes for selection, for balance, for synthesis and proportion and reserve."[18] While a restatement of the classical idea, the dynamism of Cortissoz's thought differed from that of Kenyon Cox, who emphasized restraint and introspection over the kind of controlled action that suffused Cortissoz's ideal. Cortissoz was always careful to separate technical skill from creativity. Many uninteresting and unmoving art works were skillful but lacked the ability to produce a dynamic interchange with the viewer.

These views comprised an open-ended connoisseurship that was available to any sensitive person. It was thus a kind of expertise based ordinarily sensitive denizens of No Man's Land . . ." offered thought-specialized or arcane; it was grounded in intelligent and ordered feeling rather than simple factual knowledge. He would have agreed with the aesthetician Walter Pater, who said in 1873:

> What is important, then, is not that the critic should possess a correct abstract definition of beauty for the intellect, but a certain kind of temperament, the power of being deeply moved by the presence of beautiful objects. He will remember always that beauty exists in many forms; to him all periods, types, schools of taste, are in themselves equal. In all ages there have been some excellent workmen and some excellent work done. The Question he asks is always: In whom did the stir, the genius, the sentiment of the period find itself? Where was the receptacle of its refinement, its elevation, its taste? "The ages are all equal," says William Blake, "but genius is always above its age."

Cortissoz often quoted his own favorite maxim derived from Blake: "Art is a means of conversing with Paradise."[19]

Like Cox, Cortissoz thought art central to society. He also believed that all creative acts represented basic human needs and were linked, whether expressed in words, music, paint, or bronze. This being so, the critic was obliged to know of many things and to see their connections. "Art criticism is not a matter of casual and capricious impressionism," he insisted in midcareer, "but a reasoned activity of the mind."[20] This required constant curiosity in both critics and observers, and Cortissoz steeped himself in a wide variety of art. He ultimately wrote not only about painting but also on jewels, rare book designs, architecture, furniture, and interior decoration. In the 1920s he wrote an elegant essay on the work of the sculptor Edward McCartan, who designed the large rooftop clock for Grand Central Station. Cortissoz pointed out the difficulty of the assignment, given its distance from the viewer and the tendency of hurrying passersby to ignore yet need it. The result was striking and appropriate. McCartan had made time, so vital to the traveler, dignified, noble, and an organic part of the building's design and purpose.[21] The essay typified Cortissoz's idea that beauty was where one found it and always spoke to the sensitive mind.

Cortissoz considered both creativity and appreciation to be matters of tone as well as fact, and his definition of tradition was equally broad.

He understood the academic demand for training and learning, but in the end the process of sustaining tradition was intangible. The intelligent viewer could not be an expert on art and had to rely on cultivated taste and familiar emotional reactions in appreciating it. Tradition was "a striving toward perfection that filters down from generation to generation. It germinates creative ideas. Also it subtly inculcates a feeling for restraint and measure. It discloses ideals of sound proportion. It stabilizes judgment and purifies taste," he said in later years.[22] He would avoid formulas that might stifle creativity but agreed with Edwin H. Blashfield that "all good art of the past is pertinent to any moment that comes later."[23] In a study of Blashfield's work, Cortissoz called tradition "the tribute which the genuine artist pays to the wisdom of the finer souls in the art of all ages."[24]

Cortissoz saw the painter as a special personality, able to condense and unify experience; but he was wary of egotism, or feelings and gestures that did not speak intelligibly to others. Yet he tolerated individualism more than Kenyon Cox did and was inclined to let the painter speak in verbs instead of nouns. In avoiding any fixed commitment to formulas or appearances as evidence of traditionalist intent, he kept the door open to innovation. If the genuinely creative person had something to say that was indeed special and well done, Cortissoz rather thought the result would be within the grand tradition. He also knew how hard it was for the constructive innovator to emerge from established taste and procedure. In the end, he focused on tone and intent in judging such departures from the norm and saw creative genius as having "a zest for what is fine and inspiring, a kindling joy in grace, color, charm, and the indefinable thrill that we get from nature or great music or any noble thing."[25] But like Cox and other traditionalists, he always demanded of the new the password of familiarity in both form and purpose. Change was welcome, but there were no sharp breaks in tradition; and the artist could not abandon some agreed-upon sense of nature and retain an audience.

The American painter John La Farge seemed to Cortissoz the best example of the artist who joined a moving personal style with the ongoing tradition. He dealt with reality but infused it with mood, mystery, and ambiguity that extended the viewer's sensibilities. La Farge was "a type of intellect governing and coloring imagination and emotion and expressing itself with a certain natural tendency toward the grand style."[26] Cortissoz was also fascinated with Elihu Vedder,

Albert P. Ryder, and Arthur B. Davies, who evoked the unknown and unknowable, the unseen but felt, and the allegorical. These "extraordinarily sensitive denizens of No Man's Land . . ." offered thought-provoking mystery and intriguing suggestion. Theirs was the murmur in modern painting, not the shout he associated with other practitioners.[27]

This combination of common sense and high purpose informed Cortissoz's approach to criticism. He wanted a certain intellectual rigor and honesty in criticism but was skeptical about the new scientific approaches that affected art studies in the late nineteenth century.[28] He welcomed historical research that exposed fakes or established attribution but thought such work had little to do with appreciation. He did not think that art history, esthetics, and criticism could be reduced to facts or procedures any more than could painting and sculpting. He also feared that narrow expertise would make art seem complex and forbidding to potential audiences. "Your latterday expert takes himself with appalling seriousness and stands up so straight that now and then he falls backwards," he wrote in 1905. "He is afraid to take a natural human view of his subject, being fearful that if he does so he will be regarded as an amateur."[29] This was a shrewd warning to a generation increasingly captivated with the expert and discrete facts, at the expense of feeling and intuition.

Cortissoz continued to speak for catholicity and common sense. "In advocating the use of common sense in the study of art I am only urging the reader to keep his head and his sense of humor, to be wary of the esoteric qualities commended to him by the pundit of whatever artistic or critical persuasion, to look at a work of art in a natural human way, with an open mind," he wrote in 1913. "Let prejudice and pedantry go hang. Beauty is all. And is it not the enjoyment of beauty that we are all driving at?"[30]

Cortissoz wrote in an engaging manner. In a typical essay, he took the reader through a gallery, studio, or single work as if he were an eye and a voice, explaining appearances and meanings. Each essay had something about the artist, since Cortissoz believed the work expressed the personality. The approach was elevated, but the tone was genial and accessible to any literate reader. He could be acerbic, as in dealing with the moderns, but seldom lost his informality and emphasis on common sense. Cortissoz always appealed to a great many Amer-

Royal Cortissoz in mid-life wearing the Order of
Leopold of Belgium. (Detail. William H. Zerbe,
photographer. Archives of American Art, Smithsonian Institution.)

icans who otherwise might never have looked at art, because he seemed to be a comfortable and human expert.

From the 1890s onward, Cortissoz wrote about a wide variety of American and European art. He followed the exhibitions and activities of the National Academy of Design, the chief custodian of academic ideals. He also watched the development of special groups such as the Society of American Artists that diverged from certified taste and showed controversial work. And he knew many of the artists and their studios. He tried to spend some summers in Europe touring the great museums and looked at contemporary painting in dealers' galleries. He also read widely and took advantage of the increasing number of reproductions and photographs which advances in publishing made available. In the first stage of his career, Cortissoz was well informed about most developments in art. He made less of an effort to analyze or accept the modernisms of his later years.

A major challenge to reigning taste in painting came from impressionism. He first encountered it in the show that the Paris dealer Paul Durand-Ruel brought to New York in 1886, which included examples of the leading impressionists. It compelled critics to confront and judge not only this particular approach but also broad changes that were clearly affecting the art world.[31]

The reaction of a great many American critics, as was the case in Europe, was negative, but Cortissoz reserved final judgment. He realized that painting had been in the process of changing both its appearance and intellectual purposes for some time. Modern democratic societies clearly desired an increasingly dynamic art. The tendency to depict mundane and informal subject matter in terms that people could easily understand was also strong. Even conservative critics realized that the academic approach had to accommodate the growing demand for light, color, and informality in painting. The great issue was how to attain this without abandoning either technical skill in depicting nature or important ideas.

Like many art lovers, probably Cortissoz came to impressionism via the Barbizon school. Only twenty years earlier, the works of Corot and Rousseau had been considered modern French art. A strong American following for them developed. Their technique, which blurred natural forms and concentrated on tonal effects to produce a poetic mood, at first seemed radical but quickly appeared to match their purpose, what Cortissoz called "imaginative naturalism plus individuality."[32] These two qualities, fidelity to observed nature expressed in understandable individualism that provoked unifying thought, were the hallmarks of Cortissoz's idea of change within tradition. In a broad sense, the Barbizon style prepared viewers for some kind of loose effect and blended tones.

Most early attention focused on the impressionists' treatment of landscape and the outdoors in natural light. Cortissoz appreciated this step but had several reservations. Like many early critics he saw impressionism as perceptual rather than conceptual, oriented toward the eye instead of the mind and memory, and enamored of depicting transitory and perhaps unimportant effects instead of enduring truths. The impressionists emphasized the painter's role and vision, and the style seemed to presage a divisive individualism. In his 1894 essay "Egotism in Contemporary Art," Cortissoz allowed a fictional impressionist to state his case:

> This is as *I* see nature. You may tell me that this is an oak, and that those flowers are daisies. Yonder bush may be one of roses. Mais que voulez-vous? I am no maker of catalogues. I do not pretend to tell you just what is there. I tell you what I see there, and what I see is so much tone. I leave it to your cleverness to translate my tone, my beautiful pigments back into natural facts. Presto! I have looked quickly, because a change in the atmosphere will make me see another thing ten minutes later. There is my picture!

This was all very well, and Cortissoz did not dismiss either the technique or the aim. But he found the willful disregard for ideas and palpable form troubling. The approach was "not imaginative, not based on spiritual insight and the formative power of a genius passing loosely related facts through the alembic of his art, to bring them out knit closely together, a marvelous totality. It is pure ocular synthesis, a synthesis founded on the baldest visual experience." It seemed to be a legitimate form of realism; he appreciated its color and light, its obvious vitality and interest in the world. But he also feared that impressionism "marks a step in the wrong direction, in the direction of personality resting satisfied with its own outlook."[33]

In time Cortissoz's views softened. By 1906 he saw the once-controversial Edouard Manet as a kind of classicist, with "a deep general interest in simplicity, in the direct handling of pure color, in the cold and truthful manipulation of values."[34] He came to like the works of Mary Cassatt and admired those of Edgar Degas, though he did not always enjoy them, because they too retained a good deal of formality and emphasis on subject.[35]

He finally considered Claude Monet the most successful of the impressionists. His obvious efforts to record the truths of nature as he saw them was admirable. But in a lengthy, thoughtful review in 1896 of fourteen of the famous series of the facade of Rouen cathedral at different hours, Cortissoz questioned the impressionist approach:

> Imagination, so these pictures seem to say, is a faculty of no consequence whatever. For him [Monet] there is no mystery about the gothic pile which he has attempted to portray. If there is, it is the mere mystery of a mass of stone partially obscured by atmospheric conditions. The poetry of the thing, the fantastic charm of this wonderous structure, the indescribable potency which leads the imagination from base to pinnacle and prepares the observer to accept almost any marvel of pictorial art in the interpretation—these elements he misses altogether.[36]

Cortissoz would have agreed with Kenyon Cox that in painting a subject such as Rouen cathedral, an artist must make some effort to invoke its symbolism, the history behind it, and the human aspirations it involved. To the impressionist it was less, a subject that absorbed or reflected light in certain ways.

Cortissoz continued to appreciate Monet's handling of light and atmospherics. He even liked the diffuse renderings of water-lilies, or *Les Nymphaes,* that occupied Monet's last years. But he still questioned the lack of form and tendency toward mere coloration in some of the master's works. "Better the pedestrian statements of his earliest, most realistic essays than this splash of paint that is not color but only paint," he said of some works in a 1914 retrospective show.[37] At the same time, good impressionism more and more looked like part of the European art tradition. And it seemed beautiful in comparison to what followed. "Beside the vagaries of the Cubist or Futurist it seems very like some ancient academic formula," he wrote in 1912.[38] Whatever his doubts about impressionism's emphasis on appearance and its lack of ideas, Cortissoz accepted its large impulse to depict nature truthfully. "The important point about impressionism is that it kept its eye on the object and painted with absolute directness," he wrote in 1921.[39] But he also regretted that the acceptance of this last major innovative style that was accessible to a large public crowded out a good many other important painters.

Like Cox and other traditionalists, Cortissoz praised the American painters who combined impressionism's technique with an interest in form and composition. J. Alden Weir and Childe Hassam blended immediacy, informality, and rich color effects with a concern for mood and reflection. On the whole, he thought that the American painters' hard-won respectability and recent maturity made them skeptical of fads and innovations that did not endure.[40]

Yet Cortissoz understood as the new century developed that something far-reaching was in the air. He was familiar with the symbolist experiments in poetry, literature, and drama that had affected the intellectual world in the 1890s. There would be some counterpart in the plastic arts. This in turn would have broad social effects, especially relating to the roles of artist and the public.

Any trip to a major exhibition served notice that the earth was beginning to shake. This was especially true in Europe, where the gallery goer was likely to see a broader range of work than in the United States. In 1900, Cortissoz visited the Paris Universal Exposition and found the lavish national art exhibitions both boring and disturbing. The English school, always noted for love of anecdote, the pious tale, carefully arranged landscapes, and animal pictures, seemed not to have heard of modernism in any form.

The French appeared little better in different ways. No one disputed their technical skill, but official support and academic training had produced little that was arresting. Large *machines du Salon* proved the painter's ability to spread pigment if nothing else. Clearly, "the French school of the day will go down to oblivion beneath a chaos of officialism, mediocrity, and mere canvas and paint."[41] The realistic works appeared equally formalistic and repetitive. The lesser national schools, even those of Italy and Germany, with their illustrious heritages, seemed imitative of the French and provincial, lacking any special local character.[42] This sense of stagnation troubled Cortissoz. It revealed how hard it was for traditional approaches to change. It also suggested a coming revolt against official and corporate methods that would deeply affect the artist's role in society.

In the summer of 1906, Cortissoz toured the important European art centers in an effort to judge the current status of painting and to discern its likely directions. The experience was not a happy one. The English had not changed. Most canvases, "conscientious beyond words and ineffably flat," seemed to recapitulate the English interest in anecdote, historical incident, and sanitized landscape. "Criticism beats in vain against that fortress of reaction," Cortissoz said of the Royal Academy. "There is something pathetic and droll about the efforts made to disturb its inertia. One thinks of Sidney Smith and the boy who scratched the turtle's back to give it pleasure. 'You might as well stroke the dome of St. Paul's to please the dean and chapter.' "

Across the Channel the scene was not much better. As always, the French painted well but seemed superficial. "Smart dexterity is at a premium, and the instinct for beauty seems to have lost a good deal of its vitality, when it has not suffered absolute atrophy. The average French picture suggests that modern taste has been transformed into a part of the nervous system and is concerned altogether with sensation, not with principle." Impressionism had long since ceased to shock or to innovate, and most painters had learned the wrong lessons from it. "Impressionism has filtered its way down into modern painting, and the younger men have learned the value of sunlight, if they have learned nothing else, from the revolutionists of the sixties and seventies. Not so many of them, on the other hand, have known just what to do with their new resources; they do not create, they mark time."

He liked the works of Ettore Tito and a group of Italians called Young Etruria, who painted scenes from daily life in a vivid manner that emphasized local color and individual character. He continued to admire much modern Spanish painting, including that of Joaquin Sorolla, famous for outdoor scenes, especially at the beach, that combined intense sunlight, color, and figures. In Germany, he liked the work of Adolph Menzel, Max Liebermann, and Franz Lehnbach, but realized that they belonged to the preceding generation. He found the Secessionist works an appalling forecast of things that might come. These new painters drew in heavy outlines, used strong, often clashing colors, and relied on thick paint rather than formal drawing to create design. Their subjects were often contorted or anguished figures. Theirs was an intense expressionism of *angst,* clearly meant to shock. Cortissoz understood their energy but disliked their techniques and purposes. ". . . the Secessionists riot in nerveless, brutal drawing, in gaudy or morbid color, in thick opaque tones, and in the most dubious taste." Their energy was merely destructive, and "the mission of [these] German painters seems to have been to set the teeth of the connoisseur on edge." A wedge of change had entered the scene. What lay behind it was anyone's guess.[43]

Back in the United States, Cortissoz more and more heard the names of Henri Matisse, Pablo Picasso, and other modernists whose influence seemed to be gathering power. He was a good friend of the modernist champion Alfred Stieglitz, though they often disagreed violently. He saw numerous modernist exhibitions at the famous 291 gallery on Fifth Avenue. He also apparently saw some advanced painting, including that of Cubists, in Paris in 1911, but was reluctant to write about it. He suggested to one editor that "I think you would do well to wait a little while until we have had more of the stuff *shown over here.*"[44]

Cortissoz understood the younger artists' demands for change and for attention to their work. This was only natural in any arriving generation. But there was a sense of larger realignment in thought and perception. He too wished to move on but dreaded the direction. "On the one hand, you have entrenched authority, usually committed to academic formulas and usually rich in mediocrity, preventing the rise of anything new," he noted in 1910. "On the other hand, you have youth and originality, sometimes genius, and always generous ambition."[45] As modernism gained momentum, Cortissoz wanted to like it and understood that the inherited tradition was adrift. But he did not see why this work had to be so ugly in form or violent in intent. It was struggling to express something powerful, perhaps vital, but would find no audience unless it spoke in a civilized tongue. How to be familiar and yet striking was the question.

The modern trends came together for Americans at the famous Armory Show in 1913. Cortissoz knew of the plans for this elaborate exhibition of examples of advanced European and American work. It involved those painters, especially the French, who had moved beyond impressionism into varying kinds of new painting. Each of the many strains in this work had an *ism* after its name, something Cortissoz found disturbing, since its specificity indicated that art was becoming fragmented. His traditional views permitted individual interpretations but involved a basic core of beliefs about technique and subject matter, which he feared the new modernism would destroy, thus weakening the prestige of art in society.

Cortissoz dealt with the broad tendencies common to all the varieties of modernism. These included emphasis on the painter's effort to express feeling, often in exaggerated terms, rather than what he saw in a subject. Most of the new painters abandoned traditional illusionism and perspective, treating the canvas as an arena for interacting planes, colors, and forms. Some, like the Cubists and Futurists, were fascinated with depicting simultaneous states of motion and perception. Others manipulated color in patterns and designs that allegedly heightened a sense of reality that was not obvious to the eye. Some of the work reflected interest in African and Oceanic artifacts, whose exaggerations the moderns thought expressed basic forms and intense feelings that were superior to refined and inhibited western ideas of nature. In general, the moderns wished to condense the impact of nature and action, to attain the elemental in feeling, to allow the artist's gesture to determine form, and to emphasize the uncertain and unknown. As Cortissoz had said for some time, this artistic mode was part of a large change of sensibility in thought and culture, oriented toward the intense gesture from the unusual personality who did not necessarily wish to communicate with a broad audience.

By now, Cortissoz was widely read, and the show's organizers and friends worried about his reaction. Frank Crowninshield, an editor of *Century Magazine* and supporter of the moderns, spoke with Cortissoz about an article he was preparing for the magazine. Cortissoz proposed to deal with modernism in general, since he had watched it for some years, and to review the Armory Show once it opened. He said frankly that "he will be critical and impartial but that he will never be a whole-hearted enthusiast about the movement."[46]

When the show opened, Cortissoz tried to appear detached. He praised the Association of American Painters and Sculptors for staging the exhibition as a service to the interested public. He thought the arrangements superb for showing the development of the general movement and of each artist represented. He went out of his way to praise the committee for displaying American painting, which he thought superior to that of the Europeans because it was less shocking.[47]

Of course, he never hid his opposition. Kenyon Cox, like Cortissoz a leading traditionalist despite their occasional disagreements, stopped at Cortissoz's apartment, hoping to discuss the show. Cortissoz was out but later wrote Cox a lengthy letter explaining his tactics. "I was in strong sympathy with the Armory Show, as a show, and I've been really glad that it included these horrors." For one thing, he hoped the contrast with familiar works would provoke a reaction. For another, he did not want the moderns to benefit from any American defensiveness about comparisons to European art. "Consider what would have happened if they had not been brought over. The crazy disciples over here, constantly appealing to the sanction of things 3000 miles away, would have had the strategical advantage of citing documents unknown to people here, and people would not have been in a position to talk back. Now everybody *knows* and can properly discount the pompous nonsense of the hierophants. In my opinion this completely counterbalances the harm that might nominally seem to have been done." He had talked with the prominent realist painter William Merritt Chase, who was "exercised over the effect of all this upon the student," who might now think that training and study were secondary to mere self-expression. Cortissoz hoped not; familiarity should breed contempt. "It is better for the freaks to have come here and got discredited, than for them to have profited by the glamor that distance lends."[48]

In the intense debate over modernism that dominated the art world in the spring of 1913, Cortissoz spoke for the intelligent, middle-class art lover. He may have started with a certain sobriety, but as the press sensationalized the show, and as the partisans of modernism became more and more shrill, Cortissoz's rhetoric sharpened. He attacked the moderns on both technical and cultural grounds. As a connoisseur he found most of the abstract work ugly, and he disliked its slapdash appearance and rejection of traditional design and craftsmanship. Forms meant nothing unless they were recognizable; the artistic act was useless if it did not communicate to others; spontaneity was mere chaos without a broad cultural point. He also disliked many of the moderns' sober colors and weak light. This seemed an odd return to the studio, though he understood that the moderns rejected impressionism as merely another form of realism that depicted surface effects and did not deal with essentials of movement and meaning. And he especially disliked the distortions of forms and figures. He granted the artist more freedom of expression than did Cox but demanded that a picture resemble reality as seen through a special temperament that affected an audience.[49]

He objected to the moderns' insistence that a picture had internal conventions and rules and need not depict reality. This approach, in his view, saw all subject matter as a set of formal problems. The landscape, figure, or still life thus became unimportant, either as aspects of nature or human activity. Such art turned away from society and humanity, despite the talk of intensifying experience or finding the supposedly real qualities of nature in abstract forms and arrangements. The

79

change in technique involved a new sensibility. The moderns "simply stand for a sharp, and on the whole, sudden break with the existing order of things."[50] This was not necessarily bad, but any movement that proposed to replace millennia of art should have better credentials than he saw in the new painters. He focused this belief on a dislike of the "egotism" he saw among them, which he thought would destroy art's cultural influence if it triumphed. "What chiefly impresses me about him [the post-impressionist] as a type is his conviction that what he chooses to do in art is right because he chooses to do it."[51]

The militant adversarial stance the modernists took against other painters and critics was also offensive. He did not think they were gods descended from the sky to dispense a new order of thought. Those who disagreed were not all blind or ignorant. "The playgoer who does not like dirty plays is denounced as a prude; the music-lover who resents cacaphony is told he is a pedant; and in all these matters the final crushing blow administered to the man of discrimination is the ascription to him of a hidebound prejudice against things that are new because they are new."[52] This apparent arrogance reinforced the basic fear that Cortissoz shared with Cox: the public would connect art with the irrational and bizarre, and the artist would lose whatever prestige and authority the preceding generation had gained.

Cortissoz saved his harshest words for cubism, which he thought either a bad joke or mere sensationalism. He could not believe that its apparently arbitrary jumble of planes and generally muddy coloration represented any sense of reality:

> It is like the monstrous potato or gourd which the farmer brings to the village store to see if his cronies can make out in certain "bumps" which he indicates the resemblance that he has found to General Grant or the late P. T. Barnum. It is even more like what one would contemplate if a perfectly respectable wombat, finding himself in the midst of one of those gigantic colored vessels which stand in a druggist's window, should suddenly go quite mad, thrashing about him and causing great havoc.[53]

In other cases, he granted the artist a certain sincerity and striving to communicate, even if he did not think the results successful. This was roughly true of Cézanne, an artist who puzzled traditionalists. Many of his canvases bespoke an impressive monumentality and concern for interpreting the basic forms and forces of nature. He had moved beyond impressionism to a quest for essentials and aspired to a grandeur derived from classical sources. And he had an important artistic attribute, the power to disturb. But his paintings seemed unfinished, halting efforts that fell short of realization. Cortissoz attributed this to lack of ability; "he simply did not know his trade."[54] He continued to doubt Cézanne's abilities or the merits of his new viewpoint, even as the painter became a major influence in art history. Cortissoz wrote in 1929 that "there has always seemed to us a measure of uncertainty about him, as though he somehow lacked the technical authority to transmit his vision in full-rounded perfection."[55]

He was less uncertain about the work of others. "Picasso, too, the great panjandrum of the Cubist tabernacle, is credited with profound gifts. Why does he not use them? And why must we sit patient, if not with awestruck and grateful submissiveness, before a portrait or a picture seemingly representing a grotesque object made of children's blocks cut up and fitted together? This is not a movement, a principle. It is unadulterated 'cheek.' "[56]

Vincent Van Gogh seemed to epitomize the "egotism" that so offended Cortissoz. He recognized Van Gogh's immense energy and desire for expression. But the raw crudeness in Van Gogh's paintings well illustrated the dangers in abandoning technical and intellectual approaches that permitted coherent expression:

> But as he grew more and more absorbed in himself, which is to say more and more indifferent to the artistic lessons of the centuries, his pictures receded further and further from the representation of nature, and fulfilled instead an arbitrary, capricious conception of art. The laws of perspective are strained. Landscape and other natural forms are set awry. So simple an object as a jug containing some flowers is drawn with an uncouthness of the immature, even childish, executant. From the point of view of the Post-Impressionist prophet, all this may be referred to inventive genius beating out a new artistic language. I submit that it is explained rather by incompetence suffused with egotism.[57]

But Cortissoz reserved his harshest judgment for Henri Matisse, an artist he pursued for the rest of his life. Matisse already had a following in Europe and had abandoned traditional principles of design and draftsmanship in favor of strong colors that often clashed, bold outlines, and motion indicated through distortion. His figures were recognizable but were often drawn with broad sweeps of paint. He also enjoyed arranging colors and unusual forms in patterns. This was hardly unique among moderns. But the high colors that interested other critics seemed garish and untruthful to nature to Cortissoz. The playfulness and energy in many of Matisse's canvases struck him as shallow. On the whole, Matisse seemed to be a clever decorator whose works lacked ideas or complexity. They might be attractive but were never moving. He had "proceeded to paint his nudes and his studies of still life not with the naïveté of a child, but with the forced simplicity of an adult playing a trick."[58] He thought this especially disturbing since the approach seemed to devalue art.

Cortissoz devoted most of his criticism of the Armory Show to the much-touted Europeans because he assumed that their work would create the greatest interest and need the strongest refutation. He benefited from a residual American desire to see European culture as decadent if not depraved. As a counterpoint, he praised the native works at the exhibition for their sobriety and technical skill. After the show closed, he began urging the public to buy American artists as an expression of confidence in their ability to compete with the Europeans.[59] In any event, he believed that his views had their impact for the good. "Let me add, by the way, that I have been greatly tickled over the reception given to 'The Post-Impressionist Illusion,' " he wrote an editor. "From every direction I have heard the most sympathetic things about it."[60]

The debate over the new art subsided by 1914, when the world war turned public attention to larger issues, but Cortissoz kept up a steady drumfire against modernism. Like Cox, he seemed to fear that for some unfathomable reason it would triumph. In 1915, he continued the attack in reviewing the works of Picasso, Duchamp, Derain, and others. In company with many observers, he found their survival odd. "We cannot believe in their staying power. It is ill repeating a tasteless jest. In time, we are sure, the new experimenters will come to themselves."[61] As the world entered a new era after 1920, Cortissoz summarized his dislike of modernism: "I disbelieve in modernism because it seems to me to flout fundamental laws and to repudiate what I take to be the function of art, the creation of beauty. If modernism has anything legitimate to substitute for the experience of the past it is under obligation to make a convincing demonstration; the burden of proof rests with the innovators."[62]

As with all creative movements, the first wave of modernism had a powerful impact but spent itself rather quickly. It left a curious and divided immediate legacy. Something styled *modernism* infused the arts of the 1920s, but abstraction did not dominate. Instead, an emphasis on simplicity of form emerged among many new painters. Older artists generally continued their familiar styles but steadily eliminated detail. This paralleled a trend in the popular advertising arts, which fostered a modish tone of *chic* that rested on technical simplicity. Subject matter was wide in range, with renewed attention to urban themes and types that reflected changes in the nation's economic and social development. The classical emphasis on allegory, whether in murals or easel works, faded but occasionally took new forms in public buildings. And an attenuated yet often beautiful impressionism recorded the country's landscape and attained a wide following.

Contemporary foreign work was regularly exhibited and drew considerable comment. But there was a curious ambivalence in the art world of the 1920s, which strove simultaneously for some kind of understandable painting that reflected an individualistic and dynamic current life, with its bases in machine technology and democratic tastes, and for continuing interest in the inherited tradition. Between 1920 and 1940, when another great war dominated events, the American art world saw an impressive number of retrospective exhibitions of all kinds of painting. The struggling heroes of the late nineteenth century often became the old masters of the mid-twentieth. Cortissoz had some reason to believe that modernism would become merely another historical style. The wish no doubt fathered his thought that at least it would not dominate. During these years he treated modernism rather like an unwanted relative who came to visit and threatened to stay. He was not entirely negative about some American modernists and kept up his relationship with Alfred Stieglitz. But many of those whose works had so agitated people before 1913 already seemed remote. He thought that most modernists, like the enthusiasts in any movement, would disappear in time.[63]

Yet he kept ready a sharp eye and pen, especially for the Europeans. He developed a distaste for the German expressionists, who struck him as crude and barbaric, qualities he had attributed to German culture in general during the world war.[64] His review of a major show of contemporary German work in 1923 was typical. "We do not see in them pioneers, inventors, the carriers of a new and valuable gospel.

We see in them only a company of ill-equipped and tasteless artists, the best of them, such as [Emil] Nolde, giving away their birthright for an egotistical and sadly ill-mixed mess of pottage."[65] He thought their art reflected a decadent culture, toward which most such expressionism pointed, another form of the alienated egotism that had no moving message for others.

The French school remained an inviting target, and he continued to attack its drift toward abstraction and introspection and lack of apparent references to life. "If a new heaven and a new earth were ushered in by the Armory Show thirteen years ago it is high time that they exposed some eligible sites," he wrote in 1926. "Instead of which we are vouchsafed a work like M. [Francis] Picabia's 'Peinture,' wherein what we must assume to be trees have their trunks fashioned of what looks like spaghetti, with heads made of feathers. Wearily we ask again, what of it?" On the whole, despite modernism's striking effects and many varieties, it already seemed repetitive and predictable. "Our own impressions are of a yeasty fermentation getting nowhere."[66]

The Americans remained more cautious than the Europeans. Cortissoz appreciated the continuing insistence on formal design, rich effects, and action; but this too seemed unsatisfying. Bryson Burroughs, Edward Hopper, and Jerome Myers were among many painters whose work he reviewed at a typical exhibition of 1928. It was all very interesting, though not very exciting. "But leaders of distinction are not readily discernible, and in no quarter does there seem to be anything like genius stirring." Perhaps this absence reflected deeper social change and was evidence of the artist's turning inward. "The creative energy of the period, so abundantly manifest in the fields of science and engineering, is apparently in abeyance where the painter is concerned."[67] Thus neither the moderns dealing in abstraction or symbolism nor the traditionalists attempting to retain recognizable interpretive art were satisfying. There was a general sense of marking time. But the great enemy was still the alienated moderns. "I fight them steadily because I believe they are downright harmful," he wrote a friend in 1927. "Sooner or later these silly egotists will go to the scrap heap. But in the meantime they are ruining the younger generation."[68]

The 1930s were a time of troubles for the world. A crushing depression and political turmoil compelled a reexamination of both the individual's fate and the nature of society. The arts inevitably reflected efforts to explain the failure of the gods of materialism and progress and to chart directions. Dada, which began earlier in the 1920s, received renewed interest. This movement, which emphasized the random aspects of life and sought to cast off the past and cautious rational thought in favor of whimsy, the unpredictable, and spontaneity, troubled Cortissoz.

He found the Museum of Modern Art show, Dada and Surrealism, in 1936 both irritating and disturbing. The works were certainly unusual, the various manifestos even more so. "And what do we see?" he asked. "For one thing, an actual wire cage containing lumps of real sugar, a masterpiece by Marcel Duchamp which is entitled 'Why Not Sneeze?' It might be argued that this is an extreme case, but in essence it is representative of the blague which prevails in this exhibition." But he thought that Duchamps's avowed stance as an "anti-artist," a term that meant he rejected past formulas and dogmas, was ominous. "That is what the exhibition essentially stands for—anti-art—in standing for distortion and willful obscurity, for the grotesque and preposterous. Its influence, if it has any, can be only of a disintegrating nature."[69]

Surrealism posed additional challenges. Cortissoz rather liked Salvador Dali's technique, which was in the great tradition of meticulously finished painting. He was clearly talented and "capable of extraordinarily skillful miniaturistic effects. He is also capable of a certain breadth, and his 'Puzzle of Autumn,' with its fine landscape and luminous sky, is undoubtedly the best thing in the show."[70] But the meaning of these extraordinary canvases, with their limp wristwatches, swooning telephones, silken clouds, and bizarre figures was another matter. They were in a grand tradition of disturbing allegory that went back to Heironymous Bosch, but they spoke in symbols that seemed deliberately obscure. "What meaning have the paintings?" he asked in reviewing a Dali show three years later. "So far as I can make it out, no meaning whatever. They are supposed, I gather, to express various movements of the subconscious mind, but those movements wander inconsequentially from a telephone receiver to a landscape, from one fantasticality to another. He is, by the way, distinctly addicted to the telephone. But I am afraid it persistently vouchsafes him only the wrong number."[71]

Surrealism reflected the continuing effort of many artists and thinkers to find hidden meanings and motives in life and the personality and to accept unpredictability and irrationality. It had great impact on many art forms. But Cortissoz and other critics found it distasteful because it emphasized uncertainties, ambivalences, and tensions in both individuals and societies. It seemed morbid and decadent, perhaps understandable given the times but hardly a viable substitute for traditional ideals that promoted harmony and unity.

Cortissoz had suggested for years that the final stage of modernism would be emphasis on pure color and line, an abstractionism that arrived with some force in a Museum of Modern Art show in 1936. He had watched the trend away from interpreting familiar form since the 1880s, when impressionism focused on light effects. This latest departure from nature and familiar illusionism into individual expression through abstract forms did not impress him. He thought it had few links with human culture or personal life. It seemed lifeless and contrived, detached and machine made. Piet Mondrian and Kasimir Malevich said nothing to him except that they could produce lines and masses not found in nature.[72] When he celebrated his fiftieth year as an art critic in 1941, he said candidly of nonobjective painting: "I'm not interested. I think it leads to an impasse."[73] He meant that art could not abandon natural forms and that the public would not forgo the depiction of natural and human actions for abstractions. This trend, in his view, would only increase the separation of artist and public.

During these years Cortissoz reviewed a good deal of American art with relief. Many American modernists were as advanced as their European counterparts, and Cortissoz dealt them the same criticism. Others sought new moods and aims with more traditional techniques. Cortissoz remained a fan of Arthur B. Davies, whose allegorical nudes and mythical animals in exotic landscapes placed him in the tradition of La Farge, Ryder, and Vedder. His work was symbolic but understandable, a "fusion of tangible and intangible things."[74] He liked the paintings of Guy Pène du Bois, whose decorative scenes of street and café life retained realism, action, and character in smoothly painted, rather flat, outlined figures.[75] He praised Georgia O'Keeffe's ability to express emotion and power through impressive familiar forms. "And modernist, though we suppose she is to be designated, she shows in this picture that one may be representational and yet remain a true artist. All that is necessary is to turn the bald fact into beauty, which is done in 'Taos Pueblo.' "[76] That building, reduced to elemental and strongly stated architectural forms, resonated with the power of both the landscape and the Indian culture it represented.

The shock of the depression and its effects on inherited values and attitudes turned many artists inward to private musings and anxieties. But it also revived a broad interest in familiar subject matter and realistic methods. Many artists returned to older themes and values. Even in 1930, before the depression's full effects were obvious, Cortissoz had praised the developing regionalism typified in the works of John Steuart Curry and Grant Wood. He thought their designs striking, well made to evoke unifying memory, a sense of place, and personality. He especially liked Wood's portrait *American Gothic*.[77] He also thought it good to celebrate America's diversity.

In 1934 he reviewed a show at the Museum of Modern Art of 135 pieces of federally supported art drawn from 15,000 examples. He saw little genius but thought the level of technical performance strong. And the works spoke to a continuing high level of public interest in familiar art.[78] A second show of New Deal art at the Whitney Museum in 1936 revealed how much this strong current of American art had returned to depicting daily life and locales. It was homely narrative painting by and large, but it occasionally revealed flashes of originality and the power to evoke sound ideals from the American past.[79] The New Deal murals for public buildings were equally interesting, though Cortissoz missed any sense of real grandeur or exalted purpose in them. They tended to deal with daily life, which seemed curious to one who had matured on the works of Cox and Blashfield. But perhaps the world had lost faith in such older ideals; the reassurance of the normal and homely was enough for now.[80]

Much of Cortissoz's art criticism in the 1930s showed a sense of marking time, of having had his say. This was partly a matter of aging, no doubt. But it also reflected the simple fact that cultivated Americans and artists no longer seemed to have the strong sense of working toward important purposes that had informed art in his youth and middle years. Modernism had certainly baffled a good deal of the potential audience for culture, but it was in his view only one force that dissipated art's momentum as a cultural force. The arts had to compete now with more democratic forms of expression, such as movies, radio, and popular writing. Cortissoz never believed that the mass of humanity would turn to high culture. But as the century wore on, he thought support for creative artists and for art in general declined.

He wrote in a different tone about his first love, architecture, which attracted much of his attention in the 1920s and 1930s. He knew New York City best and naturally focused on its development in analyzing architecture. He recalled vividly how the city had struck him as a young man working for McKim, Mead and White, while dreaming of a career in journalism. The city radiated the energy in American life, with rivers of traffic, colorful people, and a fascinating commerce and industry. But his eye was always on the esthetic, and he perceived even as a youth that the city's architecture and general appearance did not really match its vitality and ambition. The traditional American aversion to planning, plus New York's remorseless crowding and verticality, often as not made it seem confused and threatening rather than challenging and exciting.

Many streets had rows of buildings in clashing styles. Others, at the opposite extreme, presented a monotonous line of brownstone or cast iron fronts. Individual houses varied in style from the eclectic Queen Anne to mock colonial to various French and Italian mélanges. Tall buildings were often covered with inappropriate ornament or did not take advantage of their one great attribute, the sense of upward thrust that symbolized the city's ambitions. Statuary often seemed designed merely to occupy otherwise unusable sites. Aside from Central Park, parks appeared to be afterthoughts or false oases in the endless bustle. Cortissoz had no quarrel with an enlightened eclecticism and did not want a city of uniform buildings. But New York did not please the eye or exhilarate the mind. A directionless individualism seemed the norm.[81]

Of course, it was hard to say what historical urban precedents best suited the American experience. Cortissoz did not believe that most American cities, and certainly not New York, lent themselves to the style of development typified in Paris, with huge formal plazas, elaborate monuments, and wide boulevards. In any event, this was impossible where basic street plans were long since established. Older cities such as New York, Boston, Baltimore, or Philadelphia had developed in bits and pieces, with strong neighborhoods. He thought that planners should try to develop schemes suitable to the functions and histories of such districts and neighborhoods.[82]

Cortissoz thought Italy exemplified the best combination of tradition and changing urban needs. That country's smaller towns retained their historic charm and local importance. Some of the larger ones, such as Venice, were picturesque but functional. Rome boasted a great variety of buildings and had changed over the millennia, yet it retained a sense of intimacy. Its monuments impressed but did not really over-

awe the viewer. Their materials had aged well and gave the city a rea-
sonably unified and pleasant appearance, despite congestion and decay.
Human scale and human needs prevailed. The Italians had tried to
unify the arts in civic expression, and churches, public buildings, monuments, even housing in varying degrees involved the artist. "In them
you see architecture, painting, sculpture, cooperating in the production
of one effect, all working in the grand style, all aiming at nobility of
conception, largeness of execution, and that simple canon of perfect
equilibrium which is at the root of beauty," he wrote in 1895.[83]

At the same time, Cortissoz liked some of the large-scale approaches
to urban development of Daniel D. Burnham and other architects.
These City Beautiful plans, with large axial designs, groups of monumental buildings, parks, and statuary, could work where there was
room to grow. They should retain a human scale and try to make the
city part of the larger landscape.[84] Urbanites like Cortissoz tried to
make cities more than just places to live or conduct business. They
sought a mass and sense of power that did not overwhelm people and
an orderliness that was not monotonous. Above all, they wanted an
architecture and cityscape with historical associations that would give
city dwellers a sense of being part of the larger world of culture, as well
as that of current business. Americans needed an urban ethic to complement their long-standing emotional, or sentimental, regard for the
rural setting. With a sense of history, decoration, and human scale,
cities could become urbane as well as urban.

This approach involved a strong sense of tradition, which Cortissoz
defined as loosely for architecture as for painting. He wanted architects
to study historical models but not to adopt formulas. They must seek a
sense of past and present times, of the culture that produced the buildings, not merely the component parts. The "essence of good architecture is a flexible searching for grandeur of effects, an aim incompatible
with any rigid adherence to academic rule," he noted in 1895.[85] The
innovative architect made a personal statement within this tradition,
derived from the Greeks and Romans, as modified in the Renaissance.
This allowed a good deal of eclecticism, as in the case of a favorite
architect, Charles Adams Platt, who worked in a simplified classicism
for both public and domestic buildings. But the resulting tone, as with
Cortissoz's conception of traditional painting, emphasized harmony
and continuity.[86] In the 1920s, Cortissoz insisted that Henry Bacon's
Lincoln Memorial was appropriate to its subject. It did not represent

Grecian architecture so much as Grecian ideas. It was quite suitable to Lincoln's character and to his insistence that the United States belonged to the ongoing ages.[87] Cortissoz continued to preach the need for architecture to express continuity as it adapted to modern demands and tastes and for buildings to symbolize their functions. For both architect and viewer, the successful building involved "an atmosphere, a stabilizing habit of mind, a fundamental principle," he said in 1940.[88] Building was a public act that affected surroundings and people even more than painting or sculpture. And buildings were more permanent than paintings, obliged to outlast the moment of their construction.

For Cortissoz the work of McKim, Mead and White best combined traditional and modern architectural forms and ideals. He had admired the partners since working as their office boy in the 1880s. Stanford White was a genius at decoration and design, while William R. Mead guided the firm's office and financial affairs. But the soft-spoken, reflective Charles F. McKim developed the firm's architectural projects and left his mark on American building. Much of their early work was in domestic architecture for the wealthy, especially in the fashionable seaside resorts of the northeastern coast. But by the 1890s the firm was noted for its public buildings, especially in New York City. Cortissoz thought that the perceptive McKim had studied the city's architectural chaos and determined to change it. He believed that the wealthy individuals, societies, and corporations that dominated the city's cultural life were ready for refinement rather than mere display.[89]

Richard Morris Hunt had popularized modified French architecture, especially seventeenth-century château style, chiefly for the homes of wealthy patrons. Henry Hobson Richardson had adapted the romanesque, emphasizing mass and strong forms in rough-hewn granite. Both had sought to integrate American ambitions and taste into world architecture, with appropriate emphasis on the country's wealth and power. McKim in turn opted to combine elegance and a suppressed sense of authority in a modified Renaissance Italian style that seemed suitable for some businesses, and especially for colleges, clubs, museums, and government offices. McKim thought that this style would promote order, retain human scale, and provide esthetic pleasure with its proportions, appealing stonework, and interior decoration. The style had served the great Italian Renaissance commercial centers well and seemed appropriate as a way of shaping the expansive American spirit of enterprise. "Pure line, deftly balanced mass, graceful and not too lavish decoration, with a perfectly rationalized aim underlying them all, would win us from the nondescript and the uncouth, from meaningless form and redundant color," Cortissoz remembered. "We would yield the more readily, too, as this reign of law was humanized, made not only significant and authoritative but beguiling."[90]

McKim, Mead and White's greatest buildings were successful because the partners' talents were so harmonious. They were outstanding examples of Cortissoz's belief that a group of individualists could function without becoming a formalistic school. They treated each building as an artifact that must match the site, symbolize its avowed use, and represent traditional institutions and ideas. Cortissoz said of McKim something that could apply to the body of this firm's work: "When he built a library or a church, a club-house or a state capitol, he left it a building with a soul."[91] McKim steadily reduced ornament until the buildings fitted the modern interest in mass. Their proportions, graceful appearance, and careful decoration all tempered the American urges toward display and bigness.[92] The firm did not simply adopt historical appearances; it stated the tradition in each building. Cortissoz thought this style superior to the revived Gothic that was also popular because the latter was too closely identified with church architecture. He also thought the Parisian Beaux-Arts style too grand and official for most American buildings, though he often admired it. Modified classical and Renaissance styles were more appropriate to the sense of secular power in modern, democratic societies, even as their grace and rationality tempered that power.[93] Especially for public buildings whose functions had historical roots, Cortissoz continued to favor traditional styles, which would survive for more than one generation. He admired the simplified classicism of John Russell Pope, who designed several major official buildings and monuments in Washington, including the National Gallery of Art and the Jefferson Memorial. And he liked the similar appeal of Cass Gilbert, who also sometimes used a more informal Mediterranean style.[94]

The twentieth century brought a prosperity that lasted with only brief interruptions until the Great Depression of the 1930s. Large cities such as New York witnessed a building boom that supported a succession of architectural styles. Cortissoz understood that cities were like great beasts, forever molting or shedding their architectural skins in favor of something for a new taste and need. He did not expect a uniform style of building but hoped that each generation's architecture would reflect tradition while serving its own immediate demands. But he deplored the thoughtless destruction of famous landmarks such as Hunt's Vanderbilt houses or Stanford White's Madison Square Garden, [95] and he found the rush after efficiency and cost-effectiveness shortsighted. Buildings were more than places to work or live; they must answer community needs for some kind of inspiration. The great days of Hunt, Richardson, and McKim yielded in favor of too many architects who seemed to be engineers and accountants rather than designers. By the 1920s, Cortissoz had enough cultural authority, not to say bald candor, to tell the members of the Architectural League to their faces that such technicians were shirking social responsibilities. "They stand for an alliance between the sketchbook and the checkbook," he said in 1923.[96]

Cortissoz paid special attention to skyscraper design, which dominated any city's appearance and ambience and for which an apparently endlessly expanding New York was a laboratory. He realized that each skyscraper was the equivalent of a neighborhood, requiring internal power plants, transportation and maintenance systems, and office and service space. Each must also in some way express the importance or purpose of its workers. For him the great esthetic problems in skyscraper design were to avoid subordinating people to the building's mass and to provide decorative forms and facades that logically evoked historical associations.

The skyscraper, though it well expressed the American drive for the practical, powerful, and energetic, nonetheless should not overwhelm occupants or observers. As these buildings approached fifteen or twenty stories in the early part of the century, he praised Daniel Burnham for combining decorative stonework and window treatment with an impressive bulk in such structures as the Flatiron Building in New York. Yet he knew that skyscraper design was esthetically difficult simply because of the scale involved. "Are any of them beautiful, in the strict interpretation of the word?" he asked in 1907. "Hardly that. Theirs is the beauty of fitness. They are beautiful as a great warship is beautiful."[97]

The problem of combining appropriate decoration and efficiency increased in the 1920s as the technology of steel skeletons permitted higher and higher buildings. The dizzy prosperity of that decade reinforced the notion that "the American skyscraper is an expression of the genius of a people."[98] Could it also combine a sense of history with the current generation's often blatant concern for material progress? Cortissoz thought this was possible in the hands of a master designer. One answer was to be creatively eclectic, combining ornament with basic modern forms in a way that captured the spirit rather than the mere appearance of different eras. He liked the Tribune Tower in Chicago, which boasted Gothic ornament, including a crown with flying buttresses. Though later disparaged among architects, this building was widely praised at the time. Cortissoz thought the modified Gothic was appropriate since it expressed the soaring spirit of that prior age as well as the present. He liked the American Radiator Building in New York. This striking building rose in a dramatic sheath of black bricks; the Gothic ornaments that marked its setbacks were touched with gold terra-cotta. The total effect was one of appropriate upward motion and historical associations. The coloration made it seem one unified structure; and the architect, Raymond Hood, avoided the bands of windows that made so many new buildings seem monotonous.[99] Cortissoz also praised the Empire State Building, the latest word in simplicity. It rose from the street with perfect ease and great dignity. Carefully proportioned setbacks gave it a sleek, powerful appearance. It was unornamented, but metal window frames and a mooring mast crown kept it from seeming bare or monotonous. Its great height dominated midtown Manhattan, a kind of decoration in itself.[100]

But Cortissoz remained uncomfortable with the prospect of a city filled with skyscrapers. They could express power and ambition, efficiency and utility, and might even produce a certain exhilaration; but they would always diminish people. He also distrusted the growing tendency toward sheer bulk and the aversion to ornament in skyscraper design that grew during the 1900s and 1930s. New York City's height ordinance of 1916 had caused architects to develop a style that set back tall buildings at given heights to increase air circulation and sunlight for the street below. This hastened the tendency toward external simplicity, as in the McGraw-Hill Building of 1931, the city's first truly modern skyscraper. It rose from the street, with windows running in unadorned horizontal bands, the entire structure recessed at several levels. A colorful terra-cotta sheathing enlivened it somewhat, and it had a clean-cut, boxy appearance that seemed ultramodern to some but very strange and bare to the traditionalist.

Cortissoz liked the sense of power and cleanness in many of these buildings, but not their impersonality and banality. He feared that the city would end up with artificial walls or clusters of such "vertiginous verticality" that they would obliterate older, more comfortable, structures and increase the city's already unfortunate impersonality.[101] They would also diminish the architect's role in favor of a corporate blandness. "These buildings have a majesty of sheer bulk to commend them, but it is a terribly bleak majesty, and it is gained at the expense of one transcendently important element, that of artistic individuality and character," he wrote in 1930. "The architect, to my mind, is nothing if not an artist, a sensitive creature, full of imagination and personality. How much of him is left by these bald, factory-like facades, reduced to a common denominator which makes the work of one firm look astonishingly like the work of another?"[102]

Nor could he believe that the occupants of these skyscrapers were comfortable. "What a vivid sense they give us of the prosperity and efficiency of which we are so proud!" he wrote in 1930. "But what does the businessman, the occupant of, say, Room 5682, think of it all?" Cortissoz thought he knew. While walking past these new buildings, he saw trucks unloading Oriental carpets, marble fireplaces, Tiffany lamps, carved moldings, paintings, and statuary for offices and lobbies. Controlled temperatures, swift elevators, even the view from the fiftieth floor, all had their place. But there remained the basic human need for color, variety, and contact with the great traditional styles.[103]

In his attention to the dominant skyscraper mode, he did not forget more intimate and eccentric buildings. He often walked past McKim's Gorham Building, done in his usual Italian manner in modest height, which suited its commercial functions and also made it a delightful place to visit or work in. He spent much time in the Bowery Savings Bank across from Grand Central Station. This splendid building boasted a lavish lobby with huge columns of different colored marbles, mosaics, a coffered ceiling, and other decorations that delighted the eye and somehow seemed appropriate to a countinghouse. The Cunard Building in the financial district, with its tiled floors, elegant murals, and fine brasswork, was the perfect anteroom to an exciting sea voyage.[104]

It was not surprising that he disliked the first designs for Radio City, which became Rockefeller Center, in 1931. This massive group would displace blocks of familiar buildings from Cortissoz's youth. He thought the proposed structures overweening and too plain. More to the point, they would likely become the model for the next generation of architects. The final design did provide more open spaces, walkways, and decorations both inside and outside that tempered the center's formality and scale.[105]

Cortissoz remained skeptical in responding to European architectural modernism. In 1932 the Museum of Modern Art exhibited models and drawings of works in an unadorned manner emanating chiefly from Germany, soon called the International Style. This approach was already well known among advanced thinkers in Europe and reflected many twentieth-century social and esthetic trends. Its German spokesmen, such as Walter Gropius and Ludwig Mies van der Rohe, believed that architecture should embody a democratic sense of equality. Overt ornamentation or spectacular effects were bourgeois or aristocratic and had no place in modern building. In esthetic terms, the style, whatever its variants, represented similar urges in painting and literature for condensed forms and simplicity, which its practitioners saw as a new kind of classicism based on unadorned mass and fundamentals. The approach also celebrated modern machine technology; glass, steel and aluminum, plastics and other such materials should replace traditional stonework. Each structure must develop organically and express its purpose and circumstances through materials appropriate to modern times. History must yield to contemporaneity, with the suggestion, or dogma, that modern civilization was in the midst of a fresh dispensation that required new expressions, an idea that Cortissoz had rejected in dealing with the first generation of modern painters. Though these architects built some small-scale and domestic works, attention naturally focused on their industrial, commercial, and office buildings.[106]

Cortissoz had hoped that the American approach to a new architecture, especially for large buildings, which had been developing in the 1920s would become a world style. It steadily simplified appearance but employed stone and tiles for coloration and texture and used ornament with appropriate historical allusions.[107] The new European approach now incorporated all the tendencies he had hoped to avoid. "This modern architecture marks the abdication of the architect as artist and his subjection to a mode of international standardization," he wrote in reviewing the Museum of Modern Art show in 1932. "He accepts a common denominator of expression, employs metals and glass, or stucco and glass, in long, low horizontal lines, rarely allows himself so much as the ghost of a cornice, and eschews decorative detail as though there were something evil about it. If he has any ideas of beauty they lie in the profundities of 'functionalism.' " The definition of this quality was exceedingly narrow. The "positive acres of glass" in most of the buildings might appeal in Germany but would intensify glare and heat for the unfortunate American occupants. Flat roofs posed another problem for most of the world's climate. *Bleak* was an adjective he used several times to describe the result. "These architects are evidently unaware that architecture is a thing to contemplate as well as to use, and what is ordinarily meant by 'beauty' is mysteriously absent from their productions."[108]

His dislike rested on more than mere pique. He did not believe that the twentieth century marked a new dispensation. It was part of the ongoing tradition and needed references to the past. Any esthetic that relied on contemporary technology and its forms risked producing art and architecture that would be stranded in time when people moved on to other things or recapitulated the past. He especially doubted that the penchant for the unadorned would satisfy most people. This puritanism would fail in the face of mankind's love of color, variety, and display, no matter how technically efficient it seemed.

The European theorists thought the new architecture celebrated democracy and equality in easily readable forms. Cortissoz thought it would rapidly express impersonal business and governmental power. He dreaded the anonymity such buildings would bring to congested cities. Nor did these structures gain importance or authority from symbolizing their functions, a cardinal rule of traditional architecture. The office tower, courthouse, museum, factory, and college gymnasium all looked alike, as if architects were afraid of the historical functions behind them.

He thought this was a cyclical change of taste, and as with so much of modern painting, doubted that it would command long-term popular allegiance. Architects, like painters, might go their way, perhaps for some time; but would the public really follow? He was skeptical, holding as usual that there were no sharp breaks in tradition and that the new had to prove its merits. "I am a traditionalist, long convinced that the historical styles have been developed by slow evolutionary processes and that an impalpable element called 'beauty' has tinctured them all," he wrote in 1933. "I likewise believe that the results of sudden, theoretical experimentations are to be approached with very careful consideration. On the other hand, my mind is open to new ideas and I have no more prejudice against the new movement in architecture than I have against the precession of the equinoxes."[109] He continued to think that these buildings had "the bare majesty of a packing box, with arbitrarily broken horizontal lines."[110] By the time the International Style appeared, Cortissoz was old enough to see that it would go through the usual cycle of creative efflorescence, repetition, and decay. But there was less content in this style than in most, less chance to vary its basic formulas. The classical and Gothic lent themselves to cyclical refurbishment and modification. This style did not. It would end in banality, like the abstract painting he disliked.

Cortissoz wore his credentials as a cultural spokesman lightly, however authoritative and sometimes outrageous the tone of his writing. He was a genial and respected figure in the cultural world of New York City and beyond and had a wide range of acquaintances in journalism and the arts. This lion of the galleries and showrooms was a lamb at home and at the office, an authority in print but not among friends and coworkers. He retained the regard of many with whom he disagreed, such as his friend, the militant modernist Alfred Stieglitz. Cortissoz was also a good friend of the expansive critic James Gibbons Huneker, a major spokesman for the early moderns. Huneker once wrote a thank-you note: "My Dear Royal. Both by name and nature so."[111]

Cortissoz's workspace revealed the genial side of his nature. His office in the Tribune building was stacked with books, clippings, photographs, and papers. He eagerly showed his modest but excellent collection of drawings to any willing visitor. His longtime secretary remembered him fondly, while despairing over his work habits. Facing the overflowing office, he would remark: "We must be neat by being ingenious!" He visited galleries and shows before noon during the art season, then lunched with friends and reported to the office for work. He wrote by hand but also used the Dictaphone, carefully spelling out difficult words for her. He wrote smoothly, with little revision.

He was an engaging talker both in private and public, full of puckish wit, with a fondness for elaborate puns. He once attended a dinner at the Players Club and rose to make a few remarks as a mock bishop. Instead of the usual blessing "Benedictus, Benedictus," he playfully said "Benedictine, Benedictine," only to have a fellow guest gently pull him down on the assumption that he was tipsy. When his invalid wife died in 1933, his circle of friends became that much more important, for Cortissoz had no family. He encountered many famous people and usually took them in stride, but was occasionally awestruck in the presence of celebrities such as the actress Billie Burke.[112]

Golf was his great private passion, an outlet for tension and a means of exercise. It developed for him, as for many other people, an almost mystical quality, properly seasoned with good humor. He even wrote a paean to the game in 1922 entitled *Nine Holes of Golf.* "If golf were only a game it would not appeal to the meditative man," he wrote. "But it is, far more, like Platonism, a habit of mind. Hence its lure. In tennis you are confined to one spot and exhaust yourself in acrobatic exercise like a squirrel in a cage. In baseball you sit in the bleachers and howl. In golf you do not loaf, not by any means, but you invite your soul."[113] This passion resulted in a good deal of banter with his more sedentary friends. He lunched often at a special table at the Coffee House, which boasted a silver plaque at his seat: *Hic Sedet Regius Cortissoz in Cespitibus Audax in Asperia Hilaris.* (Here sits Royal Cortissoz, audacious in the fairway, hilarious in the rough.)[114]

Despite a remorseless writing schedule, Cortissoz became a well-known figure in other roles. He lectured to many groups in the East and Midwest that were interested in art. He had an informal conversational manner and often employed slides and photographs. He usually enjoyed the lecturer's role and needed the income but in time wearied of the work.[115]

As his cultural authority increased, he was sometimes called upon for unusual duties. His gift for clear language made him popular as a writer of mottoes for monuments and organizations. The most important such occasion came when his friend Henry Bacon, architect of the Lincoln Memorial in Washington, asked him to devise an inscription for the space on the wall behind Daniel Chester French's great seated statue of the sixteenth president. Cortissoz, of course, was a fervent Republican and a great admirer of Lincoln. He had some doubts about finding the proper words. But after much thought and a moment of inspiration, he wrote out an elegant text that captured Lincoln's striking combination of simplicity and grandeur:

IN THIS TEMPLE
AS IN THE HEARTS OF THE PEOPLE
FOR WHOM HE SAVED THE UNION
THE MEMORY OF ABRAHAM LINCOLN
IS ENSHRINED FOREVER

Bacon thought the words inspired and secured their adoption, ignoring some changes that President Warren G. Harding suggested.[116]

Despite his cheerful demeanor, Cortissoz sometimes reflected on the inevitable discord and occasional enmity that followed in the wake of any critic. Judgment necessarily caused anger as well as friendship.[117] The insulated world of art, like that of politics or perhaps any other profession, held its grudges. On being nominated for the Century Club in 1920, he worried, needlessly as it turned out, about being black-balled.[118] His friend Edwin H. Blashfield thought him a "predestined protagonist" but admired his consistency.[119] As time passed, Cortissoz had few regrets. "As an art critic, I have been a 'square shooter,' knowing neither friend nor enemy," he wrote late in life. "My belief, as an art critic, has been, briefly stated, that a work of art should employ an idea, that it should be beautiful, and that it should show sound craftsmanship. I have been a traditionalist, steadfastly opposed to the inadequacies and bizarre eccentricities of modernism."[120] All in all, "What happy years they have been."[121]

Cortissoz celebrated fifty years as an art critic in 1941 and continued to write for the *Herald Tribune*. He kept to a demanding writing schedule and professed to enjoy his work, which kept him interested in the world as well as in art. He was effectively retired when World War II came; and time inevitably took its toll, marked in the passing of friends and the accumulation of ailments. His energy declined, and he went to fewer and fewer shows and social gatherings.[122] He was mortified to break a leg in 1943 on the golf course "of all places," as if this were sacred and immune ground. He wore an uncomfortable cast for some time, then hobbled about on a cane.[123]

At the time of his death, on 17 October 1948, Cortissoz was clearly a figure from the past. The art world was poised for another cycle of modernism. Like Kenyon Cox a generation earlier, he would have found no home in the postwar world. He often counseled friends of like mind that history had its long as well as short cycles of taste. The modernism they disliked might triumph for a time, might even produce some lasting work; but tradition as they knew it would not cease. As he told a friend in 1933, "old ideals are really not superseded. Don't worry about being 'old hat.' Take it rather as a matter of pride and honor. It means fidelity to what is right and fine."[124]

His sense of history must have shaped any reflections on the value of his life's work and legacy. He had been an enthusiastic supporter of many current trends when he began art criticism but became a nay-sayer as modernism dominated art discussion after about 1910. It was always easier to be enthusiastic than admonitory. Cortissoz warned against easy acceptance of the new and untried because he did not believe that humanity changed its tastes or needs as much as modernists held. His criticism rested on coherent principles which he believed would endure precisely because they were rooted deeply in human experience. These were chiefly the need for order and familiarity while progressing and an insistence that the art experience unify rather than disturb. And while genius had its claims, art had broad social responsibilities; the true creator must not abandon either tradition or the public.

Cortissoz was wrong in his judgments about the impact of many moderns. His dislike of Cézanne, for instance, rested on an inability to see that this painter had changed the terms of the debate about art. Cortissoz would have been surprised at the following that developed for Picasso and would have doubted its depth. The art world's acceptance of nonobjective painting after 1945 probably would not have seemed so surprising, since it was the logical culmination of devaluing the object and observed nature. He would have doubted that this art appealed to any broad public.

His apprehensions about the general impact of twentieth-century modernists on art appreciation and on culture in general retained considerable validity. The art critic ceased to be cosmopolitan and spoke to and for a small number of followers. Formalism replaced taste as a guide. The painter gained acceptance within that small world but was likely to attain mere celebrity or notoriety in the world at large, which seldom understood or patronized the works involved. The alienation of the twentieth century brought the occasional artist foward, but in a diminished social role, as traditionalists had foreseen.

Cortissoz's long effort to find harmony and unity rather than unsettling innovation in the arts reflected a belief that tastes and needs changed slowly and broke with unifying precedents at their peril. His catholic taste allowed him to see the value of art in almost every corner of life. He also realized the tenuous nature of most social relationships, especially those that benefited from the order the arts brought to civilization. He dreaded a culture without a sense of its past because such a void necessarily meant a lack of direction. A society that lacked esthetic taste or that did not support culture was most likely composed of atomized individuals and at the mercy of destructive swings of temper and mood.

Pablo Picasso. *Nude,* 1910. (Charcoal on paper, 19¹⁄₁₆ x 12⁵⁄₁₆ in. All rights reserved, The Metropolitan Museum of Art. The Alfred Stieglitz Collection.) This is typical of the abstract works shown at the Armory Show which the traditionalists could not take seriously.

Cortissoz spoke for more people in his lifetime than any other American art critic, though numbers are no yardstick to immortality or correctness. Yet the long historical cycles he spoke of may yet favor his belief that people will not accept art that fails to interpret nature in ways they can understand. Modernism of all forms at its best will always be a great addition to the arts, but perhaps not the dominant and certainly not the final word.

FRANK JEWETT MATHER, JR.

The Humanist as Critic

Frank Jewett Mather, Jr., was an educator and scholar, then became a widely known art critic, and ended his career as an art historian and museum director. He considered all of these roles educational in the best sense of the word, a purpose that befitted his descent from one of the sons of the famous Reverend Richard Mather, who settled in New England in 1635. He was born on 6 July 1868 in Deep River, Connecticut, as his father was before him, who must have influenced his children a great deal. The elder Mather studied briefly at Brown University, then at Albany Law School. He practiced corporate law in New York City during a long and successful career, traveled in the South and Midwest on business, saw a good deal of Europe, and met many of the famous people of his day. He bequeathed to his namesake a strong interest in nature and never fully accepted the changes that people made on the tangled and romantic landscapes of his youth. He had a deep sense of living through confused and exciting times, which saw revolutions in technology and thought as well as politics and economics. Whether or not this was progress he could not say. A fatalistic sense of the tenuous nature of civilization befitted his puritan heritage. All of this doubtless reinforced the son's interest in history and in the problems of social development that ultimately led him to study art, even though the father candidly admitted to lacking an interest in art. The senior Mather also passed on a sense of detachment and good humor. At the age of 92 he finished a memoir with the wry observation: "Meanwhile, I sit beside the sea and await the muffled oar."[1]

The son had a keen intellectual curiosity and chose a path to scholarship and college teaching. He graduated from Williams College in 1889, then entered graduate school at the new Johns Hopkins University in Baltimore. This institution was already famous for programs in both the sciences and humanities that were modeled on German examples. This meant for the Ph.D. candidate a specialized regimen. Mather chose German studies, English, and the history of philosophy, with a special interest in linguistics and Anglo-Saxon language and literature. He took the much-discussed and praised seminars of inten-

sive and individualized study for which Hopkins was noted. His dissertation, "The Conditional Sentence in Anglo-Saxon," argued that this
dead language deserved study for its own sake, as well as for its influence on modern English. This viewpoint was important to those who
sought to modify the importance of Latin on English and to emphasize
the significance of nonclassical languages for modern tongues in
general.[2]

Mather received his doctorate in 1892 and published his dissertation
the following year. His personal interests were more catholic than the
curriculum revealed. In looking back on the graduate grind, he was
grateful for the credentials of scholarship but retained a sense of
humor about the process of getting them. He had "followed the
straight and narrow road to a Johns Hopkins doctorate, had emerged
from the mill, to change the metaphor, with much of the juice squeezed
out of me, but with enough left to know that I had been squeezed."[3] He
soon developed strong doubts about both the practical and intellectual
merits of the increasingly narrow Germanic approach to academic
study and learning. He thought German educators overemphasized
detailed research at the expense of analytical thought in the student
and ended up relying too much on methods and theories that fragmented knowledge. "You may crack a filbert with a trip-hammer," he
said in 1901, "you may put *wissenschaftliche Methode,* too, to the most
trivial uses." He hoped that German academic leaders would return to
the emphasis on general knowledge that had characterized the preceding generation's approach. "It meant, besides unsparing industry in the
mere accumulation of facts, a certain constructive quality of mind
which mastered the facts and set them in philosophical relations."[4]

He was a good scholar, displaying flashes of wit and insight, and
already wrote gracefully. In 1892 he was one of two Johns Hopkins
students representing the university at ceremonies marking the three-
hundredth anniversary of the founding of Trinity College in Dublin.
Academic life continued to beckon and in 1893 he began to teach literature at his alma mater, Williams College. He developed an additional
interest in French and studied a year in 1897–98 at the Ecole des
Hautes Etudes in Paris with the famous Gaston Paris.

The collegiate generation he taught was small, mostly the children,
usually the sons, of affluent parents who, like their offspring, were
interested in the prestige of going to college rather than in learning. At
first Mather was as naive as any other young, new professor, certain

that his subject and his interpretation of it were paramount in intellectual life. But he did have a sense of history and of humor and focused a rather bewildered criticism on the attitudes of mind he saw in the charges who sat through disquisitions on the origins of language and the importance of literature. They were supposedly more knowledgeable about the world than was his own generation. Editorial writers and commentators on education often noted their alleged open-mindedness. Mather thought these conditions existed but warned that the student mind opened only toward the future. These young people saw the past as a huge reservoir of error that their generation, with improved instincts and opportunities, would avoid. Science and technology would continue to bear them away from these dark ages. "There was neither admission of any achievement in the past nor any charity for its too evident shortcomings," he recalled. "It was simply wrong—a thing to be thrown overboard as soon as youth should get its rightful control of things." This was characteristic of any new generation but seemed especially strong in the one he taught. "The future, on the contrary, was going to be completely bright and right. For this good reason the up-to-date mind should open only in that direction."[5]

He detected energy and optimism but little if any interest in ideas or analytical thinking. Like most Americans, youth focused on solving isolated problems with little sense of complex causes or processes. Optimism and belief in automatic progress would see them through to success. He worried over this and later devised an ideal program that required basic but broadly conceived courses, strict faculty counseling, and tough grading and deemphasized the social life that attracted students. But as time passed and he had the perspective that alternative employment provided, his senses of proportion and humor also governed. "I have found that a faithful professor may hope to do much good to a few students, that he may so conduct himself as to do no palpable harm to the rest, and that they all quite apart from lectures and classes do a lot of good to each other," he said in a Phi Beta Kappa address at the University of Cincinnati in 1920.[6]

Then there was the other, separate world of scholarship. His hope that academic life fostered cultural and intellectual development wilted rather quickly under the hot suns of administrative decisions and faculty conclaves that were far more interested in the minutiae of status and procedure than the life of the mind. He lamented the growing trend toward specialization, which his own training epitomized. It compartmentalized learning, inhibited communication, and too often made professors antagonists rather than colleagues. It also steadily separated scholarship from society. He was already a good traditionalist, emphasizing continuity rather than change in human affairs, preferring the general to the specific, seeking a unifying emotional experience as well as intellectual stimulation from his studies. Scholarly specialization and faculty life worked against all of this with a vengeance. "The great divisions of knowledge have not changed since Aristotle; ten thousand young men represent no more needed types of education than do one hundred," he said in his Phi Beta Kappa address in 1920. "Indeed, their need to cultivate a certain elevation of mind and to acquaint themselves with the best that has been thought and said and done in the world, is absolutely uniform," he noted, perhaps unconsciously paraphrasing Matthew Arnold's famous dictum about the best.[7] Education, like art, had a large social mission to sustain general thought, especially as the world drifted steadily into a divisive complexity.

Mather quickly realized that little that was truly creative would come from college life. Its routine also countered his curiosity and a desire for some expansive emotional satisfaction from solving intellectual problems. He supplemented this mental fare with large doses of nature. Like his father, he was, in the tradition of Emerson and Thoreau, acutely conscious of natural beauty and nature's processes. They shared a mystical, expansive reaction that enlarged consciousness and satisfied an urge for beauty, while at the same time reassuring the mind that life's processes endured. "When teaching at Williams College I had the habit of climbing the nearby hills toward sundown to see the glory fall and die on the great rimming mountains," he remembered. "On such solitary strolls, I often met a charming German colleague. He always beamed and with solemnity and regularity of ritual would say, 'We must do this, else we die.' "[8] Mather transferred this need for an expansive but reassuring emotional experience to art when the time came.

That moment arrived in 1900, when he left academic life. "In six years I wearied of such well-doing and escaped into New York journalism," he recalled.[9] Mather left teaching with few personal regrets. He had liked many students and colleagues and had pursued his studies. But teaching simply did not offer the unified emotional experience he had sought in academic life. He was not dissatisfied with intellectual life, the pleasures of analyzing problems, or of solving puzzles. He simply found college life cossetted and predictable.[10] But it marked his development as a critic. It had emphasized how slowly people change habits and patterns of thought and how insensitive they could be to intangible experiences. *Ars longa, vita brevis* was a fair motto for the connoisseur as well as the artist.

Between 1901 and 1906 he was an editorial writer for the *New York Evening Post* and an assistant editor for the *Nation*. The *Post* had a distinguished history under the great journalist Henry Villard. The equally famous Edwin Lawrence Godkin had founded the *Nation* in 1865 and, as editor until 1899, made it one of the country's leading independent journals. From 1883 to 1900 Godkin was also editor of the *Post*. Both publications were noted for independence, a touch of eccentricity, and excellent coverage of cultural affairs. Mather's father had a tenuous connection with the *Post* and may have helped secure his son's appointment.[11] In addition to writing editorials and other news coverage between 1901 and 1906, Mather was the *Post*'s art editor in 1905 and 1906, and again in 1910 and 1911. He was also the American contributing editor for the English *Burlington Magazine* from 1904 to 1906.

Mather's interest in art grew steadily, and he reviewed the season of 1905–6 for the *Post* under his own byline. Making the rounds of galleries and exhibitions was sometimes wearing, but he got a thorough understanding of current production and hints of things to come. This steady exposure to a cross section of American and European art widened Mather's horizon and allowed him to be properly skeptical of the inflated claims of new artists and their dealers. Like Royal Cortissoz, he learned not to see a new dispensation in every manifesto. Work as a newspaper critic gave him a strong sense of the largeness and complexity of life, while reinforcing a belief in long-term historical traditions and cycles in art and taste.[12]

Newspaper work was inevitably hectic, and for Mather city life only compounded the rush. Some time in 1906 he suffered an attack of typhoid fever and decided to leave journalism. He had married Ellen Mills in 1905, and the couple decided upon at least a year's stay in Italy, where living was inexpensive and the cultural surroundings pleasing. The truth was that Mather's physical illness coincided with a period of exhaustion and nervous debility that prevented him from planning, let alone completing, any extensive or complex projects.

Frank Jewett Mather, Jr. Apparently a passport photograph, taken c. 1906–10. (Courtesy of the Princeton University Library.)

His wife had a small income which, together with his earnings as a freelance writer, allowed them to live modestly in Italy. He rose late, ate simply, basked in the sun when possible, and walked miles to see ruins and monuments. He also allowed his mind, no doubt wisely, to live out the view of Italian culture that appealed to many thoughtful Americans. Like Kenyon Cox a generation earlier, he admired the ease with which Italians wore their artistic heritage. It seemed part of their culture, rather than a thing apart which people had to be persuaded to see, as in America. He enjoyed the sense of cultural continuity, despite all the wars and revolutions, in Italian life. Art spoke on every street. "I believe it is a good life too," he wrote his friend the philosopher-critic Paul Elmer More, literary editor at the *Post* and *Nation*. "The sense of being in an [elaborate?], fixed, and authoritative social order purges one of the vague unrest that besets one in our mobile society. One drops the vicious assumption of energy as a mere bad habit."[13] Endurance, purpose, harmony were Italy's meanings for him at a critical moment in his life, and these ideas remained the basis of his view of art in society. Small wonder that he referred to Italy as "my second *patria*."[14]

At times he seemed ready to return to the *Post* yet did not. "But visions of a freer life haunt me," he wrote More. "I only begin to realize the awful wastefulness—from the literary viewpoint—of the journalistic routine—the strain imposed by the effort merely to keep pace with the machinery. If there is a corner of the world where one can, by an easier form of self-expression, keep a roof over the head of one's family and bread and wine on the table—is it wrong to occupy that corner?" On other days his sense of malaise and of living at the edge of some abyss were almost overwhelming. He suffered from headaches and thought he had heart trouble.[15]

Mather remained in Italy, enjoying the culture and preparing, perhaps unconsciously, for more intellectual pursuits. Yet he was also a good reporter and wrote brilliantly on one of the century's most dramatic stories. On 28 December 1908, one of the worst earthquakes in history literally leveled the city of Messina and its surroundings in Sicily, killing more than 100,000 people. Mather was among the first foreign journalists to reach the scene and began sending a series of excellent dispatches to the *Post* the day after the disaster. These revealed his ability to see significant details, to generalize, and to speak clearly even in tragedy. He wrote with an artist's eye of the ruins, the survivors' courage, and the fear of disease and famine. The series won him a good deal of praise in journalistic circles.[16]

Paul Elmer More urged him to return to the *Post*, but Mather hesitated. "Whether to come back uncomfortably at 41 to a peripatetic criticism that I may not want to continue for more than 5 or 6 years is a question," he responded in the spring of 1909. "Over here I do at least a little work that somebody might want to read a few years from now." The idea of returning to college teaching was safe but certainly not exciting.[17] He equally feared the ceaseless pressure of journalism; the mere idea made his head ache.[18] Then there was his "Franciscan poverty," a style of life that was pleasant but hardly fair to his wife; nor was it pregnant with better prospects. He whimsically suggested that he might turn to selling pictures, a common enough fate for many expatriates. "There are constant opportunities and aside from a pen which wins more compliments than cash, it is my only moneymaking faculty," he wrote More. "When you come over here a very famous author, you will perhaps find me a portly shopkeeper ready to impose dubious old masters upon all your friends."[19]

It did not come to that, chiefly because Mather met Allan Marquand. This curious figure played a large, if not determining, role in Mather's life and, despite his dislike of notoriety, had a major impact on American art studies. The son of a wealthy New York banker who was also an art patron, Marquand was graduated from Princeton in 1874, then turned from the ministry that had seemed his destination to the study of philosophy and the arts. He received a Ph.D. from Johns Hopkins in 1880 and taught briefly at the College of New Jersey. He then went to Rome to study and became a major patron of the American School of Classical Studies. Wealth allowed Marquand to study in place the art that interested him and to amass a research library. In due course, he focused his attention on the sculptures of the Della Robbias, about which he published several basic works. He also funded many projects in art history and archeology at his alma mater, Princeton, and saw to the establishment of a viable program in these two disciplines there.[20] He liked Mather and in 1910 persuaded him to go to Princeton to teach art history.

Under Marquand's patronage, Mather settled into a long and basically happy association with Princeton. This second academic career was more challenging than the first one at Williams. Princeton was a comprehensive university, with good collections and a graduate program. The university affiliation also added a certain prestige to Mather's byline. He wrote chiefly for the *Nation,* which retained its influence with the educated middle class. Occasionally he professed to miss the excitement of newspaper work. "I regret that I am out of journalism," he wrote Kenyon Cox in 1912. "It is the 'firing line' after all."[21] But he did not miss it enough to return to regular newspaper writing. Instead, he steadily developed a scholarly, thoughtful, relatively calm approach to art and to criticism in the years that saw the battle between modernism and traditionalism peak in the United States.

Much of Mather's influence rested on his mature approach. He agreed with Royal Cortissoz that connoiseurship, catholic taste, and common sense were the true bases of art appreciation and criticism. Mather was essentially a scholar, given to analyzing long-term historical trends in the arts. But he retained an unpretentious air of learning and expertise. His typical review of an exhibition took the pictures seriously, set them in the historical and contemporary context of art productions, and judged both their skillfulness and ideas. His essays and studies were descriptive and presented artworks as expressions of an artist's personality and times, rather than as formal esthetic phenomena. He wrote with a genial, relaxed tone, even while treating complex subjects, and was adept at bringing the reader into the discussion. He could coin epigrams, as in noting that Emile Bernard had not benefited in art history from friendship with Vincent Van Gogh: "It is perilous to fly with a comet; men remember only the blaze."[22] He could be sarcastic, as when reminding moderns that they were not the first to see a promised land. And he was skeptical in discussing subjects that had become arcane, believing as he did that art appreciation, whatever its complexities, was open to every thoughtful person. He never lost the sense that both he and his audience genuinely wished to understand and appreciate the work under discussion as an emotional experience. He often suggested that critics sometimes abandon their technical analysis and simply say what they enjoyed and why. Above all, he understood that critics were often wrong and that good art outlasted bad comment. There were no monuments to critics. In an essay on Kenyon Cox, he remarked, "To read contemporary criticism after fifty years is usually to thank God that we are not as other critics were."[23]

Mather held these catholic and commonsense views in large measure because the authority of criticism was always uncertain. This partly reflected the steady democratization of culture in his lifetime, a point for critics to remember. "The study of painting and sculpture lies pretty far from the interests of the average cultivated man," he wrote in 1910, "and is accordingly invested with the suspicion bred of mystery." He feared the separation of critic and public quite as much as that of artist and public, since he viewed the art experience as a unified whole. In too many cases, critics widened the gap. "It [criticism] has suffered from an assumption that it claims a dogmatic authority, and the critic has been represented as a rather fatuous person who pontificates concerning taste." It was no accident that artists saw critics as pretentious nuisances or that the public often rejoiced in their fall from grace, as in Ruskin's losing case with Whistler.[24]

Mather did not believe that artists were generally able to explain their works and saw the critic as a necessary guide.[25] He understood that the critic and the public both needed informed comment, accuracy, and grounding in history and esthetics. But he did not see why acquiring these skills should make critics a caste apart from their audience. "The art critic, whatever the impression to the contrary, lays no claim to esoteric qualifications," he noted in 1910. "Unlike the poet, he is not born, but made. His curiosity in the direction of art determines his vocation, the rest is training and experience." Just as no artist ever did the final work, so no critic ever had the last word; and humility about the process of judgment was in order. "In short, every bit of our business, save the very small portion that falls under the exact sciences, is conducted simply by the guidance of experienced persons sufficiently united to offer what we call the best professional opinion," he wrote again in 1910. "We act not on certainties, for even the best professional opinion may err, but on probabilities. We know that the advice of the expert is fallible but take it all the same, for we know also that it is the best we can get."[26] Mather was always acutely conscious of the role and final authority of the audience that both artists and critics served. Neither could afford obscurantism or arrogance that alienated that audience. He also knew that Americans cheerfully used experts as long as they appeared to be democratic and as readily disavowed those who took on mandarin qualities. The tendency of modern life was toward complexity of facts and subtlety of effects, whether in business, science, or art. The critic needed a wide, humanistic context to explain esthetic changes and meanings in terms the ordinary cultivated person could understand.

Mather, like Cortissoz and Cox, believed that the artist's creation, the viewer's response, and the critic's analysis were all part of a unified art experience that was both emotional and intellectual. He noted in mid-career that the works of Irving Babbitt, the traditionalist critic and philosopher, had "taught me that enjoyment of art is a responsible act in a life, that its tendency is a function of the work of art and as such a proper subject of criticism."[27] Like all traditionalists, Mather thus sought an intense emotional reaction to art, but one safely focused on harmony and positive expansion that united the artist's efforts and the viewer's needs. As a professor, historian, and curator, Mather continuously sought to bring the cultivated public into the processes of creation and analysis. "We want to be read not only by our academic colleagues," he wrote in 1913, "but by all who seriously love the beautiful objects to the study of which our best energy and enthusiasm are applied."[28] He thus meant to help build appreciation and to secure a place in national cultural life for both artist and critic.

The artist naturally was the center of the cycle of creation and appreciation. Like other critics, Mather saw the artist as an unusual personality who explained nature and life through careful selection and interpretation. Mather studied esthetics and psychology fairly systematically but always enveloped the artist and art appreciation in some mystery. "The true artist is the aristocrat of the eye. He makes his bold exclusions and his stern selections," he noted in 1909. "He looks deep into appearances and is wary of their immediate appeal. Thus he reveals things that the rest of us are too hurried or too untrained to see at all."[29] This gift for selection, symbolism, and intensification depended upon innate personal qualities but also on a wide-ranging view of life. The great artists of the past had studied humanity and nature to see continuity while expressing themselves. To be able to depict wholeness, the artist had to seek it and had to draw upon a personal tradition of broad taste before expressing one in formal art.[30]

Art was a form of thought and feeling that required selection and integration. "An artist is merely a gifted man possessed of a strong and fine emotion which he is impelled to express in his chosen medium and thus communicate to other like feeling men," he wrote in 1913. "This strong and fine emotion, of course, grows out of his own experience—in the case of the painter out of what he has actually seen—tho [*sic*], of course, such experience may be variously recombined and transformed in memory and imagination."[31]

This demand to create order and understanding in the name of harmony made Mather dislike the modern tendency to emphasize the transitory and the superficially dramatic.[32] Beneath appearances there were meanings that could move people beyond themselves and daily life. To elucidate them was the artist's proper role, and the art experience was a process rather than a fact or isolated state. This idea was part of the traditionalist's desire for coherent change expressed in understandable forms that did not separate art and artists from society. Mather understood the modernist's desire to seek first principles and to emphasize forms rather than details. But he feared that this process would fragment both creativity and appreciation. "As a matter of fact, most of the new painting, though it has its happy audacities, remains trivial," he wrote in 1914, "the product of a sophisticated dualism which attempts to isolate the artist from the whole man."[33] Both modernists and traditionalists saw the artist as a special sensibility, but the traditionalist emphasized the need to communicate in familiar ways; there was no genuine creativity without appreciation.

That appreciation involved the ability to understand essentials and to feel their emotional meanings. "To feel quality is the chief business of art appreciation," Mather noted in 1910.[34] Like Cortissoz, he believed that the painter succeeded when he satisfied the viewer's desire to experience perfection and produced the sense of a gesture well done. Like Cox, Mather found art exciting, but its purpose was not to disturb or shock. It extended the imagination toward some ideal of perfection with the feeling of completeness and harmony. "For me the sense of beauty admits all manner of excitement," he noted in an essay on El Greco, "but always an excitement contained within an enfolding serenity." He accepted the traditionalist's basic idea that art unified the personality of both creator and viewer:

> Within limits many degrees of keen emotional experience are possible. But the moment the sheer excitement perturbs the serenity the impression of art is tottering; the moment it prevails the sensation is no longer of art at all. Contrariwise, when the excitement departs, the serenity becomes void of content—a complacency splendidly null. If this be true, the sense of beauty is akin to the feelings that we have at moments of greatest physical and mental efficiency.[35]

That efficiency, of course, represented some personal standard of perfection and progress. An art based on traditional ideas of continuity thus offered the prospect of expanded consciousness and intense feeling without the risks of social disorder or personal eccentricity. Integration triumphed over disintegration. As he put it in an essay on the English painter George Frederick Watts, "Great painting may arouse and calm one as great poetry does or noble music."[36]

Mather amplified these themes in his only book on esthetics, *Concerning Beauty* (1935). He believed that all art appealed to the sensitive personality because it completed unfinished ideas and emotions and corresponded to certain rhythms inherent in nature and human culture. A painting could fulfill through mystery, imagination, and thoughtful design a desire for completeness that no facts could satisfy because the observing mind joined the process. He always believed that "art is a process or a transaction, a becoming—a state of mind in the artist becomes a picture; the picture in turn becomes a similar state of mind in the spectator. . . . The important thing is that the work of art continues to evoke certain exalted experiences."[37] Always there was the desire for productive harmony, the sense of unity that followed creating order:

> The art lover's sense of beauty has a transporting function. It takes him out of a world where nothing is secure and much is confusing and troublesome and makes him free of [in?] a world where rules a secure, orderly and serene activity. This world is mostly of his own making, but of this he is generally unaware, and he gives thanks humbly to those works of art and revelations of nature through which he has found dynamic peace.

Nothing better illustrated the traditionalist's goal of intense yet harmonious action than the words "dynamic peace."[38] For Mather, this process occurred only when creator and viewer employed a common language of symbols, memory, and gestures that aimed to establish harmony and a sense of completeness.[39] This also made the viewer the artist's equal:

> The central figure in esthetics is really the art lover. In the realm of beauty everything proceeds from him and ultimately returns to him. For the artist is only the art lover become creative, while the work of art finds its chief reason for being in the art lover's experience of beauty. Anything like continuity of appreciation, taste as a social and historical factor, depends on the unfailing succession of generation after generation of sensitive and discriminating art lovers.[40]

The modernists' emphasis on individual gesture threatened this tradition for both artist and patron.

Mather was a western man but saw great traditional ideas in many other societies. Like Cox, he believed the basic human urges codified in these ideals were universal and timeless. He knew something of Islamic art. Japanese prints had influenced western painters since about the mid-nineteenth century. Mather thought that Japanese art was robust, sometimes crude, sometimes subtle, yet aimed to retain traditional forms and subjects. But he found Chinese painting the most interesting of the Oriental arts. It seemed to rely basically on the thoughtful, calculated masterstroke, partly because the media of paper, silk, and ink did not permit easy revision. But the Chinese artist, in Mather's view, sought to express personal feelings only in traditional ways. Unlike western art, that of China did not depend on either realism or formal allegory for effect. Its chief aims were refinement, harmonious emotion, and subtle feelings that highlighted complexity, all aimed at the universal rather than the particular.[41]

But as a critic and connoisseur, Mather naturally turned to western art in discussing modern developments. Italy was the great country of his imagination, and her art, especially of the Middle Ages and Renaissance, continued the great ambitions of Greece and Rome. Mather wrote a basic text as a testament to his love of Italian painting.[42] He greatly admired that society's ability to accommodate a multitude of individual talents within unifying styles and traditions over long periods of time. This partly reflected the peninsula's fragmented political development, which fostered localism. But most Italian artists of any stature had tried to express themselves within the unifying direction of major ideals, whether religious or civic, that transcended localities.

Mather wrote a steady stream of comment on modern developments, most of which were ephemeral. But he thought that several great personalities had continued the grand traditions in his own lifetime, sometimes in unexpected ways. Like Cox, he saw Jean-François Millet as a major figure in art history because he combined intense emotions that reflected both social and individual memory, with means that emphasized action and the contemporary. He joined the realistic and allegorical in a powerful sense of unbroken development. Millet obviously had an intensely personal artistic vision yet did not allow it to dominate his desire to be part of the larger tradition. "What seemed wonderful to him was the immemorial existence and toil of the peasant, not himself as perceiving it."[43] Millet's work radiated the assurance that man would survive as part of nature, that history would continue, and that individual lives mattered in that scheme. This regard for Millet occasioned one of Mather's most acute and moving pen-portraits, in discussing the famous painting *The Sower* (1850):

The night when man cannot work is falling, and the Sower lengthens his pace and swings his hand with a fuller pride. Only the tired uneasily upright head tells of exhaustion. The powerful strewing hand seems sacramental; the land rises to a pale sky against which the oxen prepare the field for the morrow. The scale and authority of the figure are like some Grecian metope. It has with the specific beauty of painting, the simplicity and dignity of sculpture. The appeal is heroic. One of an apostolic succession of toilers who have made possible the ever recurrent harvest, looms suddenly and unforgettably before us. We assist at the immemorial act which marks man as man. Nothing human antecedes the Sower, and nothing can supersede him. It is to have made such an eternal symbol out of a mere observation— in his own words "to have given character to the type"—that marks the humanistic greatness of Millet, attuning his particular vision with all the most valuable perceptions and reverences of the race.[44]

Mather saw occasional touches of this ability to create a sense of enduring tradition in some Americans. Like Cortissoz, he admired John La Farge's gift for nuance and mystery in expressing large ideas.[45] He came to respect, often without really liking, the work of Thomas Eakins. His search for character, for essentials rather than mere appearances in both nature and people, placed Eakins squarely in the great tradition of emphasizing enduring ideals and types.[46] And Mather admired Winslow Homer, who somewhat bewildered many American critics who recognized the energy in his work but often disliked its lack of refinement. Mather saw that Homer was interested in the relationship of human beings to the power of nature. His "defects in arrangement and tone" yielded to an obvious ability to depict elemental force and drama and to highlight the human condition that endured even before nature. "A *farouche* quality is in most of his works," Mather admitted, but they had a great presence. "They are as disconcerting as they are powerful and compelling. They agree ill with other paintings, or even with each other. Mr. Cox justly remarks that you might as well let the sea itself into your drawing room as a Homer marine."[47]

Against this concern for endurance and with a personal as well as cultural need for harmony, Mather confronted the procession of styles that engaged him as a critic. The generation of his youth had focused on developing painterly skills, critical acumen, and public appreciation. This produced a potent sense of positive direction and some stability even as fresh ideas and methods infiltrated the art world. In the last quarter of the nineteenth century, certain academic or traditional modes seemed dominant in international art. But the same era witnessed the emergence of various kinds of realism and then impressionism. The new gradually took center stage in art as it did in economics, politics, and social thought. Mather realized that the broad tendencies in new art during his youth involved efforts to answer the modern democratic society's need for excitement, color, and mundane subject matter.

Impressionism was no longer a new idea or method when Mather became a professional critic, but he devoted a good deal of time to analyzing its intentions and results. Like most critics, he took the first impressionists at their word and saw their method as an effort to intensify transitory experience and to exalt momentary perceptions of nature's effects. "Impressionism means, not as is so often maintained, a procedure, but a peculiar kind of seeing," he wrote in 1910. "The artist endeavors to transcribe a scene grasped in the twinkling of an eye. He deliberately excludes memories of similar scenes and all data contributed by other senses than that of sight. He draws as fully as he may upon pure sensation. . . . Such a man is said to have regained 'the innocence of the eye,' and is, whatever his technic [*sic*], an impressionist. The whole issue is not of veracity but of immediacy."[48] This approach created excitement in "reducing the life artistic to a series of keen but disconnected emergencies."[49] It appealed to the apparently endless modern appetite for sensation, for the unusual and the new, and the love of appearance over analysis. "A single, intense moment of sight, and its swift, unmodified record—such are the laws and gospel of impressionism," he held in 1913. "Or more familiarly, the ideal impressionist would be a man without a memory seeing the world from an express train that never repeated its route, and setting down its more vivid impressions during occasional stops."[50]

Critics such as Mather probably overstated the impressionist emphasis on the unreflective eye. The impressionists depicted mood and personality, a process that required reflection and prior knowledge, as well as some kind of composition. But impressionism did exalt immediate sensation and change at the expense of traditional ideals of continuity. This discontinuity disturbed Mather, who held above all that the artists and their work must exemplify integrated personality and harmonious goals. This required discrimination and analysis in treating nature and life. The mind had to control the eye, for the "wise artist learns to bring the whole man—and the most and better part of man is memory—to bear."[51] Mather disliked the impressionists' belief that one moment of nature was as significant as another. Psychology as well as common sense told him that no artist could in fact depict an isolated moment.[52] "There can be no visualization of emotion completely or even largely detached from the whole of the artist's experience. To reject our stored impressions of the visual world is impossible."[53] In any event, this was not a major aim for the high calling of art, which emphasized reflection, analysis, and fidelity to the meanings as well as the appearances of nature. Painting was not a camera. "But the task of the artist will be, as it has ever been, to revise, combine, and articulate these impressions. In such a process there should be not merely no attenuation but actual enrichment."[54]

Mather liked the work of Manet, who retained a strong sense of form and hidden meanings in his best art. He admired much of Monet's output, while disliking his tendency to depict ever more fanciful color and light. He also liked Degas and a few other first-generation impressionists. But he realized that the style would become as formulaic as any other, a tendency which its lack of substance and fascination with the moment intensified. He thought that concern for surface effects, color and light, and the transitory were stages in artistic development. "Impressionism itself is rather a means than an end, a desirable stage in every artistic experience, a crowning stage only in the artist whose life is imperfectly intellectualized."[55]

Later painters took the formulas to their logical conclusions, as Mather thought he witnessed in the work of Joaquin Sorolla. This Spanish painter had an immense vogue in Mather's middle years and was famous for scenes with highly colored and broadly painted figures and forms in strong sunlight. Mather thought these works were attractive but inconsequential. "A great relish has gone into them, but no thought and little selection. They are random sections of a vivid and continuous panorama. He sees much as the kodak or picnicking mankind see, and that is surely the ground of his enormous popularity." The lack of solidity in the forms or of thought in the design made the scenes trivial and decorative. "The picture gives a thrill, and one is content never to see it again. There never will be anything more in it than one has grasped in the twinkling of a casual eye."[56]

Despite his skepticism about impressionism's value or innovations, Mather saw it as a major force in modern art and a logical part of art history, "less an innovation than a revival of beautiful methods of painting which persisted well into the eighteenth century." For all its modernist impulses, impressionism was in the broad tradition of rich color and sumptuous brushwork of the Venetians, Fragonard, and Rubens.[57] He also knew that the "main business of Impressionism was after all simply to let in the light," a welcome process that had transformed all kinds of painting and one which had forced even studio artists to reconsider nature.[58]

But ultimately, like Cox and Cortissoz, he found impressionism wanting because it lacked ideas and did not seek first causes or results. "Possibly the devotion of the early impressionists to mere cuisine has been somewhat exaggerated by the critics, including myself," he admitted in 1934. "But it is certain that they spent an inordinate energy in finding equivalents in paint for the coruscation of light in nature."[59] He preferred an art of reflection and careful composition that aimed to create a harmonious mood and creative imagination. "One may concentrate on the architectonics of a natural scene—and I believe the highest esthetic pleasure from nature lies in this direction—or one may rather follow passively the adventitious epidermal splendors constantly given and taken away by the circumambient light and air," he said in 1935.[60]

Impressionism had its appeals but was part of a larger tendency toward dissolving form and eliminating realistic detail that Mather realized would dominate art in many different ways. He read about European developments and reviewed the growing number of exhibitions of contemporary work. He knew that for better or worse this generation would mark some kind of watershed in the appearance and intellectual content of painting.

On the home front, he found various independent painters interesting. Like so many critics, he did not quite know what to make of James McNeill Whistler, a painter of great skill who obviously sought to elucidate mysteries and moods in nature. Mather found the style unsatisfying; yet he sensed an important ambivalence in Whistler, an alternation between the eye and the mind, the moment and memory, some kind of collective life and an intensely individual viewpoint. He was not sure that Whistler's work would survive but thought that his example might. Whatever his intellectual intentions, Whistler was likely to influence painters with a kind of technical negation that favored mood and dissolved form. In this sense, Whistler's work was part of the broad movement toward abstraction.[61] Mather also praised the mystics such as Elihu Vedder and Albert Pinkham Ryder, who were seeking exalted or complex meanings beyond the mundane. In a curious way, they were part of the traditional approach that looked beyond appearances for first causes.[62]

He also spent a good deal of time in analyzing the popular realists around Robert Henri, whose gospel was action. The group known as the Eight painted with bold strokes and colors that subordinated appearances and structure to a sense of vivid action. They also took art into the city streets as well as the countryside, depicted people in a variety of pursuits, presenting themselves as contemporary and democratic.

Mather generally praised the objectives of these artists, even while hoping for more reflection and finish in their paintings. While these rebels thought themselves a vanguard, Mather more correctly viewed them as rebellious academicians, somewhat like the Munich school or the Society of American Artists painters of the 1870s, who had diverged from the National Academy and certified taste without abandoning many traditional goals. With his usual wryness, Mather suggested in reviewing one of their major shows that "there is more green, yellow, and red sickness about than positive talent." Even so, he preferred this vigor to "the somewhat faded fragrance of attar of roses and new-mown hay that pervades the Academy." He presumed that these talented painters would proclaim their freedom from academic restraints and then become more thoughtful in their work. "Otherwise, Henri, Glackens, Sloan, Myers, Bellows, are merely seeking the forceful notations, the speedy and economical formulas, that, except in time of decadence, have always found favor among born draftsmen," he noted in 1910. He then offered some advice: "There is a note of impatience in much of their work, and often a rather scornfully detached attitude toward the thing delineated. They are overafraid of being sentimental, and they miss some of the brooding qualities that go to make lovely paint and pictures of manifold charm. But at least much of their work is vigorous. It represents us in certain human realities; it is idiomatic, and it tends to offset the impression made by much official art that we are chiefly wearers of good clothes and wanderers in green fields."[63] As he said in 1916, the paintings of the Eight "have always made me sit up. I get the feeling of seeing something for the first time and keenly—of a discovery. Many pictures leave my sitting up muscles unaffected."[64]

This new work was modernist in tone and vigor rather than in markedly altered appearances. Paris offered more unusual changes than did New York. Mather's sense of historical development told him that the arts were approaching some kind of dramatic denouement, which had been emerging for some time. He thought that three profound changes in viewpoint and technique had dominated contemporary painting since his youth. The first was the *premier coup,* or painting directly on the unprepared canvas at the expense of thoughtful composition. This inevitably emphasized individual gesture and the immediate. The second was the concern for light and strong colors, which turned attention away from subject matter to effects. The last was painting in masses and dominant tones that emphasized pictorial composition rather than nature.[65] Altogether these stressed the individual artistic act and eroded the traditionalists' concern for harmony, familiarity, and analysis.

Mather held no brief for formulas and understood the desire to move beyond reigning conventions. But like Cox and Cortissoz, he thought that these developments would forever alter the artist's relationships to society and to artistic tradition. The impressionists had disturbed conventions but remained social in their approach; they had depicted a changing natural scene in individualistic terms yet focused on the real world and hoped to communicate with an audience. Their successors, dubbed postimpressionists after about 1910, appeared to reject the insistence of both realism and impressionism in depicting understandable reality. Whatever their individual differences, these painters opted for personal statements in unusual ways, whose validity both as art and thought rested on their intense feelings. The inner rather than the outer world dominated.

For Mather this was a logical step in the long process of dissolving perceived form and unified ideas. "Already art had been reduced to a vividly quick transaction between the individual soul and nature," he noted in a major article of 1911 on ferment in the arts. "Now nature is abolished and the soul communes spasmodically with itself." The effort to find new technical means of expression flowed from this intense desire to condense basic emotions in striking forms. "Color, for Matisse and his disciples, is no longer representative of anything in nature, but is an immediate symbolic expression of an inner emotion. Beyond this, the Post-Impressionists seek utmost simplicity of contour." This search for new means of expression became circular. The artist felt increasingly separated from tradition and the public and as a result increased an already rebellious expansiveness. Eccentricity became a mark of individualism, and thus the separation increased. The unified cultural life and search for expression within recognized tradition became secondary to personal expression, whose validity the artist determined. This fractured the art community. The entire process gained momentum because of the contemporary ability to publicize and sensationalize the unusual. Whatever sound intentions lay behind the modern impulse, "the tendency of the past generation, emphasized today by the Post-Impressionists, has been towards an individualism wholly self-sufficing and anarchical."[66]

Mather respected the power and potent sense of searching in many of these works. But he feared that the appearance of eccentricity would alienate artist and public and reduce the cultural authority of art. Like Cortissoz, he also resented the apparent arrogance behind many assertions of uniqueness and cautioned moderns to temper their certitude. "But the gospel of simplicity and immediacy may be and is a useful leaven in an art ever threatened by a narrow doctrine of imitation and a false practice of unreflective realism," he agreed in 1912. "Only, in weighing the more assertive works of the Expressionists, we may well insist that vehemence and sincerity, brusqueness and immediacy are not necessarily equivalent. A drawing by Rembrandt is far more simple and immediate than a drawing by Matisse, and also far more refined and powerful. With all Gauguin's energy there is a certain blatancy involved. We should be careful not to mistake mere assertiveness for power."[67] Common sense also told Mather that much of this ferment was cyclical and represented generational changes that time would temper. As he said in 1913, "modern art is staggering boisterously along in untrodden paths because it has found the old high road intolerably dull."[68]

Mather understood that certain basic attributes were common to all the modernist *isms,* but as a practicing critic he naturally treated leading artists whose works summarized these various energies. He spent a great deal of effort analyzing the art of Paul Cézanne. Like Cortissoz, but more perceptively, he realized that Cézanne was a powerful artistic personality seeking to express great verities in new ways. Long isolation and absorption in his own techniques testified to this quest. "Cézanne was a true archaic, painting as if the world began with him," Mather said in 1910.[69] He thought that Cézanne "always remained in intention a naturalist." He wanted to reinterpret nature in some striking way within the grand tradition. "What he wished was to lend classic stability to the rather attenuated visions of the Giverny school. In this he succeeded admirably. No modern painter has so keen a sense of mass. Really to see a fine Cézanne is to have one's eyesight permanently improved," Mather wrote in 1912.[70]

That granted, Mather thought that Cézanne's work remained unsatisfying. There was something austere and passionless about Cézanne, an absorption with formalities and technique that overrode the effort to create a powerful emotive link with the viewer. His typical canvas also had a raw, uncompleted look that indicated more an inability to fulfill his intentions than any new esthetic approach. The fascination with nature's basic forms and actions did not always produce a new synthesis of reality. It was all very well to talk of volumes, contours, planes, and perspectives; but Cézanne's work did not in fact show how either the caring eye or mind perceived nature. His canvases led Mather to suggest that Cézanne failed to satisfy emotionally because "he did not really care greatly about nature. He cared tremendously to be right about nature; his own rectitude was what engrossed him." He added: "In all the Cézanne paintings it is the same time of day and no time of day. He presents only significant structure. He cares as little for specific coruscations as he cares for specific textures."[71] This was a shrewd comment on the practical problem of balancing reality and abstraction and the sacrifice of reality in any fresh definition of pictorial or esthetic purposes in the new painting. Mather concluded that Cézanne failed in his great effort to redefine classicism and to depict first causes in nature. This failure partly reflected technical limitations, but it also revealed the shortcomings of modernism's tendencies toward abstraction, which could not in fact reproduce nature's workings or satisfy the traditional human longing to understand the world in familiar art.

Mather was equally ambivalent in his early criticism of Henri Matisse. This painter and his followers, dubbed *les Fauves* (the wild beasts) in France, seemed further outside tradition than had Cézanne. He made no apparent effort to reproduce nature, and arbitrarily used color, patterns, and masses to suggest familiar forms. Mather found his aim limited, welcome only as it challenged orthodoxy.[72]

Mather praised Matisse's early drawings, especially from the nude. The painter's interest in action and reaction was appropriate to treating the figure. "Matisse conceives the body as a powerful machine working within certain limits of balance," he noted in reviewing a show of his drawings in 1910. "The minute forms of the tackles and levers does not signify for him; what counts is the energy expended and the eloquent pauses which reveal the throb of the mechanism. The important thing is that muscles should draw over their bone pulleys, that the thrust of a foreshortened limb should be keenly felt, that all the gestures should fuse in a dynamic pattern." This vision placed Matisse in the "great tradition of all art that has envisaged the human form in terms of energy and counterpoise"; and it allowed him to suppress naturalistic details and emphasize energy with outlines and touches of paint. Mather, who at this point knew little about Matisse, expected him to influence other artists. He saw his work essentially as a restatement of the classical concern for the eternal verities that the figure represented.[73]

But this regard weakened as Mather became more knowledgeable about Matisse, "whose more ambitious things strike me as so many gravely compiled puerilities."[74] Matisse could not seem to extend his technique into a grand statement, but Mather still thought he delineated motion and energy well. "As to Matisse, I am quite likely wrong, but at bottom we mean different things about him," he wrote Kenyon Cox rather defensively in 1912. "I never have said, or at least have never meant to say, that his drawing was constructively fine. . . . What I do admire in Matisse is what Vasari call *furia,* a dynamic impression that I take it is compatible with very faulty construction. . . . But you see I could admit what you say about Matisse's ignorance, indeed I do accept it, and [still] find him a kind of power *quand même.*"[75]

By the time of the Armory Show in 1913, Mather thought Matisse a failure, chiefly because of his deliberate distortions of form and artifical view of nature and perspective.[76] In the late 1920s he still praised Matisse's early drawings and lamented his paintings, which were "garish and unsteady, splotched with conventionally sharp colors, like a tomato salad with mayonnaise, which are exciting without being really decorative." He thought that Matisse betrayed "no sign of develop-

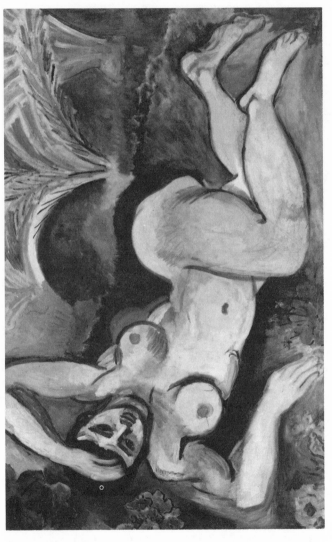

Henri Matisse. *Blue Nude* ("*Souvenir de Biskra*"), 1907. (Oil on canvas, 36¼ x 55¼ in. The Baltimore Museum of Art. The Cone Collection, formed by Dr. Claribel Cone and Miss Etta Cone of Baltimore, Md. BMA 1950.228.) This work, shown at the Armory Show in 1913, is typical of the heaviness of treatment and distortion of figural values that traditionalists disliked in the work of Matisse and other moderns.

ment or maturity. It is the penalty of any counsel of pure lyricism that one cannot grow old gracefully on it."[77] Like other traditionalists, Mather finally concluded that Matisse covered his superficiality with striking patterns of color and arrangements of objects. Unlike Cézanne, he had never even sought to understand or depict nature's complexity. "The declension of Matisse to a merely technical virtuosity seems to me even more marked," he wrote in 1934. "With extraordinary gifts as a colorist and an impeccable decorative sense, he soon drifted into a gypsy eclecticism, to end in a monotony exquisite, to be sure, but expressing nothing save essentially superficial decorative formulas. At bottom he remains merely a fine mannerist."[78] Perhaps Matisse's great sin was to lend a sense of joy and sensuality to the process of destroying the formality and analysis that the traditionalists valued so highly.

Given his study of contemporary art, Mather found the Armory Show both exciting and anticlimactic. Like Cortissoz, he was determined to treat the new art seriously. He wrote a widely read review for the *Nation* that was sober and responsible, though studded with pithy remarks. He praised the Association of American Painters and Sculptors for offering a good cross section of the much-discussed contemporary work, both European and American. The retrospective canvases in the show, designed to reveal modernism's antecedents, were sound. Like many American critics, he feared that the European works would overshadow the American art.

Mather took his readers through the exhibition artist by artist, working toward a general statement about the cultural and artistic tendencies they represented. He found Van Gogh's powerful expressionism interesting and a logical offshoot of some Dutch art, but too raw and individual. Gauguin was a potent abstractionist but a marginal figure. Cézanne already looked like an old master; his canvases did not excite the eye or stir the imagination as they had even five years earlier. Matisse remained effective, sometimes stunning, in figure studies and eccentric and often distasteful in other works. Like most other critics of the time, he reserved harsh words for the cubists. "Upon the Cubist works of Picasso, Picabia, and Marcel Duchamp I cannot dwell," he said curtly. "We seem to have to do either with a clever hoax or a negligible pedantry." Cubists talked of seeking basic forms, depicting simultaneous motion, and rearranging pictorial design. Mather thought the result was simply bad painting, jumbled, muddy, savoring of the studio and of a self-conscious desire to shock, all bearing metaphorical titles that the works did not fulfill.

All the painters were clearly powerful individualists, differing in techniques and aims, but all represented certain changes in intellectual perception and artistic procedure. In one way or another, they assumed that the artist's immediate, intense perceptions of nature were superior to studied compositions. They believed equally that some kind of symbolism better represented the powers and meanings in nature than did any kind of realism. They saw modern life as especially intense, chaotic, and impossible to depict accurately in familiar ways.

Mather disagreed on most counts. He saw this work as an offshoot of the symbolist poetry and literature of the 1890s which he thought ended in decadence because it was divorced from common life. The demand to interpret nature in nonrealistic ways seemed to him a misreading of recent art history.

> The trouble with pictorial art never has been and never can be too great devotion to nature; the trouble with art has been merely weak or undisciplined or dull personalities. The utmost degree of naturalistic representation possible to painting will always be, however limited, wholesome. It will at least celebrate the lovely variety of the world and the joy of the seeing eye, and it will ever serve as the firm base from which imagination may take its flights. For dull or faltering painters, and their feeble symbolism, it is no remedy to throw nature out of the window; public neglect may hasten reform, but the death of the dull artist is the only real remedy. One well managed St. Bartholomew's would do more to set things right than a century of hothouse spontaneity.

The much-touted individualism would simply narrow the artist's vision and make for morbid self-consciousness. If every artist and every viewer saw nature uniquely, social and cultural cohesion, which it was one of art's great roles to support, would vanish.[79]

A week later, Mather devoted another review to the American works in the Armory Show, again fearing they would become lost in the controversy surrounding the Europeans. Like Cox and Cortissoz, he praised the Americans' retention of recognizable form, even while they adopted many modernist techniques. He made several interesting comparisons. He thought that Cézanne and John H. Twachtman were working toward the same ends. Twachtman, an American who died in 1902, was famous for his landscapes, especially those of winter, which flattened and abstracted basic forms in muted colors. Both painters reduced nature to abstract elements, but Twachtman retained an understandable realism and lyrical handling. For Mather the traditionalist, he created a reflective and analytical mood in the viewer without tricks or distortions. Mather thought that Maurice Prendergast's hatched paintings resembled those of advanced Europeans but retained comprehensible form. The Eight were represented, and he continued to praise their dynamism and rich effects. The Americans were clearly more cautious than the Europeans but seemed more intent on retaining ties to the public through recognizable art, whatever their individualistic aims. Mather once again praised the exhibition's promoters and, despite a distaste for sensationalism, appreciated that the show had brought art to the front pages. "There is nothing of the somewhat funereal and dutiful atmosphere that habitually rules in our large stated [staged?] shows," he noted approvingly. "In the Armory people fall into talk, wrangle amiably, readily exchange enthusiasms. To a critic who has been accustomed to see his ministrations accepted with the resignation appropriate to those of the undertaker, all this is inspiring." He urged the art public and painters to attend with an open but skeptical mind and to compare the modernists with their predecessors. "If after such comparisons you honestly feel that the older painting is in any sense put down, and find you crave the new, why, you are entirely welcome to it."[80]

In late March 1913, Mather dutifully reviewed the National Academy of Design's annual exhibition. He took these works as seriously as he had those at the Armory Show. If nothing else, they represented an honest striving for technical skill and interpretation in the grand tradition. The canvases bespoke how much American artists had grown in his lifetime. The landscapes, still lifes, figure paintings, and genre studies all testified to the ability to interpret and depict nature. Yet Mather's review was valedictory. The pictures were competent but seldom moving. The Academy simply preserved "a dwindling tradition" that might return in better times.[81]

Mather's continuing criticism focused more on the new art's social and cultural implications than on specific works. The egotism of the modernists disturbed him, since it willfully separated the artist from the controlling realities of nature. He also disliked the tendency toward morbid introspection, which traditionalists thought had unhealthy social as well as individual effects. He believed that "the layman may well dismiss on moral grounds an art that lives in the miasma of morbid hallucination or sterile experimentation, and denies in the name of individualism values which are those of society and of life itself."[82]

The isolated artist, contemptuous of society or the times, was a familiar romantic image, and there was a powerful strain of romanticism in the new art. But Mather saw a profound difference between the modernists and the romanticists of the early nineteenth century. The earlier romantics, whatever their alienation, continued to analyze and depict the real world and to try to communicate with society. "His [the romantic's] volcanic and imperative emotions he drew, after all, from his reactions to the immense variety of nature, to the extreme joys and horrors of the world of man," Mather insisted in 1914. "Here the Post-Impressionist parts company with the mere Romantic. The Inner Need may grow out of the artist's wider experience, but preferably should not. It is an isolated specialized stress which finds within itself both the motive and the materials for creation." Mather also already saw in the most radical modernists a desire to abandon reality in favor of an abstract painting of lines and colors. He thought this especially ominous since it would divorce the artist from both society and nature and lead to the dead end of self-absorption. He did not consider valid the comparisons of a new kind of painting with music that many modernist thinkers made. Painting could not in fact adopt the allegedly abstract attributes of music and remain expressive. In any event, for Mather music was not abstract in the way these theorists supposed. Music on the page had its formal conventions and abstract qualities. But it was performed as a human act of interpretation, just like painting. "Music itself does not play with fixed abstract terms such as Kandinsky wishes the color to be," Mather insisted in 1914. "An oboe, for instance, is neither a sad nor a glad instrument; it all depends on circumstances. The cello and even the double bass are highly serious or most playful instruments, according to context." There really was no abstract music, only players and instruments—the "nature" of the form.[83]

A curious calm followed the Armory Show and the outburst of deeply felt criticism on all sides. The world war erupted in August 1914, and people turned to more pressing questions. But modernism's effects seemed suspended in the calm that often follows a fierce quarrel. Mather noted the loss of momentum among modernists in reviewing the Forum Exhibition of 1916, which leading figures such as Alfred Stieglitz, Robert Henri, and the militant modernist critic Willard Huntington Wright sponsored. The show was designed to promote American works. It included the advanced paintings of pure colorists, such as Stanton Macdonald-Wright and Morgan Russell, and the works of well-known painters, such as John Marin, and less familiar ones like William Zorach and Marsden Hartley. Mather thought it curious that the moderns, already ingrown and repetitive themselves, attacked academies for being exclusive. Their claim to be important for being serious, spelled out in elaborate catalogues and manifestos, failed to impress him. "Many persons are most seriously convinced that the world is flat, the poor whites of certain southern states are most seriously convinced that clay is a delicious comestible. But their seriousness doesn't matter, and I think the seriousness of these modernists matters very little." It was also ironic that modern works which were supposed to communicate intense experience required extensive explanation. He sensed the drift in modernism that followed the first striking manifestations of any creative impulse. "In short, there is every symptom of an inverted sort of academicism, and none of an unfolding art in its spring-time."[84]

The war that abated the debate between modernists and traditionalists had an unexpected impact on Mather's life. From the first he was an outspoken opponent of Germany. Like most American intellectuals and artists, he saw France and Great Britain as the upholders of western culture and democratic ideals. He thought that Germany's cultural tradition had weakened in the last century as her leaders opted for political and economic power. The individual German seemed subordinate to the demands of the state, a situation that inhibited the free exchange of ideas and the imagination. Prussia had ruthlessly dominated the other Germanic states at the expense of their cultures.[85]

He saw German militarism as a real threat to American interests. The Allies were "merely engaged in a gigantic and most difficult police enterprise against a power which has wantonly broken the peace of Europe," he noted when the conflict was just two months old.[86] Militarism made the new German Empire seem a throwback in history, despite its obvious modern political and economic power. "To be militaristic in this twentieth century is to be an outlaw," he held early in 1915, "and Germany is plainly destined to the fate of a declared outlaw in an aroused and indignant community." The answer was Germany's sound defeat and "conversion from militarism."[87]

As the war developed, Mather accepted the stories of German atrocities in Belgium and other occupied territories. In June 1915, he wrote a letter to the *New York Times,* refuting with great umbrage the observations of another reader that war was hell and the Germans had done little that Sherman had not done in the South. "Major Bigelow is able and lucid, and will be far too shrewd to reply when I ask him simply if the annals of our entire Civil War afford a single realm parallel to the massacres of Aerschot, Dinant, and Louvain?"[88] He welcomed the entry of Italy into the war; one more civilized nation was opposed to Kultur and atrocities.[89] He also challenged those who held that the Allies were exaggerating or manufacturing stories of German atrocities; he steadfastly believed the worst.[90] In any event, he recognized the influence this image of Germany as destroyer of culture and committer of atrocities would have in America. "Where we felt ourselves really champions of humanity was much less in future arrangements for peace than in making the black past impossible, whether in peace or war," he wrote in the retrospect of 1919, analyzing the propaganda effects of war posters. "The artist who silhouetted a Hun leading off a little girl thoroughly understood the thinking of the average American soldier and sailor."[91]

Mather readily joined various academic groups committed to assisting the Allies with their propaganda while the United States was neutral.[92] But it was not enough to talk and write. The forty-seven-year-old professor and art critic took the preparedness course at Plattsburgh, New York, in August 1915. He left an amusing account of the fate of the overage and shapeless patriots like himself who vowed to prepare for service in a conflict they thought the country would soon enter. He did not believe that the usual volunteer army would be ready or adequate immediately after war was declared. Reality required a substantial and well-trained cadre. He found the experience exhilarating if exhausting. As a result of early roll calls, poor food, long marches, and physical training he came to a major conclusion for the art critic: "On their stomachs before the foe all fighting men are aesthetically equal."[93]

Mather was a reflexive patriot but had a well-elaborated view of the world that mixed an idealism about democracy and progress with at least a minimal understanding of why nations behaved as they did. Personally he liked the idea of action in a cause that he thought would save the high culture to which he had devoted his life. He had no sympathy with pacifist academics such as the Columbia professors who opposed American entry into the war.[94] In due course, he underwent training as a member of the United States Naval Reserve and saw modest sea duty off the Atlantic coast.[95] He viewed this service with pride but as usual was wry in judging its intellectual effects. In 1920 he referred to "an obscure eighteen months in the American Navy, where sometimes my associates were men almost without letters, [a condition that] may have helped abate the professor in me."[96] In this wartime duty, Mather represented the intellectual who alternated between reflection and action and between the desire for cultivated high ideals and a taste of worldly reality.

Although hardly in a position to affect national policy, Mather was a well enough known cultural figure to command an audience. His desire for American intervention was well known before 1917, but he also discussed numerous peace plans, all designed to disarm Germany and prevent future conflicts. At the end of 1915, with a deadly stalemate on the western front, he opposed any compromise peace that left Germany a major power. "It seems to me folly to speak of any military conclusion short of a permanently enfeebled Germany, of any moral conclusion short of a Germany honestly repentant and willing to make reparations." True to his professional and personal concerns, he insisted that Germany return any art works taken from France and Belgium and restore the monuments and historic sites destroyed in battle.[97]

When the United States did enter the war, as he knew it would, Mather hoped the Allies would see it through to complete victory. And he wanted an overseas expedition of Americans committed to battle in the trenches, for "the absence of our flag from the blood-stained trenches, where strangers are supplying a human bulwark, would be a notice to all mankind that we are, indeed, a nation of shopkeepers and money changers, truly Pharisees and 'not as other men.' "[98]

In the later, tangled debate over the League of Nations in 1919, he thought the opposition Republicans were "stupid in the extreme." He suggested that the Senate simply vote on the peace treaty, amendments and all, and send it to President Wilson for his approval or rejection.[99] Instead, all parties were intransigent, the League failed, and most of the high ideals Mather had hoped to attain disappeared in the aftermath of what was then the greatest war.

In later years, Mather reevaluated his wartime positions. He never revised his low opinion of German imperial culture, or Kultur as he styled it, or his distaste for German militarism. But he agreed that many Americans like himself had been naive and ill informed about power politics and the dynamics of modern warfare. No one had foreseen the appalling chaos that followed the destruction of the old European order or the appearance of bolshevism and fascism. But Mather remained a patriot, even as he grew more cautious about the world's affairs. He believed that the United States required more modern defense systems than it possessed and that in any event it could not be isolated from the world.[100]

During these busy years when Mather was earning a reputation for insightful traditionalist art criticism, he also pursued several parallel literary and creative interests. Among these was a regard for Herman Melville, known in Mather's youth as the author of *Moby Dick,* "usually regarded as a good whaling book spoiled by a crazy streak of allegory."[101] The poet and litterateur Edwin Lucas White one day read a passage from *Moby Dick* to the young Mather, who instantly found the style and tone irresistible.[102] With his usual curiosity, Mather pursued the subject and saw Melville as a major writer. He found in him the qualities he looked for in good painting. "He combined in an extraordinary degree impressionist delicacy and precision with emotion and mental vigor, and withal a robust humor; he was both drastic and refined, straightforward and deeply mystical, precious and delightfully homey," Mather remembered. And he had a special impact for the traditionalist seeking harmony and unity: "He felt keenly the task of harmonizing so many opposites."[103]

In about 1904, Mather located and visited Melville's daughter, Elizabeth, who cooperated eagerly with this potential biographer. Mather read the family documents in her possession and helped her collect other endangered materials. She in turn gave him two rare pamphlets of her father's poetry, which completed his collection of first editions. Mather then approached several publishers, only to find that none considered Melville significant enough to warrant such a book. He abandoned the project but remained a militant partisan of Melville and had the satisfaction of seeing recognition of this great writer begin to rise in the 1920s.[104] He saw in Melville a great power to disturb, which made the sensitive mind analyze grand themes of the individual's relation to humanity, nature, and the cultural tradition. He saw Melville as a tragic figure in his failure to gain recognition but also as a very human writer, endowed with humor, a great gift for description, and insight into a variety of human types. He admired Melville's ability to write in a style that expanded the imagination and satisfied the reader's desire for grandeur, while remaining rooted in reality.

Mather was also interested in collectors and collecting. He spoke and wrote from personal experience, since he began collecting prints in a modest way as a sophomore in college. During his first trip to Europe in 1892, he picked up some good examples of modern European prints and drawings and also bought some Japanese items. This was a time when prints and drawings lacked prestige, and it was possible to buy good examples of major artists for very little, and fortunately so, given Mather's financial state. His taste was eclectic, but he liked the Italian primitives, as well as many nineteenth-century European artists. Among Americans, he especially favored John La Farge, Albert Pinkham Ryder, Homer Martin, and several Hudson River painters.[105]

This personal interest joined with Mather's ongoing survey of the art world to produce considerable comment on the American collector. The initial generation of collectors focused on well-established masters whose value was known. The first moderns to appeal to them were the Barbizon painters. Many specialized in the works of a single fashionable artist or a school of painters. Impressionism had reached the American consciousness at a moment when many wealthy patrons were open to its appeals, and by the time Mather started writing criticism, it was an important style for collectors. Many such persons also purchased arms and armor, rugs and textiles, glass and porcelain, and sculpture.

Mather began his study of collecting with laments about the apparent lack of discrimination among wealthy collectors. Rather than adopting some unifying principles, they too often bought in job lots, driving up prices and adding dross to otherwise sound collections.[106] At the same time, Mather saw much potential good in such collectors. He merely wished for more common sense, good taste, and willingness to rely on sound advice among them. As he remarked in 1910, "the grievance against the plutocratic collector is not that he affects Rembrandts, but that he does not love those he owns. Any kind of honest love of art must work for the aesthetic good of the country. A fine work of art, we think, is never expatriated where it finds a lover."[107]

The results of all this were evident in the numerous art museums the wealthy founded or endowed with their collections in the generation before the world war. "The time has come," Mather correctly noted in

1913, "when no European student of art history can write exhaustively of any subject without considering examples owned in America."[108] Though he understood that some motives for collecting had little to do with the love of art, he thought the public benefited. There was, after all, no national governmental support for the arts, and little enough at the local level. Any great collections for viewing or study of necessity had to come from private individuals. In any event, this was "vast wealth seeking a novel, interesting, and ideal outlet."[109] In 1934 he reviewed the politically radical Diego Rivera murals at the New Workers' School in New York City. Their depiction of plutocratic capitalists oppressing workers seemed incomplete to him. He held no brief for great wealth but had a nonpolitical view of the collections some of these men, such as J. P. Morgan, had built. "If they rest on blood money, it was blood money well spent."[110]

This interest prompted his one foray into fiction, a series of short stories published as a book, *The Collectors,* in 1912. These were profiles of various types in the art world.[111] There was one on the collector whose prize acquisition might be fake. Another dealt with the famous scholar who destroyed evidence rather than see his pet theory challenged. In others the experts on attribution, the innocent but possibly intelligent connoisseur, the obsessed collector all figured.

The stories were elegantly written and deftly captured the personalities and moods in the world of dealers, connoisseurs, and collectors. They won a small but significant readership and were a welcome creative diversion for Mather. But they also had a serious purpose. They argued that collectors must in the end be public benefactors; those who would not take this responsibility were merely selfish. The love of art was always a superior guide to mere expertise. The art experience was not a preserve for aristocrats or scholars; the captain of industry could become an appreciator of art. The stories also dealt with the various motives behind collecting, whether love of display, desire for social prestige, compulsion to possess and organize, or simply enjoyment.

These interests paralleled Mather's concern for museum development. The late nineteenth and early twentieth centuries witnessed a boom in museum construction, as many cities established or expanded museums. Universities developed special holdings in the arts. Wealthy patrons also founded smaller institutions to care for and display their collections. These new museums testified to the enlarged holdings of art and artifacts in both public and private hands. Part of the effort to make cities attractive centers of culture, they reflected the desire of many Americans to make the country culturally as well as economically competitive with Europe. And they spoke, as did education, to the modern need to codify, analyze, preserve, and use knowledge.

Museum management was a critical aspect of the interconnected art world. Mather noted a divergence of ideas about how to develop museums as early as 1905. The established ideal focused on custodial care, preservation, and the research use of art and objects. The British Museum and its German counterparts exemplified this exclusionary approach. But a new generation of people concerned with museums had different priorities. They believed that museums were essentially educational, engaged primarily in raising the level of public awareness of art and taste, in turn developing sound long-term support for the arts. This meant that a museum showed only its best pieces in ways carefully arranged to create public interest and that it avoided the forbidding atmosphere that often made many amateurs shun the arts. This approach inevitably brought public exhibitions to the forefront. It also introduced a wide range of expertise into museum operations, with special departments and staffs, publications, reproductions, and advertising.

Mather liked most aspects of the new public-oriented policy, which emphasized the patron's role and which he thought suited the present state of American holdings.[112] He also favored the novel idea of traveling exhibitions that in effect allowed institutions to borrow each other's materials. This defied the custodial tradition, but he counseled museum personnel to stop behaving like old-fashioned librarians who disliked allowing the public actually to use their books.[113] He also applauded the establishment of small museums, usually the gift of a single donor with specialized material, such as J. P. Morgan or Charles Lang Freer. The displays and exhibits in these intensified experience and gave an accurate context for the collection involved. Smaller museums were a welcome alternative to the comprehensive institutions that served the general public. "And the art life of a city is richer when, besides its great museums, it has here and there many little galleries which represent, not so much art history, as the personal enthusiasm of some collector of taste, and are a kind of visible counsel of perfection to the entire art-loving community."[114]

He was more ambivalent about other innovations. He agreed with the Metropolitan Museum's policy of accepting copies of famous works, as long as they remained on view only until originals or works of equal merit appeared. He also suggested developing holdings in industrial design, crafts, and furnishings. Beauty was where one found it, whether in wood, pewter, ceramics, or gold and marble. He did caution against making a museum a dumping ground for unrelated artifacts. He disliked the then-current penchant for rebuilding period rooms, chapels, or courtyards inside museums, thinking it false in both tone and content, and preferred models as teaching aids.[115]

Mather later amplified these ideas as director of the Princeton University Art Museum from 1922 until 1946. He continued to favor small, specialized museums to offset what he called the Jumboism of the great comprehensive institutions. These museums might specialize in one large field, such as armor or arms, or they could focus on the art of a period or country.[116] At the same time, he did not want to make the art experience easy or diluted. He insisted that museums were repositories of the evidence of greatness and should maintain an appropriate tone. "One goes there to gain contact with personalities far greater than those we meet in ordinary life. It is no light matter to make the acquaintance of Rembrandt."[117] He was still suspicious of the reconstructed period room or interior because it could seldom reflect the sense of particular time and place that made it. Any art work suffered on being moved; but lighting, good context, and explanation could also enhance its "museum values" and might actually heighten its impact. "The primary value is imperishable: the passing of a high creative impulse to an understanding soul—all this is intact. Indeed, through a degree of generalization and the dropping away of local associations, there has often come a new value of universality."[118] These were all technical matters with important intellectual overtones that any museum staff had to manage pragmatically. But Mather always focused on the primary aim of the art experience, a transfer of creative impulse and enhanced sense of unity to the sensitive viewer. This was especially true in teaching museums such as the one he directed. It was necessary that the staff there introduce art to young minds slowly and logically, with items of genuine quality, and give students access to original materials rather than to books or photographs only.[119]

For one who always professed to dislike the pressures of journalism, Mather had written a remarkable amount of excellent art criticism between 1901 and his wartime service, which started in 1917. The postwar years brought new priorities and activities. Mather returned to teaching and later to directing the university museum at Princeton. He remained a prominent figure in the art world and was a gifted lecturer. He wrote book reviews and essays but concentrated on larger projects that added to his reputation as an art historian. His *History of Italian Painting* (1923) became a standard text for college use. *Modern Painting* (1927) was a popular overview of the nineteenth and twentieth centuries, written with wit and clarity. *Venetian Painters* (1936) and *Western European Painting of the Renaissance* (1939) also became basic works.

Like Cortissoz, Mather sensed a curious calm, almost a stagnation in the art scene of the 1920s. The moderns retained their champions and gained some public support. Many individual artists were accepted as major figures. But the American art world also saw a steady procession of revivals of older painters, retrospective exhibitions of traditional schools and styles, public interest in old masters, and a considerable moderation of both style and content among surviving modernists. Mather attended to these events and welcomed the diversity of the art scene as evidence that modernism had not swept all before it. But he also sensed a lack of deep public interest in cultural questions. His turn to formal art history came, no doubt, from weariness with the critical wars and from a need to trace the grand traditions for yet another cycle that needed them.

The twenties witnessed broad social and cultural changes that often depressed Mather. After a short postwar recession, the economy expanded to feed the public dream of automatic prosperity, though few people seemed to know what to do with material success. New industries and businesses provided leisure and convenience for an expanded mass market. The motion picture, the radio, and the phonograph opened fresh vistas of entertainment. But the tastes and ambitions behind all these developments seemed trivial and banal, the antithesis of the kind of thought and experience that Mather and other traditionalists, or modernists for that matter, had tried to develop in the prewar period. In that earlier time, the arts had benefited from interest in large questions and from an audience willing to read and analyze issues, whether in economics, politics, or culture. That now seemed a remote era, and the arts appealed only to specialized groups.

Disillusionment with technology and science and dislike of the mediocrity and triviality of democratic taste made the New Humanism attractive to Mather in the late 1920s. This philosophical and critical movement rested on foundations which his friends Irving Babbitt and Paul Elmer More had laid earlier in the century. Babbitt, who taught literature and criticism at Harvard, attained considerable fame as a steadfast critic of most intellectual trends since the Enlightenment. He argued in the classroom and in a series of books that modern civilization was adrift and must return to classical order and restraint. Science and its methods had fragmented the world into specific and often irrelevant facts and had made humanity merely another part of nature. Popular evolutionary doctrine emphasized the contemporary environment rather than long-valued historic ideals and tastes. Above all, modern times had become promethean in emphasizing expression over thought, sensation over analysis, individualism over collective balance. Human nature was torn between the egotism that desired to dominate the world and the need for familiarity and order in a viable society that required restraint. Democracies accentuated disorder in refusing to curtail individual ascendancy and in disavowing standards of taste and conduct drawn from historic models. Technology bombarded people with clichés and slogans that promised happiness through endless sensation that did not require analysis and an easy, mechanized life that did not need thought.

Mather had taught with Babbitt at Williams College in 1893–94, and the two liked each other, though they did not always agree about specific points in what became the New Humanism.[120] In 1910, Mather reviewed Babbitt's seminal book, *The New Laokoon,* in a lengthy *Nation* essay. Babbitt argued that the confusion and lack of critical standards in the arts resulted from Rousseau's emphasis on individualism at the end of the eighteenth century. This romantic ideal held that feeling was all and that reflection, analysis, and critical standards derived from the past inhibited legitimate expression. Babbitt thought that spontaneity and individualism were self-referential and thus condemned the arts to flux, always making the new seem good. Like other traditionalists, he argued that the romantics following Jean-Jacques Rousseau had abandoned their cultural and social responsibilities.

Mather believed that Babbitt was often correct, though he overstated the specific case against Rousseau. Mather's view of this essentially philosophical issue did not differ much from his ideas of art activity. "The mind should control the passions, but with a constant delicate scrutiny and criticism of its own overlordship," he noted. Babbitt really sought to restate Aristotle's golden mean, moderation in all things.

The artist must individually express ideas, but only in recognizable forms that emphasized ties to society and aimed to unify, rather than fragment, experience. Babbitt was "advocating a kind of sweet reasonableness that expresses itself practically in tempering each extreme by its opposite, in a delicate equilibration of the claims of the mind and instinct," Mather wrote. "Not the craze for liberty, eleutheromania, but the sensitive pursuit and practice of self-discipline, constitutes a whole man." As always, he feared that lack of individual restraint would harm society. "We need a conception of personality broad enough to take in both passion and discipline," he warned. "Those who admit no criticism of impulse are unwittingly preparing themselves for servitude to those impulses which are strongest—the hunger for gold and the lust for empire."[121]

Mather felt less kinship with More's efforts to develop a unifying religious sense as well as esthetic standards but admired his emphasis on the need for controlled individualism and social cohesion. "It is plain that the doctrine of limitlessness is the popular one," he had written More from his training barracks in New Bedford, Massachusetts, in 1918. "I hope you will keep on showing that art is not anarchy, and poetry simply effusiveness."[122] On many later occasions he spent time with Babbitt or More, or both, debating the merits of their views and the most effective tactics for spreading them.[123]

These ideas did not win public recognition until late in the 1920s. Opponents attacked them as antidemocratic and negative and saw Babbitt and More as foes of innovation and human progress. But the New Humanism gained considerable attention in the intellectual community because it raised important and often troubling questions about the alleged shallowness of democratic taste. And for whatever reasons, intellectual and artistic life needed a fresh sense of balance and self-criticism.

Mather agreed with the broad aims and indictments of the New Humanism but as usual was in the middle ground of the fierce debate. He disliked dogma and absolutes. He also thought that the New Humanists, like most critics, were excessive in indicting many modern trends. He saw science and technology, the bugbears of New Humanism, as both logical and inevitable developments in history. Nothing in them was necessarily inhuman or divisive, only the uses people made of them. Science had never offered moral values, merely the prospect of a certain kind of material progress.[124] He was also wary of trying to make the New Humanism an alternate religion. He thought it useful as an attitude of mind and guide to action rather than as a body of prescriptive rules. If humanism became a substitute for religious feeling or emphasized one religion over another, it would become embroiled in humanity's oldest quarrels and would lose its power to engender cultural unity. "In short, unless the New Humanism is of universal value it interests me very mildly," he told More in 1930.[125]

Integrating the New Humanism with democracy posed the greatest challenge. Whereas Babbitt and More candidly disliked democracy and the ordinary tastes it reinforced, Mather had held that the art experience was no group's special preserve, but open to anyone of imagination and curiosity who sought it. But he thought the New Humanism might elevate democratic taste indirectly through pointing out the failure of materialism to satisfy human need for large ideals and certainties. As he said in 1930, "the Humanist is not heartlessly unmindful of the common man, but rather works in his interest, if by indirection." On the more mundane level of reform and education for the masses, Mather was firmer. "The Humanist is not hostile to that improving of the environment which the socialist urges, but he is skeptical of any permanent moral gain arising simply from material betterment," he wrote in 1930.[126] But the New Humanists had to accept the fact that their views were not readily attractive because they required restraint and obedience to authorities, qualities that ran counter to American ideals. "But it was hard teaching to put over on a people that since Andrew Jackson's time had made it a virtue to deny indignantly any inferiority that was actually theirs, and to conceal scrupulously any superiority that a few of them might really possess," he wrote in 1941, when the movement had lapsed.[127]

Mather's chief concern in discussing the New Humanism was naturally for the arts. In analyzing the art problem, Mather restated his basic belief that the artist had been adrift since the eighteenth-century emphasis on individualism began to affect serious thought. Industrialism had ended the craft ideal, whose concerns for traditional forms sustained the desire to be part of an ongoing history that tempered individual expression. The church and aristocracy lost their power as patrons to emphasize history and symbolism, and the developing middle class focused more on novelty than on traditional styles and themes. Democracy, the disorder in modern life, and communication that emphasized the sensational and transitory all weakened the old view of the artist as a special sensibility with an enduring ideal in favor of the image of artist as rebel. "And the rebel, in a manner perfectly familiar to the neurologist, built up his compensations, by which he extolled that isolation, which was really his sore misfortune, as his superiority and his advantage, until after three generations it has become a common conviction among artists that their proper task is self-expression in a void, that there should be no desire to communicate and, obviously, no need to be understood." In yet another reinforcement of this new chaos, society devalued the art experience, seeking to make it easy rather than challenging or moving, sensational instead of thoughtful.[128]

As always, Mather focused on the interchange between artist and audience in trying to counter these trends. He had never opposed self-expression or individualism, only the assumption that they had no cultural obligations beyond self. Once again, he insisted that the true artist speak to people of like mind. "The humanist artist will feel that it is a vain thing to have expressed himself, however gorgeously, if nobody knows that he has expressed himself, and he will also admit that the mere feelingful and urgent self gains richness and value only when it is measured by other selves in society," he wrote in 1930. On the part of society, he wanted a rule of reason and an expectation that the arts rise above sensation. Any "humanized art would imply in practice a central authority lightly and genially imposed, a just offishness towards the artists who too overtly repudiated the tradition, withal a somewhat skeptical hopefulness towards experiment and innovation, a hospitable desire to understand the artist even when his communication is obscure, a wish to have its own ideals expressed through the arts."[129] Perhaps this last injunction was the most important. A society must seek quality before it could receive it and must expect to challenge rather than reassure or amuse itself with the results.

Mather admired much about the New Humanism but was uncomfortable with its dogmatic and often exclusionary tone. The great personal problem of his youth and middle years had been to balance conflicting psychological drives for action and repose, the basic issue in traditionalist thought. In due course, he accepted this duality and saw thinking and feeling as compatible aspects of daily life, provided that they formed a coherent pattern. One did not exclude the other.[130] He sympathized somewhat with the charge that New Humanists were negative and dour; they were too often "tummyachey and life-diminishing."[131] In addition, he was simply more catholic in tastes and a more genial personality than most of the New Humanists. As he said in gently dedicating *Modern Painting* (1927) to Babbitt: "You will find me more indulgent than yourself towards the pleasanter by-products of error, less hopeful, perhaps, of truth's prevailing through polemic, but you will also find me fighting beside you for such art as is humanistic, traditional and socially available."[132]

Mather came to expect little sustained analysis of anything serious from modern society. He hoped to provide or identify avenues of expression and recognition for interested individuals; perhaps their efforts would sustain tradition. In the meantime, he adopted a rule of reason. "The humanist technique is self-examination, self-knowledge, self-control, emerging in conduct as moderation and a quest of the golden mean."[133] As the writer Van Wyck Brooks remembered: "Mather was a humanist in the older sense, the kind that is spelled with a small 'h,' a respector of impulse along with discipline, indulgent to his erring kind, with an educated palate for all the good things of life."[134]

As if to demonstrate those broad interests, Mather undertook many unusual activities, including a trip to the Soviet Union in 1931. The communist experiment had survived its birth pangs and produced hope or fear, depending on the observer's vantage point. Mather wished to see the great collections of both traditional and modern art there. Traveling conditions were primitive because of the recent civil war and Soviet poverty, but he went with an open mind. Mather disliked the police-state atmosphere; it was clearly no place for the free-thinker. He saw enough evidence of militarism not to discount the Red Army's power or the people's determination to maintain their system. The building-sized posters, parades of workers and peasants, and ceaseless insistence on the coming world revolution were all distasteful to him, but as a tourist he found them more a nuisance than a threat. He liked the Russians, if not their system, and thought their culture would ultimately overpower the new dogma. He wryly reported on retaining his morality after sharing a sleeping compartment for both sexes and dazzled some Russians with such luxuries as a portable gas ring for making instant coffee.[135]

As a traditionalist he was glad to report that revolution had not erased art from the public consciousness. If anything, interest in painting, architecture, and music was greater than ever, since these represented ongoing Russian culture. Their current forms were not especially interesting, but this would change with time. The collections of historic works, which the Bolsheviks were careful to maintain, were striking despite the omnipresent propaganda. "If only the Director [of the museum] could keep the evidence of the Five Year Plan out of his lobby, but of course he can't, and probably he does not want to do so," Mather genially noted. "One must heartily wish the success of the plan if only to leave the Russians free to practice taste in their museums and historic monuments."[136]

He spent hours carefully studying the great Morosov and Shchukin collections of impressionist and postimpressionist works in Moscow. The experience made him modify his earlier judgments. He admitted that "I had somewhat exaggerated the breach with tradition involved in these new radical styles, or rather I had at times failed sufficiently to note that a good painting always has some kind of affinity with any good painting that has anteceded it. The early well-considered opinions I do not recant, but if I were rewriting the old essays and chapters I should give them a somewhat different and more favorable emphasis."[137]

Back in a United States in the grip of its worst depression, Mather went about his duties as professor, art historian, and museum director. He remained well known in the art world, though he wrote little about current matters. In discussing the New Humanism he had concluded that "painting and sculpture are kept alive by a sort of artificial respiration" in museums and among collectors.[138] He continued to wonder if art could survive in a world that fed on illusion and immediate sensation. "Obviously any art that requires self-control and contemplation and self-criticism must fare ill when the worship of the great god Whirl makes these meditative habits hatefully old-fashioned," he noted sadly in 1930.[139] In off moments, he thought that art might be "on its own," permanently separated from any but a specialized and dwindling audience. "If so, art will of course become merely an eccentric activity, an indulgence and luxury of coteries, hence of no more concern really to the humanist than the trade, say, of the perfume maker." But the returns were not it. "On the other hand, no one can safely deny the possibility that art may once again be profoundly integrated with society."[140]

By the mid-1930s, despite the apparently endless economic depression, he thought he detected some concern for public appreciation in the mural movement and in the development of several styles that contained ideas people could understand.[141] Despite a valedictory sense of things, he could not quite abandon the traditional ideal of a society in which art was important in maintaining a sense of orderly development and in enriching individual lives. Nor could he believe that painters would settle for a circumscribed introspection forever. He noted again in 1935 "the artist's normal desire to communicate with the art lover, which has so long and fruitful a history that its abrogation in our times seems most unlikely. A pure expressionism means a pure anarchy, a mere succession of incoherent idiosyncracies."[142]

Mather devoted much time to historical research. He completed the surveys of Italian and European painting that he had outlined a generation earlier while living in Italy.[143] He wrote for the Princeton Museum's publications and did several monographs. He was widely admired as a teacher. Geniality and ability to explain complex artistic questions simply, but without being superficial, made him a popular figure on the lecture circuit. He was something of a campus character, regularly eating with cronies at the Baltimore Dairy Lunch. This institution boasted white-tiled walls, round stools, and marble-topped tables. It served notoriously delicious éclairs and other pastries that did not improve Mather's portly figure. Mather's group was the Baltimoreans, or Balts for short.[144] His family was also a source of pride. His son, Frank III, became a well-known naval architect and marine scientist. A daughter, Margaret, married Louis A. Turner, who became a well-known physicist.

But despite these pleasures, the thirties depressed him as much as they did any other observer. The depression seemed incurable, and the rise of fascism appeared to be the greatest peril of modern times. He sometimes yielded to pessimism. "The times are awful. It's best to forget them," he wrote More in 1935. "In the supreme irrationalism of the moment, are we paying for all the false rationalism from Socrates to Voltaire? One feels the entire precariousness of all that we call culture and morality. In almost fourteen years, Mussolini has undone the civilizing work of six hundred."[145]

The outbreak of war in Europe in September 1939 seemed both predictable and appalling to Mather. In contrast to his attitude of 1917, and this time like most Americans, he hoped to remain out of the conflict. "On the war, I am a rank isolationist, whereas I was an incorrigible interventionist in the World War," he wrote Bernard Berenson as Hitler's armies overran Poland. "Of course, we should supply France and England so far as we can do so without danger [illegible] to ourselves, but nothing more." He certainly hoped to see the western democracies victorious, but the precedent of 1914–1918 indicated to him the limitations of America's power to mitigate or reform European affairs. But American entry into the war in December 1941 came for Mather, as for many other thoughtful people, as a relief from a long sense of impotent anxiety that had dominated the previous decade. At age 73, he promptly tried to enlist first in the American and then in the Canadian navies, but to no avail.[146]

Mather retired in 1946, after giving his collection of prints and drawings to the Princeton Museum. His textbooks were widely used in colleges, and he remained the dean of American art critics until his death on 11 November 1953.[147]

Mather was probably the most catholic and thoughtful of the traditionalist critics. He was more tolerant and shrewd in judging the chances of esthetic progress in modern culture than was Cox, more analytical than Cortissoz. He made a more graceful peace with human limitations than either of them. A love of art matched his belief in the need both in society at large and in individuals for the harmonizing and expanding art experience. And he carried ideas about the arts into aspects of life such as education and museology that were equally important in establishing or maintaining culture. Like most people who fight long battles against strong odds, he grew pessimistic at the end, yet he retained his ideals. In 1941 he congratulated Cortissoz on his fiftieth anniversary as a critic. "We have not always agreed, which is of [the] slightest importance," he said, "but I have always admired the way in which you have maintained a perfect professionalism with the gusto of a fine amateur."[148] It was not a bad epitaph for his own life.

Afterword

Traditionalist art thinkers had large expectations of the art experience. As befitted the classical tradition on which they drew, their breadth of thought encompassed both personal and cultural goals. Individually, they saw the art experience as a way of unifying disparate and often conflicting aspects of life, of creating harmony and purpose which did not always seem evident in daily living. The art experience thus represented imaginative actions that expanded the personality toward perfection and idealism. For them, it was a critical aspect of the examined life.

Multiplied many times through society and through institutions, these individual experiences could create a civic consciousness of the arts that helped explain human achievements within history and the directions of society. In the late nineteenth century, the traditionalists were acutely conscious of living in a period of rapid change. The era needed the organizing influences of the arts, both to temper modern industrial demands for material success and to control the sense of rootlessness that permeated the new industrial society. The culture the traditionalists defined and sought thus promised harmony and repose in a time of rapid and bewildering social change.

As critics, and sometimes as painters, they also hoped to shape stylistic changes within the arts. They did not oppose innovation but asked that the new be attached to the grand art tradition. They wanted art to depict nature and the human experience, broadly defined, in languages and symbols that sensitive persons could understand. They opposed the modernism that began to dominate at the beginning of the twentieth century because it seemed to turn away from the familiar and reflective toward mere personal expression and to speak in unknown tongues. This, in their view, would narrow the ability of art to speak in cultural terms and would separate artist and public. Catholicity of taste eroded in the art world with the advent of a modernism based on personal expression and the interpretation of private worlds. This modernism was puzzling, perhaps threatening, but it represented enormous energy that undermined the authority of inherited thought and styles. Traditionalists could not seem to produce art forms that answered the public's demands for novelty and action, while remaining within historic bounds. And their approach simply required more knowledge and thought than a democratizing art public seemed willing or able to sustain.

Various kinds of modernism steadily dominated the art world as the century developed, but traditionalists retained considerable influence with the cultivated public. In time, modernism seemed attractive only to particular critical and cultural elites, lacking a broad public appeal. Like all great movements, modernism had its cycles of efflorescence and stasis.

In what is now clearly labeled a postmodern era in the arts, when many kinds of modernism no longer fully answer needs for harmony or creative expression, the traditionalists' heritage deserves another look. Many of their views remain viable. The insistence on training artists to work with technical elegance and authority merits emphasis. The art world needs more of the historical perspective that these critics prized, both to broaden its scope and depth of feeling, and to help avoid fads. Artist and patron alike would profit from at least trying to make the artist an important member of society and the arts central to civic life.

Notes

Introduction

1. *The Classic Point of View* (New York: Scribner's, 1911), 27. This sense of unprecedented change during the last generation of the nineteenth century has been the subject of much scholarly analysis. The theme is conveniently summarized in such works as John A. Garraty, *The New Commonwealth, 1877–1890* (New York: Harper and Row, 1968); Morton Keller, *Affairs of State: Public Life in the Nineteenth Century* (Cambridge: Harvard University Press, 1977); Robert Wiebe, *The Search for Order, 1877–1920* (New York: Hill and Wang, 1967); H. Wayne Morgan, ed., *The Gilded Age: A Reappraisal*, rev. ed. (Syracuse: Syracuse University Press, 1970); Alan Trachtenberg, *The Incorporation of America: Culture and Society in the Gilded Age* (New York: Hill and Wang, 1982); and T. J. Jackson Lears, *No Place of Grace: Antimodernism and the Transformation of American Culture, 1880–1920* (New York: Pantheon, 1981).

2. The best overview of the art of this period is *The American Renaissance* (Brooklyn: Brooklyn Museum, exh. cat., 1979). There is a good deal of thoughtful material in *Art of the American Renaissance* (New York: Hirschl and Adler Gallery, exh. cat., 1985). See also Lois Marie Fink and Joshua Taylor, *Academy: The Academic Tradition in American Art* (Washington: National Collection of Fine Arts, exh. cat., 1975); H. Wayne Morgan, *Unity and Culture: The United States, 1877–1900* (New York: Penguin, 1971), and his *New Muses: Art and American Culture, 1877–1920* (Norman: University of Oklahoma Press, 1977); and Howard Mumford Jones, *The Age of Energy: Varieties of American Experience, 1865–1915* (New York: Viking, 1971).

3. Will H. Low caught this spirit well in a letter to Royal Cortissoz much later: "I think of all my brave comrades at that time who came back from their studies impressed with the fact that they must say something to justify their claims for better technical accomplishment than had heretofore been known here." (Low to RC, 15 December 1928, Royal Cortissoz papers, Beinecke Rare Book and Manuscript Library, Yale University). See also Will H. Low, *A Painter's Progress* (New York: Scribner's, 1910), 110.

4. KC, "Raymond's Theory of Art," *Nation* 58 (24 May 1894): 393–94, reviewing George Lansing Raymond, *Art in Theory: An Introduction to the Study of Comparative Aesthetics* (New York: Putnam, 1894).

5. John La Farge, *Considerations on Painting* (New York: Scribner's, 1895), 210–11.

6. KC, "Notes," *Nation* 65 (1 July 1897): 14–15, reviewing Ernst Grosse, *The Beginnings of Art* (New York: Appleton's, 1897).

7. KC, "Tolstoy on Art," *Nation* 67 (22 September 1898): 226–27, reviewing Leo Tolstoy, *What Is Art?* (New York: Crowell, 1898).

8. La Farge, *Considerations on Painting,* 42–43, 56.

9. Ibid., 126.

10. Will H. Low, "The Education of the Artist Here and Now," *Scribner's Magazine* 25 (June 1899): 766.

11. KC, "Symonds's Art Essays," *Nation* 58 (1 February 1894): 87–88, reviewing John Addington Symonds, *Essays Speculative and Suggestive* (New York: Scribner's, 1893).

12. KC, "Jules Breton," *Nation* 52 (12 March 1891): 223, reviewing Jules Breton, *The Life of an Artist: An Autobiography* (New York: Appleton, 1890); KC, "Muther's History of Modern Painting," *Nation* 63 (12 November 1896): 369, reviewing Richard Muther, *The History of Modern Painting* (New York: Macmillan, 1896). In a later review, Cox spelled this out: "The more one studies the really great figures in art, the more inadequate the theory of Taine appears, and the more one is forced to the recognition of the inexplicability and the importance of individual genius. The race, the *milieu,* and the moment may account for Botticelli, but not for Michelangelo; for Ter Borch, but not for Rembrandt; for Zurbaran, but not for Velázquez. The art of these greatest ones is colored by the race instinct and the time spirit, but is not produced by them. It is not the race or the epoch that interests us in their art; it is their art which interests us in the race and the epoch." KC, "Books on Art and Artists," *Nation* 80 (9 March 1905): 194–95, reviewing C. Gasquoine Hartley [Mrs. Walter Gallichan], *A Record of Spanish Painting* (New York: Scribner's, 1904). This was a restatement of Cox's view of the artist as a special personality, with unusual insights into life.

13. KC, "The Illusion of Progress," *Century Magazine* 86 (May 1913): 39–43, rpt. in KC, *Artist and Public* (New York: Scribner's 1914), 77–98.

14. W. J. Stillman, "Realism and Idealism," *Nation* 41 (31 December 1885): 546.

15. KC, *The Classic Point of View,* 29–30.

16. Theodore Robinson, diary, 18 February 1894, 18 February 1895, and 8 February 1896, Frick Art Reference Library.

17. See Theda Shapiro, *Painters and Politics: The European Avant-Garde and Society, 1900–1925* (New York: Elsevier, 1976), 94–100.

18. Stephen Kern provides a good deal of interesting analysis of the themes in modernism in *The Culture of Time and Space, 1880–1918* (Cambridge: Harvard, 1983), esp. 34, 64, and the introduction.

19. See the interesting comments in T. J. Clark, *The Painting of Modern Life: Paris in the Age of Manet and His Followers* (New York: Knopf, 1985), esp. 12.

20. Cox was sharp in condemning this egotism and narrowness, as he conceived them: "In the last forty or fifty years, especially, painters have been willing, for the most part, to appeal only to a professional interest in the cleverness of their rendering of the superficial aspects of nature, or to the still narrower interest of cliques and coteries in the exploitation of personal whim and extravagant theories. They have cultivated a contempt for the public and have little right to complain if, in times like these, the public neglects them and what they do." (KC, *Concerning Painting* [New York: Scribner's 1917], vii).

21. See Frederick R. Karl, *Modern and Modernism: The Sovereignty of the Artist, 1885–1925* (New York: Atheneum, 1985), esp. xii.

Chapter 1

1. Mary Rudd Cochran to H. Wayne Morgan, 2 July 1971. Ms. Cochran was the daughter of Cox's half-brother, William Cochran.

2. See Jacob D. Cox to Charles F. Cox, 23 March 1869, Jacob D. Cox papers, Oberlin College Archives; J. D. Cox to Rutherford B. Hayes, 16 September 1869, Hayes papers, Hayes Library, Fremont, Ohio; Helen F. Cox to Will C. Cochran, 8 March 1869, and J. D. Cox to T. H. Robinson, 11 June 1872, both in the collection of Mrs. Katharine Smith, Wooster, Ohio, now in the Jacob D. Cox papers. Also, Will C. Cochran, "The Political Experiences of Major General Jacob Dolson Cox," vol. 2, 1156, typescript, Western Reserve Historical Society, Cleveland, Ohio; Jacob Dolson Cox II, *Building an American Industry: The Story of the Cleveland Twist Drill Company and Its Founder: An Autobiography* (Cleveland: The Company, 1951), 43–44; William A. Coffin, "Kenyon Cox," *Century Magazine* 41 (January 1891): 334; "Kenyon Cox," *National Cyclopedia of American Biography* vol. 5 (New York: J. T. White, 1907), 321; Allyn Cox, interview with H. Wayne Morgan, Washington, D.C., 8 March 1982; Caroline Cox Lansing to H. Wayne Morgan, 12 March 1984; Allyn Cox to Henry Hope Reed, 10 January 1979, Allyn Cox papers, Archives of American Art.

3. Jacob D. Cox to Helen F. Cox, fragment dated July 1863, Kenyon Cox papers, Avery Architectural and Fine Arts Library, Columbia University (hereafter cited as Cox papers).

4. Coffin, "Kenyon Cox," 334. See also "Kenyon Cox," *National Cyclopedia,* 5: 321.

5. KC, Journal, 2 January 1876, Cox papers.

6. See KC to his father, 10 March 1876 [1877]; to his mother, 13 March 1877; and to Leonard Opdycke, 17 July 1877, all in Cox papers.

7. KC to his mother, 18 October and 1 November 1876, Cox papers.

8. For information on KC's student years, see H. Wayne Morgan ed., *An American Art Student in Paris: The Letters of Kenyon Cox, 1877–1882* (Kent: Kent State University Press, 1986).

9. See Will H. Low, "The Primrose Way," typescript, 59–60, Low papers, Albany Institute of History and Art; Eliot Gregory, *The Ways of Men* (New York: Scribner's, 1900), 108; Will H. Low, *A Chronicle of Friendships, 1873–1900* (New York: Scribner's, 1900), 158, which has the Bouguereau quotation; and "A French Painter and His Pupils," *Century Magazine* 31 (January 1886): 373–76.

10. See KC's comments on Carolus-Duran in three of his later books: *The Classic Point of View* (New York: Scribner's, 1911), 198–99; *Artist and Public* (New York: Scribner's, 1914), 153; and *Concerning Painting* (New York: Scribner's, 1917), 188–89.

11. On the Ecole and its tradition, see Lois Marie Fink, "The Role of France in American Art, 1850–1900" (Ph.D. diss., University of Chicago, 1970); and her "The

Innovation of Tradition in Late Nineteenth-Century American Art," *American Art Journal* 10 (November 1978): 63–71; Albert Boime, *The Academy and French Painting in the Nineteenth Century* (New York: Phaidon, 1971); and his "The Teaching Reforms of 1863 and the Origins of Modernism in France," *Art Quarterly,* n.s. 1 (1977): 1–39; and H. Barbara Weinberg, "Nineteenth-Century American Painters at the Ecole des Beaux-Arts," *American Art Journal* 13 (Autumn 1981): 66–84; and her "Lure of Paris: Late Nineteenth-Century American Painters and the French Training," in *A New World: Masterpieces of American Painting, 1760–1910* (Boston: Museum of Fine Arts, 1983), 16–32; and her *American Pupils of Jean Léon Gérôme* (Fort Worth: Amon Carter Museum, 1985).

12. KC to his mother, 9 November 1878, Cox papers.

13. On Gérôme, whose reputation is justifiably reviving, see especially Gerald Ackerman, *The Life and Work of Jean-Léon Gérôme* (New York: Sothebey's, 1986).

14. See KC to his mother, 2 April and 3 June 1879, and to his father, 29 October 1879, in Cox papers. See also the comments of several of Gérôme's American students, including Cox, in "American Artists on Gérôme," *Century Magazine* 37 (February 1889): 636; and Will H. Low, *A Painter's Progress* (New York: Scribner's, 1910), 165–66.

15. KC to his father, 14 May 1879, Cox papers. See also J. Alden Weir to John F. Weir, May 1874, where the young painter said of Gérôme: "He will not let one dodge about for effects, glaze, or attempt any tricks, as he terms it, but he must try to study the value of color and paint solidly." (qtd. by Dorothy Weir Young, *The Life and Letters of J. Alden Weir* [New Haven: Yale University Press, 1960], 37).

16. The principal focus here is on Bastien-Lepage, whose work produced a great deal of comment among students like Cox and other people in the late 1870s. For his career, see William Steven Feldman, "The Life and Work of Jules Bastien-Lepage (1848–1884)," (Ph.D. diss., New York University, 1973). Gabriel Weisberg, *The Realist Tradition: French Painting and Drawing, 1830–1900* (Bloomington: Indiana University Press, exh. cat., 1980), contains a cross-section of realistic work. The broader background is sketched in Linda Nochlin, *Realism* (New York: Penguin, 1971); and Robert Rosenblum and H. W. Janson, *Nineteenth-Century Art* (New York: Abrams, 1984). The sharp debate about the nature and accuracy of the term *realism,* especially as applied to Courbet and his followers, is well detailed in Charles Rosen and Henri Zerner's three articles in the *New York Review of Books:* "What Is, and Is Not, Realism" 29 (18 February 1982): 21–26, "Enemies of Realism" 29 (4 March 1982): 29–33, and "The Judgment of Paris," 34 (26 February 1987): 21–25, the last of which is critical of efforts to revive interest in Salon painting and other kinds of formal or "official" art of the period and is interesting.

17. *Cincinnati Daily Gazette,* 11 June 1879. This was one of three articles Cox wrote for his hometown newspaper on the Salon of 1879.

18. KC, "Some Books on Art," *Nation* 73 (19 December 1901): 475–76; a review of Charles Caffin's *Photography as a Fine Art* (New York: Doubleday, Page, 1901).

19. See KC, "Bastien-Lepage," *Nation* 54 (5 May 1892): 343–44; KC, *The Classic Point of View,* 15–16; and KC, "Some Phases of Nineteenth Century Painting," *Art World* 1 (February 1917): 315–20.

20. KC to his father, 16 January 1878, Cox papers.

21. KC, "What Is Painting?" *Art World* 1 (October 1916): 29–33; see also his earlier review of J. A. Symonds, *Essays, Speculative and Suggestive* (New York: Scribner's 1893), in *Nation* 58 (1 February 1894): 87–88.

22. Robinson to Cox, 19 December 1882, Cox papers; Mary Rudd Cochran to H. Wayne Morgan, 2 July 1971; and Mary Rudd Cochran to William E. Bigglestone, 10 October 1975, Oberlin College Archives.

23. See H. Wayne Morgan, *New Muses: Art in American Culture, 1865–1920* (Norman: University of Oklahoma Press, 1978), 23–25. See also KC to August Jaccaci, 12 April 1904, Jaccaci papers, Archives of American Art, which bills the publisher $100 for three small designs; and KC to his wife, undated but probably 1904, Cox papers, which refers to a $150 commission for a *Collier's Magazine* cover. Both were significant sums.

24. See KC to his mother, 12 and 20 February 1886, Cox papers. This edition of Rossetti's *Blessed Damozel* was published in New York by Dodd, Mead in 1886.

25. KC to Leonard Opdycke, 3 June 1886, Cox papers; and KC to Will H. Low, 4 February 1887, Low papers.

26. The Cox Collection of the Cooper-Hewitt Museum in New York City has a great quantity of preparatory and completed work for these commissions.

27. Secretary of the Treasury Franklin MacVeagh to KC, 10 October 1912, offered $3,000 for an approved design; and MacVeagh to KC, 1 February 1914, enthusiastically accepted the resulting effort, both in Cox papers. The *New York Times,* 5 December 1912, has a story on the note.

28. Robinson to Cox, 20 June 1883, Cox papers.

29. KC to his mother, 11 August 1889, Cox papers; and John C. Van Dyke, "The Art Students League of New York," *Harper's Monthly* 83 (October 1891): 688–700; Marchal E. Landgren, *Years of Art: The Story of the Art Students League of New York* (New York: McBride, 1940), 42, 63–66; Dan Beard, *Hardly a Man Is Now Alive* (New York: Doubleday, Doran, 1939), 277; and *New York Times,* 2 February 1908, sec. 1, p. 8, for a picture of Cox with a group of students.

30. KC to his father, 3 June 1885; and to Leonard Opdycke, 3 January 1885, Cox papers; and KC to Low, 31 July 1884 and 9 September 1886, which has the quotation, both in Low papers.

31. KC, *Concerning Painting,* 20-21; see also *The Classic Point of View,* 130–32; KC, "The Nude in Art," *Scribner's Magazine* 12 (December 1892): 747–49; and KC, "The Subject in Art," *Scribner's Magazine* 50 (July 1911): 1–13.

32. KC to his mother, 4 April 1885, Cox papers.

33. KC to his mother, undated but 1886, Cox papers; see also Charlotte Adams, "Artists' Models in New York," *Century Magazine* 25 (February 1883): 569–77.

34. KC to Mr. Fraser, 2 April 1895, Century Collection, Manuscripts Division, New York Public Library.

35. KC to White, 8 October 1890, 16 April 1892, and 19 May 1893, all in Stanford White papers, New-York Historical Society.

36. KC to Blashfield, 18 January 1900, Edwin H. Blashfield papers, New-York Historical Society. The basic coverage of this subject is William H. Gerdts, *The Great American Nude: A History in Art* (New York: Praeger, 1974). Landgren, *Years of Art,* 49–55, 87–89, has some information on the use of nude models, including the raid of

the self-appointed censor and crusader against pornography, Anthony Comstock, in 1906.

37. KC to Allyn Cox, 7 January 1918, Cox papers. A few years earlier, Cox asked an old friend to destroy one of his early nude drawings, which he would replace with something he now considered more suitable. "I don't think I ever did anything with a smutty intention, but even the most harmless and classic nude is apt to be misunderstood, as I have had evidence in an anonymous letter since some of my things have been shown here" (KC to Henry Moser, 2 and 10 April 1911, Henry Moser papers, Archives of American Art). He also apparently answered a criticism, or at least a query, from the *Boston Sunday Post* that he employed nude female models while working at his summer retreat in Cornish, New Hampshire, in 1913 (KC to W. H. Troy, 17 September 1913, Houghton Library, Harvard University).

38. FJM, "Kenyon Cox," *Scribner's Magazine* 65 (June 1919): 765.

39. See Pauline King, *American Mural Painting* (Boston: Noyes, Platt, 1901); Edwin H. Blashfield, *Mural Painting in America* (New York: Scribner's, 1913), 8; Edwin H. Blashfield, "A Definition of Decorative Art," in *Brochure of the Mural Painters* (New York: Mural Painters, 1916), 7–10; Charles H. Caffin, *The Story of American Painting* (New York: F. A. Stokes, 1907), 313–14; Cynthia Sanford, *Heroes in the Fight for Beauty: The Muralists of the Hudson County Courthouse* (Jersey City: Jersey City Museum, exh. cat., 1986), 11–12; Morgan, *New Muses,* 51–55; and Richard Murray, "The Art of Decoration," in *Perceptions and Evocations: The Art of Elihu Vedder* (Washington, D.C.: Smithsonian Institution Press, 1979), 167–239.

40. Cox's remark about always wanting to be a mural painter, which may have been retrospective, is in KC to Mrs. Lew F. Porter, 22 March 1913, typed copy, Jersey City Museum. Lew F. Porter was the state official who oversaw the placement of Cox's work at the Wisconsin state capitol in 1914–1915. Frank D. Millet's "The Decoration of the Exposition" (*Scribner's Magazine* 12 [December 1892]: 697) has an illustration of *Ceramic Painting,* since destroyed. This was apparently part of KC's group that also included *Steel Making, Building,* and *Spinning.* See also KC, *Concerning Painting,* 248–49.

41. KC to his mother, 4 July 1893, Cox papers; see also his "Paul Baudry," in John C. Van Dyke, ed., *Modern French Masters* (New York: Century, 1896), 61–72.

42. KC, "Puvis de Chavannes," in Van Dyke, ed., *Modern French Masters,* 25–26; see also his "Some Phases of Nineteenth Century Painting. II. Mural Painting in France and America," *Art World* 2 (April 1917): 13.

43. KC, *The Classic Point of View,* 186; see also KC, *Concerning Painting,* 255–56; and his "Making of a Mural Painting," typescript, Cox papers.

44. KC, *The Classic Point of View,* 76; and KC, "Saint Gaudens's 'Sherman,' " in KC, *Old Masters and New* (New York: Scribner's, 1905), 278–85.

45. KC, *The Classic Point of View,* 71.

46. Ibid., 71, 75. In a review of Jared B. Flagg's *Life and Letters of Washington Allston* (New York: Scribner's, 1892), Cox noted that Allston's heroic historical canvases failed as decorations in the mode of the old masters because they were merely inflated easel pictures. See KC, "Washington Allston," *Nation* 56 (12 January 1893): 32–33. See also David C. Huntington, *The Quest for Unity: American Art between World's Fairs, 1876–1893* (Detroit: Detroit Institute of Art, exh. cat., 1983), 99.

47. KC to Bernard Green, 2 December 1894 and 1 January 1895, which has the quotation, in Beverly Elson, "The Library of Congress: A Merger of American Functionalism and Cosmopolitan Eclecticism" (Ph.D. diss., University of Maryland, 1981), 128–29.

48. KC to his wife, undated but 1896, Cox papers. See also RC, "Painting and Sculpture in the New Congressional Library. III. The Decorations of Mr. Kenyon Cox," *Harper's Weekly* 40 (21 March 1896): 276–78; *The Library of Congress Mural Paintings* (New York: Foster and Reynolds, 1902); and Herbert Small, *The Library of Congress: Its Architecture and Decoration* (New York: Norton, 1982), 135–37.

49. Minna C. Smith, "The Work of Kenyon Cox," *International Studio* 32 (July 1907): i–xiii; and Gladys E. Hamlin, "Mural Painting in Iowa," *Iowa Journal of History and Politics* 37 (July 1939): 244–50.

50. KC to his wife, 16 April 1906, Cox papers.

51. KC to Saint-Gaudens, 10 September 1906, Augustus Saint-Gaudens papers, Dartmouth College.

52. Cox discussed these works in letters to his wife of 19 and 21 May 1914 and 5 October 1915, Cox papers. See also Stanley H. Cravens, *Wisconsin State Capitol Guide and History* (Madison: Wisconsin Department of Administration, n.d.), 15–17, 28.

53. *Boston Evening Transcript,* 18 December 1914.

54. KC to his wife, 21 April 1906, Cox papers; see also Rena Neumann Coen, *Painting and Sculpture in Minnesota, 1820–1914* (Minneapolis: University of Minnesota Press, 1976), 98–99; Neil B. Thompson, *Minnesota's State Capitol* (St. Paul: Minnesota Historical Society, 1974), 64–66; and KC, "The New State Capitol of Minnesota," *Architectural Record* 18 (August, 1905): 95–113.

55. The Winona mural is illustrated in Blashfield, *Mural Painting in America,* opp. 74. The Oberlin murals were displayed in New York before being put in place and were reviewed in the *New York Times,* 8 November 1914, sec. 5, 11.

56. KC, "Puvis de Chavannes," 569; see also KC, "The Winter Academy," *Nation* 85 (26 December 1907), 596; KC, "The American School of Painting," *Scribner's Magazine* 50 (December 1911): 765–68; and KC, "Some Phases of Nineteenth Century Painting. III. Mural Painting in France and America," 16.

57. KC to Leonard Opdycke, 23 January 1886, Cox papers.

58. Blashfield to Royal Cortissoz, 21 January 1932, Royal Cortissoz papers, Beinecke Manuscript and Rare Books Library, Yale University.

59. KC to his mother, 15 December 1886, Cox papers.

60. KC, "Books on Painting," *Nation* 73 (7 November 1901): 362–63; and his "Books on Art," *Nation* 75 (6 November 1902): 364–65, which has the quotation.

61. KC to Robert Underwood Johnson, 3 November 1910, Century Collection, New York Public Library.

62. KC to Robert Underwood Johnson, 20 March 1897, Century Collection, New York Public Library.

63. The quotation is from Low to KC, 2 May 1911; the reported conversation is from KC to his wife, 20 April 1912, both in Cox papers.

64. Most of Cox's writing develops this theme, but its best statement is in his *The Classic Point of View.*

65. For interesting background on this matter, see Lois Marie Fink and Joshua C.

Taylor, *Academy: The Academic Tradition in American Art* (Washington: Smithsonian Institution Press, 1975).

66. KC, "Academicism and the National Academy of Design," *Art World* 2 (August 1917): 426–27.

67. See KC, "Realism and Idealism," *Nation* 42 (7 January 1886): 10–11; KC, "The Nude in Art," *Scribner's Magazine* 12 (December 1892): 747–49; and KC, "Symonds's Art Essays," *Nation* 58 (1 February 1894): 87–88.

68. KC, "Design," *Scribner's Magazine* 50 (September 1911): 335–37.

69. KC, *Concerning Painting,* 62–64; emphasis in original.

70. KC, "Stillman's Essays," *Nation* 66 (13 January 1898): 31–32, reviewing W. J. Stillman, *The Old Rome and the New* (Boston: Houghton-Mifflin, 1897); see also KC, *The Classic Point of View,* 36–37; KC, "The Subject in Art," 4; KC, *Concerning Painting,* 7–10.

71. KC, "What Is Painting?" *Art World* 1 (October 1916): 29.

72. KC, *Concerning Painting,* 18–22.

73. KC, "Michelangelo," *International Quarterly* 11 (April 1905): 66.

74. An interviewer titled the story "Cubists and Futurists Are Making Insanity Pay," *New York Times,* 16 March 1913, sec. 6, 1.

75. KC, *The Classic Point of View,* 3–4.

76. For his lifelong admiration for Millet, see KC, "Jules Breton," *Nation* 52 (12 March 1891), 223, reviewing Jules Breton, *The Life of An Artist: An Autobiography* (New York: D. Appleton, 1890); KC, "Muther's History of Modern Painting," *Nation* 63 (12 November 1896): 368–69, reviewing Richard Muther, *The History of Modern Painting,* 3 vols. (New York: Macmillan, 1896); KC, "Notes," *Nation* 81 (26 October 1905): 347; and KC, "The Art of Millet," *Scribner's Magazine* 43 (March 1908): 328–40, which has the quotation. Laura L. Meixner's "Popular Criticism of Jean-François Millet in Nineteenth-Century America" (*Art Bulletin* 45 [March 1983]: 94–105) traces the changing uses to which critics and audiences put Millet's works.

77. KC, "Journal of 1876," 5 January 1876, Cox papers.

78. KC to his father, 5 September 1879, Cox papers; see also KC, "Bastien-Lepage," *Nation* 54 (5 May 1892): 344.

79. See KC, "Rembrandt," *Nation* 58 (4 January 1894): 13–15, reviewing Emile Michel's *Rembrandt: His Life, His Work, His Time* (New York: Scribner's, 1894) and Charles Knowles Bolton's *Saskia, The Wife of Rembrandt* (New York: Crowell, 1893); and KC "Notes," *Nation* 75 (14 August 1902): 135–37, reviewing Auguste Breal, *Rembrandt* (New York: Dutton, 1902); KC, "Rembrandt," *Architectural Record* 20 (December 1906): 455, which has the quotation; and his extended discussion of light effects in chap. 5, "Light and Shade and Color," in *The Classic Point of View,* 158–95.

80. KC, "Light and Shade and Color," *The Classic Point of View,* 166. Cox made an interesting observation in the same year on a celebrated work of Sargent's, which depicted a carefully disguised figure blended into dense foliage: "Have you seen Sargent's *Hermit* [1908] in the Metropolitan Museum? It is the most successful piece of pure impressionism I have ever seen, and a capital example of what modern methods gain and lose for art. It is amazingly like nature, and the hermit is as inconspicuous a part of nature as if the picture were intended for an illustration of protective coloring!

You have to hunt for him. In other words, Sargent has realized with extraordinary skill just that condition of things which convinced me, the last time I tried to paint a figure out of doors, that I did not want to paint nature as it really looks" (KC to Edwin H. Blashfield, 16 June 1911, Blashfield papers). The work is conveniently illustrated in Carter Ratcliff, *John Singer Sargent* (New York: Abbeville, 1982), 211.

81. KC, "The Winter Academy," *Nation* 85 (26 December 1907): 596; and KC, "The American School of Painting," *Scribner's Magazine* 50 (December 1911): 768. See his interesting remarks on Manet and Monet contrasted with Gérôme in using composition and design in "Brownell's French Art," *Nation* 55 (15 December 1892): 454–55, a review of William C. Brownell, *French Art: Classic and Contemporary Painting and Sculpture* (New York: Scribner's, 1892).

82. KC, *The Classic Point of View*, 166–68.

83. Ibid., 114; see also KC to Low, 3 May 1911, Low papers, in which he said: "What I object to in Monet, for instance, is not what he did but what he did not do." See also KC, *The Classic Point of View*, 168.

84. KC, *The Classic Point of View*, 171–72; see also KC, *Artist and Public*, 138–40.

85. KC and William A. Coffin ("The Society of American Artists," *Nation* 50 [8 May 1890]: 382) praised Monet's original investigations of light effects but criticized thoughtless "followers" who overused both light and color. KC, "Brownell's French Art," *Nation* 55 (15 December 1892): 455, reviewing William C. Brownell, *French Art: Classic and Contemporary Painting and Sculpture* (New York: Scribner's, 1892), again praised Monet's intentions and generally saw impressionism at its best as an extension of trends already underway before the 1870s. KC, "Notes," *Nation* 77 (3 December 1903): 444–45, reviewing Camille Mauclair, *The Great French Painters* (New York: Dutton, 1903), held that the author overrated the group, with an emphasis suitable for anyone "who cares to see what French art looks like when seen, as it were, through blue spectacles, . . ." KC, "Art: The Winter Academy," *Nation* 83 (27 December 1906): 564–65, and KC, "Art: The Carnegie Institute Exhibition," *Nation* 84 (18 April 1907): 368–70, both saw impressionism as an established, if not academic, formula and praised those, even Robert Henri, who had adapted it to more traditional means. The quotation is from Theodore Robinson, diary, 21 November 1894, Frick Art Reference Library. See also the interesting remarks in Huntington, *The Quest for Unity*, 41–42: "A generation beset by doubts sought assurance, not denial, of the soul. What was needed was not 'scientific impressionism,' but 'poetic impressionism.' "

86. As early as 1890, he thought that "the art of America already ranks second only to the art of France in the world's production." See KC and William A. Coffin, "Society of American Artists," *Nation* 50 (8 May 1890): 380–82; and KC, "American Art at Buffalo," *Nation* 73 (15 August 1901): 127–28; KC, "Art: The Carnegie Institute Exhibition," *Nation* 84 (18 April 1907): 370; KC, "The Winter Academy," *Nation* 85 (26 December 1907): 595–96; KC, "The Pennsylvania Academy Exhibition," *Nation* 86 (23 January 1908): 88–89; KC, "The American School of Painting," *Scribner's Magazine* 50 (December 1911): 765–66; KC, *The Classic Point of View*, 26–27.

87. KC to Edwin H. Blashfield, 16 June 1911, Blashfield papers. He wrote another friend: "I feel strongly in both these and other ways [that] the West is infinitely more alive than we are in New York." See KC to James B. Carrington, 20 March 1911, Carrington papers, Beinecke Manuscripts and Rare Books Library. He also wanted to

elect new people from the West to the National Academy of Design, as stated in KC to My Dear Curran [Charles C. Curran?], 13 May 1911, Cox papers. His positive view of the Chicago scene was stated in "Art: An Example from Chicago," *Nation* 92 (4 May 1911): 455–56.

88. KC, *The Classic Point of View*, vi.

89. See KC to Low, 29 April and 3 May 1911 (the latter has the quotation), both in Low papers.

90. *New York Times*, 30 April 1911; see also the earlier KC, "Books on Painting," *Nation* 72 (9 May 1901): 377–78.

91. KC, *The Classic Point of View*, 149–51; *New York Times*, 16 March 1913.

92. KC, "The Whistler Memorial Exhibition," *Nation* 78 (3 March 1904): 167–69.

93. KC, "The Art of Whistler," *Architectural Record* 15 (May 1904): 469.

94. KC, "The Modern Spirit in Art," *Harper's Weekly* 57 (15 March 1913): 10.

95. "Cubists and Futurists Are Making Insanity Pay." An editorial on the same day equated modernism with political anarchism.

96. KC, "The Illusion of Progress," *Century Magazine* 86 (May 1913): 39–43. Cox originally delivered this essay to a meeting of the American Academy of Arts and Letters on 13 December 1912.

97. The first quotation is from KC to Mather, 12 November 1915; the second is from KC to Mather, 29 January 1915, Frank Jewett Mather, Jr., papers, Princeton University Library.

98. KC, "Artist and Public," *Scribner's Magazine* 55 (April 1914): 512–20. This was published as the title essay in his *Artist and Public*. He apparently received a great deal of complimentary mail on the essay, "something the like of which has never happened to me before" (see KC to E. L. Burlingame, 11 May 1914, Scribner's Collection, Princeton University Library).

99. KC to Mather, 12 November 1915, Mather papers.

100. KC to Allyn Cox, 16 April 1918, Cox papers; and his *Concerning Painting: Considerations Theoretical and Historical*, vii–viii.

101. KC to Allyn Cox, 19 August 1917, Cox papers.

102. Louise Cox to KC, undated but 1911, Cox papers, when he was lecturing at the Art Institute of Chicago, reported a mere $300 in the bank. KC to August Jaccaci, 1 September 1911, Jaccaci papers, reported that he had had no mural work recently.

103. KC to his mother, 26 October 1901, Cox papers.

104. Low, *A Painter's Progress*, 58.

105. KC, "Rembrandt," *Architectural Record* 20 (December 1906): 459.

106. KC to Low, 12 December 1916, Low papers; see also KC, "Indifference to Art," *Nation* 75 (25 September 1902): 241.

107. KC to Blashfield, 19 December 1913, Blashfield papers.

Chapter 2

1. The pronunciation of this name must have intrigued or baffled a great many people. Cortissoz had no children and left his affairs in the hands of a favorite nephew, who wrote a standard biographical entry for his uncle. In it the name is marked for

pronunciation as "kor-tée-suz." See *National Cyclopedia of American Biography* vol. 36, (New York: James T. White, 1950), 549.

2. See his obituary, *New York Times,* 18 October 1948, p. 23.

3. Ralph Flint, "Cornices and Cortissoz," *Art News* 40 (1 October 1941): 13; and the story on his fiftieth anniverary as a critic in *New York Herald Tribune,* 1 October 1941, p. 21; and his own "Fifty Years of Art Criticism," *New York Herald Tribune,* 5 October 1941, sec. 7, 8.

4. See his report on Greenwich Village atmosphere in *New York Tribune,* 15 March 1896; RC, *Monograph of the Work of Charles A. Platt* (New York: Architectural Book Pub., 1913), iv; RC, "New York as an Art Center," *New York Tribune,* 9 April 1922, sec. 4, p. 7; RC, *The New York Tribune* (New York: Tribune, 1923), 53–54; RC, "Basis of American Taste," *Creative Art* 12 (January 1933): 20; "RC Marks Fifty Years on Tribune's Staff as Art Critic," *New York Herald Tribune,* 1 October 1941, p. 21.

5. Qted. in Flint, "Cornices and Cortissoz," 13.

6. RC to Saint-Gaudens, 30 November 1897, Augustus Saint-Gaudens papers, Dartmouth College.

7. RC, *Personalities in Art* (New York: Scribner's, 1925), 8.

8. RC, *New York Tribune,* 49; RC, *John La Farge: A Memoir and a Study* (Boston: Houghton-Mifflin, 1911), 221–22. By the 1920s, the architect Charles A. Platt could refer to RC with some justice as a "hard boiled Republican." See Platt to RC, 1 August 1928, Royal Cortissoz papers, Beinecke Library, Yale University (hereafter cited as Cortissoz papers).

9. Two letters from this period reveal his hurried life and sense of pressure: RC to Richard Watson Gilder, 25 March 1893, and to Robert Underwood Johnson, 9 May 1896, both in Century Collection, New York Public Library.

10. See Flint, "Cornices and Cortissoz," 13. Cortissoz noted his tendency to overwork and take on too many responsibilities in letters to Bernard Berenson, 21 February and 1 April 1927, Bernard Berenson Archive, Villa i Tatti, Florence, Italy.

11. Adams to RC, 20 September 1911, Cortissoz papers.

12. Reid to Hart Lyman, 30 October 1911, carbon attached to Reid to RC, Cortissoz papers.

13. RC, *American Artists* (New York: Scribner's, 1923), 13.

14. The quotation, which Arnold paraphrased elsewhere many times, is from his essay "The Function of Criticism at the Present Time," in *Essays in Criticism* (1865; London: Macmillan, 1910), 38. See also John Henry Raleigh, *Matthew Arnold and American Culture* (Berkeley: University of California Press, 1957); Arlene R. Olson, *Art Critics and the Avant-Garde: New York, 1900–1913* (Ann Arbor: UMI Research Press, 1980), 19–36; and David C. Huntington, *The Quest for Unity: American Art between World's Fairs, 1876–1893* (Detroit: Detroit Institute of Art, exh. cat., 1983), 11–13.

15. Arnold, "The Function of Criticism at the Present Time," 40.

16. RC to Belle da Costa Greene, 28 January 1930, Cortissoz papers; see also his "Some Writers of Good Letters," *Century Magazine* 53 (March 1897): 787–88.

17. *National Cyclopedia of American Biography,* vol. 36, 549.

18. RC, "Egotism in Contemporary Art," *Atlantic Monthly,* 73 (May 1894): 649.

19. Walter Pater, *The Renaissance: Studies in Art and Poetry,* ed. Donald L. Hill (Berkeley: University of California Press, 1980), xxi. Pater's book was originally published in 1873. Cortissoz mentioned Pater in *Art and Common Sense* (New York: Scribner's, 1913), 14, and *The Painter's Craft* (New York: Scribner's, 1930), 86. See also his "Art of Art Criticism," in *Personalities in Art* (New York: Scribner's, 1925), 8. The Cortissoz citation to Blake is from the *New York Herald Tribune,* 1 October 1941, 21. See also Ruth C. Child, *The Aesthetics of Walter Pater* (New York: Macmillan, 1940), esp. 22–23, 42–44, 47–51.

20. RC, *Personalities in Art,* 10.

21. RC, *The Painter's Craft,* 415–23.

22. RC, "The Hewitt Ladies," *Cooper Union Chronicle* 1 (1927): 79; see also *The Painter's Craft,* 452.

23. Blashfield to RC, April [?], Cortissoz papers. See also RC, *American Artists,* 11–12.

24. RC, Preface, *The Works of Edwin Howland Blashfield* (New York: Scribner's, 1937), [5]; see also RC, "The Vitality of Tradition," *Architectural Forum* 52 (May 1930): 635–36.

25. *New York Tribune,* 13 February 1910, sec. 2, p. 2; see also *New York Tribune,* 10 April 1910, reviewing a show of independent painters; *New York Tribune,* 2 April 1911, reviewing a show of independent architects.

26. RC, *John La Farge,* 261.

27. See RC, "Some Imaginative Types in American Art," *Harper's Monthly* 91 (July 1895): 165; see also RC, *American Artists,* 51–52, 93–105; RC, *The Painter's Craft,* 361–62; RC, *Arthur B. Davies* (New York: Whitney Museum, 1931).

28. RC, "New Aspects of Art Study," *Atlantic Monthly* 91 (June 1903): 832–42.

29. RC, "Significant Art Books," *Atlantic Monthly* 95 (February 1905): 271.

30. RC, *Art and Common Sense,* 22.

31. Cortissoz recalled this show in two stories, *New York Herald Tribune,* 18 October 1931, and 26 March 1933.

32. RC, "Egotism in Contemporary Art," 647.

33. Ibid.

34. RC, "The Present State of European Painting," *Atlantic Monthly* 98 (November 1906): 686.

35. *New York Tribune,* 4 April 1915.

36. Ibid., 11 March 1896, p. 7. He later wrote that "the truth of an unthinking perception of nature is the essential thing he [Monet] says: it is the great goal to be desired," ibid. 31 January 1899, p. 6.

37. Ibid., 15 March 1914, sec. 5, p. 7. A letter suggests that Cortissoz seems to have kept a photograph of Monet on his office wall (RC to Bernard Berenson, 23 September 1929, Berenson Archive). He also met Monet around the turn of the century. See RC, *Personalities in Art,* 262; RC, "Claude Monet," *Scribner's Magazine* 81 (April 1927): 329–36; and RC, "Auguste Renoir and the Cult for Beauty," *International Studio* 90 (August 1928): 18.

38. *New York Tribune,* 24 November 1912, sec. 2, 6.

39. Ibid., 8 May 1921, sec. 3, p. 7.

40. RC, "Exhibition of the American Water-color Society," *Harper's Weekly* 61 (13

February 1897): 162; RC, "John S. Sargent," *Scribner's Magazine* 34 (November 1903): 514–32; *New York Tribune,* 2 April 1902; RC, "The Pennsylvania Academy Exhibition," *Scrip* 2 (March 1907): 196; and RC, *Art and Common Sense,* 160–61.

41. *New York Tribune,* 12 August 1900, illus. supp., p. 8.

42. Ibid., 16 September 1900. On the tendency of French art to become the standard for other peoples at this time, see Michael Quick, *American Expatriate Painters of the Late Nineteenth Century* (Dayton: Dayton Art Institute, exh. cat., 1976).

43. RC, "The Present State of European Painting," *Atlantic Monthly* 98 (November 1906): 686, 689–91. He had a long-standing interest in both traditional and modern Spanish painting; see the papers collected in *Art and Common Sense,* 247–333; and his "The Genius of Spain in New York," *Scribner's Magazine* 49 (June 1911): 765–68.

44. See his essay on Stieglitz and the shows he saw in *Personalities in Art,* 419–22. The quotation is from RC to Robert Underwood Johnson, 11 November 1912, Century Collection.

45. *New York Tribune,* 10 April 1910; see also 2 April 1911.

46. Crowninshield to Walt Kuhn, 15 January 1913, cited in Milton W. Brown, *The Story of the Armory Show* (New York: New York Graphic Society, 1963), 117. The article in question was "The Post-Impressionist Illusion," *Century Magazine* 85 (April 1913): 805–15, which was reprinted in RC, *Art and Common Sense,* 123–38.

47. Cortissoz's newspaper reviews of the show are reprinted in *Art and Common Sense,* 141–77.

48. RC to Cox, undated but March 1913, Kenyon Cox papers, Avery Architectural and Fine Arts Library, Columbia University.

49. RC, "A Memorable Exhibition," *Art and Common Sense,* 164–65.

50. Ibid., 164. Cortissoz was not impressed with the claim of many moderns that they were descended from the masters and wished to continue or restore classical grandeur to painting. "This looks very like body-snatching to me," he later said of this view in an essay on Ingres (RC, *The Painter's Craft,* 191).

51. RC, "The Post-Impressionist Illusion," *Art and Common Sense,* 131.

52. Ibid., 126.

53. RC, "A Memorable Exhibition," *Art and Common Sense,* 148–49.

54. Ibid., 152–53; see also RC, *Personalities in Art,* 293–301.

55. *New York Tribune,* 10 November 1929, sec. 8, p. 10. The literature on Cézanne is immense; but Richard Shiff, *Cézanne and the End of Impressionism* (Chicago: University of Chicago Press, 1984), 162–74, has some shrewd and candid observations on this enduring problem of Cézanne's apparent awkwardness and unfulfilled strivings, which concerned many critics of Cortissoz's generation. Cortissoz remained skeptical of Cézanne's work but at least attended to the more favorable views of his friend Bernard Berenson. "In a nutshell, I think Cézanne is an over-rated man," he wrote Berenson in a letter of 11 April 1938; he expressed similar views in another of 6 June 1938, both in Berenson Archive.

56. RC, "The Post-Impressionist Illusion," in *Art and Common Sense,* 135.

57. Ibid., 131–32.

58. RC, "A Memorable Exhibition," in *Art and Common Sense,* 155.

59. *New York Tribune,* 23 November 1913, and 11 January 1914. See also his ear-

lier typical pronouncement in favor of American schools in "The Exhibition at Philadelphia," *Scrip* 1 (March 1906): 184–94.

60. RC to Robert Underwood Johnson, 22 April 1913, Century Collection.

61. *New York Tribune,* 28 March 1915, sec. 3, p. 3.

62. RC, *American Artists,* 3; see also RC, *Personalities in Art,* 420.

63. See his essay "291" in *Personalities in Art,* 419–22; and RC to Stieglitz, 6 November 1925, Alfred Stieglitz papers, Beinecke Library, in which he said: "By the way, I
put in it [*Personalities in Art*] that little piece of mine about '291.' The more I can do to
contribute to a record of that work of yours the better content I am." His relationship
with the prickly Stieglitz was unpredictable, and they remained friends despite some
famous arguments over modernism. In 1928, Cortissoz wrote an amusing and tart
response to some disagreement: "In the meantime, don't forget this. Tolerance is the
beginning of wisdom. You may think, as you do, that Marin is 'the greatest master in
watercolor the world has ever seen.' I may think just the opposite. And you have no
right to say thereupon that my mind is 'closed' on the subject. Stieglitz, old man,
hearken and perpend. *You* may be mistaken! *I* may be right! In either case, don't forget,
'We all have a right to exist, we and our views.' Now behave. Your unchanging friend,
RC" (RC to Stieglitz, 26 November 1928, ibid.).

64. See his anti-German articles in *New York Tribune,* 9 April 1916, 29 April 1917,
28 July 1918, 25 November 1918, 5 January 1919, and 16 February 1919.

65. Ibid., 3 October 1923, p. 15.

66. *New York Herald Tribune,* 5 December 1926, sec. 6, p. 11, reviewing the Brooklyn Société Anonyme show.

67. Ibid., 4 November 1928, sec. 7, p. 10, reviewing the prestigious Pittsburgh International Exhibition at the Carnegie Institute.

68. RC to Sergeant Kendall, 28 April 1927, Cortissoz papers. He wrote more in a
letter to Bernard Berenson. The problem in current art was "that we are in a transitional period, *lacking important leaders,* and though American art isn't exactly 'running emptyings [*sic*],' it is perilously near that sad stage. Then there is too much
French stuff on the scene, the modernistic stuff that I gather is dying out in Paris and
gets brought over here as to the last available market" (RC to Berenson, 5 February
1940, Berenson Archive; emphasis in original).

69. *New York Herald Tribune,* 13 December 1936, sec. 7, p. 8.

70. Ibid.

71. Ibid., 26 March 1939, sec. 6, p. 8.

72. Ibid., 8 March 1936, and 26 April 1936, reviewing Alfred Barr's catalogue of the
show *Cubism and Abstract Art* (MOMA, 1936).

73. *New York Herald Tribune,* 1 October 1941, p. 21.

74. RC, *Arthur B. Davies,* 7; see also RC, *The Painter's Craft,* 362–71.

75. *New York Herald Tribune,* 10 February 1929; and RC, *Guy Pène du Bois* (New
York: Whitney Museum of American Art, 1931).

76. *New York Herald Tribune,* 16 February 1930, sec. 8, p. 10.

77. Ibid., 23 November 1930, 10 January 1932, and 30 April 1939.

78. Ibid., 23 September 1934.

79. Ibid., 11 October 1936.

80. Ibid., 3 March 1940. See also Richard D. McKinzie, *The New Deal for Artists*

(Princeton: Princeton University Press, 1973); and Karal Ann Marling, *Wall-to-Wall America: A Cultural History of Post-Office Murals in the Great Depression* (Minneapolis: University of Minnesota Press, 1982).

81. *New York Tribune*, 1 May 1900; RC, "The Basis of American Taste," *Creative Arts* 12 (January 1933): 19–28; *Art and Common Sense*, 383; RC, *The Painter's Craft*, 431.

82. RC, "Landmarks of Manhattan," *Scribner's Magazine* 18 (November 1895): 531–41.

83. RC, "The American School of Architecture in Rome," *Harper's Weekly* 39 (15 June 1895): 564–65.

84. RC, "An American Architect," *Outlook* 86 (27 July 1907): 681–85.

85. RC, "The American School of Architecture in Rome," 564–65.

86. RC, introduction to *Monograph of the Work of Charles A. Platt* (New York: Architectural Book Publishing Co., 1913), xxxiii; and RC, "Charles Adams Platt," *Architectural Record* 70 (March 1939): 205. See also Keith N. Morgan, *Charles A. Platt: The Artist as Architect* (Cambridge: MIT Press, 1985), 4, 16, 19, 69, 74, and 202.

87. RC (Address to the American Institute of Architects, Washington, D.C., 18 May 1923), reported in *New York Tribune*, 19 May 1923; and RC, "The Architect," *Architectural Record* 55 (March 1924): 276.

88. *New York Herald Tribune*, 17 March 1940, sec. 6, p. 8; see also RC, "The Vitality of Tradition," *Architectural Forum* 52 (May 1930): 635–36.

89. Flint, "Cornices and Cortissoz," 13; RC, "Charles F. McKim," *Scribner's Magazine* 47 (January 1910): 125–28.

90. RC, "Charles F. McKim," *Scribner's Magazine* 47 (January 1910): 128; see also RC, *The Painter's Craft*, 431; Leland M. Roth, *McKim, Mead and White, Architects* (New York: Harper and Row, 1983); and Richard Guy Wilson, *McKim, Mead and White* (New York: Rizzoli, 1983).

91. RC, "Charles F. McKim," 127.

92. RC, "Some Critical Reflections on the Architectural Genius of Charles F. McKim," *Brickbuilder* 19 (February 1910): 23–27.

93. *New York Tribune*, 22 February 1914.

94. On Pope, see *New York Herald Tribune*, 8 November 1927; on Gilbert, see RC, "Cass Gilbert, 1859–1934: An Appreciation," *Architecture* 70 (July 1934): 34.

95. *New York Herald Tribune*, 18 July 1924; and RC, "Ghosts in New York," *Architectural Forum* 53 (July 1930); 87–90.

96. *New York Tribune*, 4 February 1923, sec. 5, p. 7.

97. RC, "An American Architect," *Outlook* 86 (27 July 1907): 683–84.

98. *New York Tribune*, 3 June 1923, sec. 2, p. 4.

99. Ibid., 10 February 1924; and *New York Herald Tribune*, 26 April 1925.

100. *New York Herald Tribune*, 2 May 1931.

101. Ibid., 9 February 1930, sec. 8, p. 10.

102. RC, "The Vitality of Tradition," *Architectural Forum* 52 (May 1930): 635.

103. RC, "The Architect and the Business Man," *Architectural Forum* 53 (August 1930): 185.

104. RC, "The American Business Building," in *Personalities in Art*, 353–67.

105. His discussion is in *New York Herald Tribune*, 31 March, 3 April, and 14 April

1931. This famous controversy somewhat resembled the fierce debate over the building of the World Trade Center towers in New York in the early 1970s, and Carol Krinsky discusses it well in *Rockefeller Center* (New York: Oxford University Press, 1978). See also Walter H. Kilham, *Raymond Hood, Architect* (New York: Architectural Pub., 1973), 113−70.

106. The literature on these developments in architecture is enormous. The text that accompanied the Museum of Modern Art show, Henry-Russell Hitchcock and Philip Johnson's, *The International Style* (New York: Norton, 1932), became famous as a statement of principles and as a guidebook. In *Architecture, Ambition, and Americans,* Wayne Andrews provides a brief summary of the style's ambitions (rev. ed. [New York: Free Press, 1978], 246−88). William J. Curtis, *Modern Architecture since 1900* (Englewood Cliffs, N.J.: Prentice-Hall, 1982) is a well-illustrated survey. There is a good deal of common sense in Paul Goldberger, *On the Rise: Architecture and Design in a Postmodern Age* (New York: New York Times Books, 1983). The most famous attack on the style is Tom Wolfe, *From Bauhaus to Our House* (New York: Farrar, Straus and Giroux, 1981), which is willfully overstated but basically sound. Margarette J. Darnall, in "From the Chicago Fair to Walter Gropius," (Ph.D. diss., Cornell, 1975), also presents a good deal of information.

107. See Deborah F. Pokinski, *The Development of the American Modern Style* (Ann Arbor: UMI Research Press, 1984) for more on this American approach.

108. *New York Herald Tribune,* 14 February 1932, sec. 7, p. 9.

109. Ibid., 12 November 1933, sec. 5, p. 10.

110. Ibid., 11 December 1938, sec. 6, p. 8.

111. Arnold T. Schwab, *James Gibbons Huneker: Critic of the Seven Arts* (Palo Alto: Stanford University Press, 1963), 185.

112. Cortissoz described his shock and loneliness after his wife's death, which followed years of invalidism, in a letter to Bernard Berenson, 24 November 1933, Bernard Berenson Archive. His secretary commented on his attitude toward some famous people in Adrienne Barry to Davenport West, 25 February 1953, Cortissoz papers.

113. RC, *Nine Holes of Golf* (New York: Scribner's, 1922), 13; see also RC to Bernard Berenson, 25 April 1927, Berenson Archive.

114. Flint, "Cornices and Cortissoz," 13.

115. RC to Robert U. Johnson, 27 April 1911, Century Collection, NYPL; and RC to Belle da Costa Greene, 3 March 1930, Cortissoz papers.

116. The story of the inscription is told in H. Wayne Morgan, "An Epitaph for Mr. Lincoln," *American Heritage* 38 (Feb.−Mar. 1987): 58−63.

117. See RC, "The Art of Art Criticism," in *Personalities in Art,* 3−23.

118. RC to Blashfield, 29 March 1920, Blashfield papers.

119. Blashfield to RC, 21 January, 1932, Cortissoz papers.

120. Qtd. in his obituary, *New York Herald Tribune,* 18 October 1948, p. 18.

121. RC to Edna Ambrose, 18 May 1942, Cortissoz papers.

122. On celebrating his fortieth anniversary as an art critic in 1931, he had written Bernard Berenson: "In spite of the forty years I continue to feel preposterously young and happy. You do, too, I believe. Who wouldn't, with a world of beautiful things to think about all the time" (20 October 1931, Berenson Archive). He noted his feelings on the approaching fiftieth anniversary as a critic in RC to Berenson, 16 January 1939,

ibid. He spoke of declining energies in RC to Charles H. Towne, 12 April 1943, Charles H. Towne papers, NYPL.

123. RC to Charles H. Towne, 12 December 1943, ibid.

124. RC to Edwin S. Barrie, 17 November 1933, Cortissoz papers.

Chapter 3

1. Frank Jewett Mather, Senior, "A Private Life," 151, typescript, Frank Jewett Mather, Jr., papers, Princeton University Library (hereafter cited as Mather papers).

2. FJM, *The Conditional Sentence in Anglo-Saxon* (Munich: C. Wolf and Son, 1893). Mather's graduate records are in the Johns Hopkins University Archives.

3. FJM, "Irving Babbitt," *Harvard Graduates' Magazine* 41 (December 1933): 67.

4. FJM, "Higher Education Made in Germany," *Nation* 72 (25 April 1901): 333. Mather generally supported liberalizing the college curriculum, though he was not in favor of an elective system without requirements. He also hoped to retain Latin and other classical studies while adding modern languages, literature, and history. See FJM, " 'The Newer Humanities,' " *Nation* 75 (30 October 1902): 341–42.

5. FJM, "Inside of the Open Mind," *Unpartizan Review* 12 (July 1919): 17–18.

6. FJM, "Aims in College Education," *Unpartizan Review* 14 (October 1920): 271–72; see also FJM, "Collegiate Confusion and a Program," *Educational Review* 74 (December 1927): 277–83.

7. FJM, "Aims in College Education," 276–78; see also FJM, "A Transit of Idealism," *Nation* 78 (11 February 1904): 104–5; and FJM, "Irving Babbitt," 67–68.

8. FJM, *Concerning Beauty* (Princeton, N.J.: Princeton University Press, 1935), 221.

9. FJM, "Aims in College Education," 271.

10. FJM, "Collegiate Confusion," 277.

11. Mather, "A Private Life," 60h.

12. See his review of the National Academy show, *New York Evening Post,* 7 January 1905, and of the Pennsylvania Academy of Fine Arts exhibition, *New York Evening Post,* 24 January 1905.

13. FJM to More, 24 March 1907, Paul Elmer More papers, Princeton University Library (hereafter cited as More papers). See also FJM to Bernard Berenson, 11 March 1908, and 18 December 1908, Berenson Archive, Villa i Tatti, Florence, Italy.

14. FJM to More, 21 May 1909, More papers.

15. FJM to More, 24 March 1907, More papers.

16. His dispatches are in the *Post,* 29, 30, and 31 December 1908, and 1–5 January 1909. He could not resist telling More that he spent more money than he earned on them; see FJM to More, 5 March 1909, More papers.

17. FJM to More, 5 March 1909, More papers.

18. FJM to More, 21 and 29 March and 21 May 1909, More papers.

19. FJM to More, 29 March 1909, More papers.

20. See Mather's entry on Marquand, *Dictionary of American Biography,* vol. 6 (New York: Scribner's, 1933), 291–92; "Alan Marquand," *National Cyclopedia of American Biography,* vol. 37 (New York: James T. White, 1951), 336–37; and Mar-

quand's obituaries in the *New York Herald Tribune* and *New York Times,* both 25 September 1924.

21. FJM to KC, 15 January 1912, Cox papers.

22. FJM, *Modern Painting* (New York: Henry Holt, 1927), 322.

23. FJM, "Kenyon Cox," *Scribner's Magazine* 68 (June 1919): 768; see also *New York Evening Post,* 28 January 1910; FJM, "The Pennsylvania Academy," *Nation* 90 (3 February 1910): 121–22; FJM to More, 21 March 1909, More papers; and Irving Babbitt to FJM, 8 September 1916, Mather papers.

24. The quotations are from FJM, "Authority in Art Criticism," *Scribner's Magazine* 48 (December 1910): 766–68.

25. FJM, "The Artist as Critic," *Nation* 85 (28 November 1907): 486–87.

26. FJM, "Authority in Art Criticism," 767–68.

27. FJM, *Modern Painting,* vii–viii.

28. FJM, "University Study of Art in America," *Scribner's Magazine* 53 (April 1913): 529–30.

29. FJM, "Two Kinds of Realism," *Nation* 89 (25 November 1909): 522.

30. FJM, "The Present State of Art," *Nation* 93 (14 December 1911): 584–87.

31. FJM, "Newest Tendencies in Art," *Independent* 74 (6 March 1913): 504–5.

32. FJM, "Realism in Art," *Nation* 102 (3 February 1916): 129–32.

33. FJM, "The New Painting and the Musical Fallacy," *Nation* 99 (12 November 1914): 589.

34. FJM, "Art," *Nation* 91 (15 December 1910): 590.

35. FJM, *Estimates in Art* (New York: Holt, 1923), 77; see also FJM, "Far Eastern Painting: Japan," *Nation* 93 (24 August 1911): 176; and FJM, "Atmosphere versus Art," *Atlantic Monthly* 146 (August 1930): 171–77.

36. FJM, *Estimates in Art,* 211.

37. FJM, *Concerning Beauty,* 33–34.

38. Ibid., 221.

39. Ibid., 131.

40. Ibid., 218.

41. FJM, "Far Eastern Painting: China," *Nation* 93 (17 August 1911): 150–53; FJM, "Far Eastern Painting: Japan," *Nation* 93 (24 August 1911): 174–76.

42. FJM, *A History of Italian Painting* (New York: Holt, 1923). This work began as a series of lectures at the Cleveland Art Museum in 1919 and 1920.

43. FJM, *Modern Painting,* 226.

44. Ibid., 234–35; see also FJM, "Literature," *Forum* 34 (January 1903): 400.

45. FJM, "John La Farge, An Appreciation," *World's Work* 21 (March 1911): 14085–100.

46. FJM, "Thomas Eakins's Art in Retrospect," *International Studio* 95 (January 1930): 44–49.

47. See FJM, "Winslow Homer," *Nation* 91 (6 October 1910): 308–9; and his review of the Homer memorial exhibition at the Metropolitan Museum of Art, *New York Evening Post,* 4 January 1911. The quotation is from FJM, "Art: An American Painter," *Nation* 100 (18 February 1915): 206–7, reviewing Kenyon Cox's *Winslow Homer* (New York: F. F. Sherman, 1914).

48. FJM, "Art," *Nation* 90 (6 January 1910): 21.

49. FJM, "The Present State of Art," *Nation* 93 (14 December 1911): 585.

50. FJM, "The Newest Tendencies in Art," *Independent* 74 (6 March 1913): 505–6; see also FJM, *Modern Painting*, 183–84.

51. FJM, "The Painting of Sorolla," *Nation* 90 (3 March 1910): 221; see also FJM, "The Post-Impressionists," *Nation* 94 (20 June 1912): 622–23.

52. FJM, "The Painting of Sorolla," 221.

53. FJM, "The Post-Impressionists," 623; see also FJM, *Modern Painting*, 202–3.

54. FJM, "Art," *Nation* 90 (28 April 1910): 444.

55. FJM, *Modern Painting*, 218.

56. FJM, "The Painting of Sorolla," 220.

57. FJM, "The Pennsylvania Academy," *Nation* 90 (3 February 1910): 122. In "Art," (*Nation* 90 [28 April 1910]) he said, "Indeed, as far as color goes, the impressionists were in the true French tradition, the Institute being astray. The weakness of the new school was its disregard of composition, form, and all the reflective qualities of painting" (443–44).

58. FJM, *Modern Painting*, 211.

59. FJM, "Art Seeks a 'Bridge to the Public,' " *New York Times Magazine*, 23 September 1934, 19.

60. FJM, *Concerning Beauty*, 93–94.

61. FJM, "The Art of Mr. Whistler," *World's Work* 6 (September 1903): 3923–25; FJM, "Afterthoughts on Whistler," *Nation* 90 (14 April 1910): 384–86.

62. FJM, "The Romantic Spirit in American Art," *Nation* 104 (12 April 1917): 427; and FJM, *Estimates in Art, Series II* (New York: Holt, 1931), 73–86, 155–80.

63. FJM, "The Independent Artists," *Nation* 90 (7 April 1910): 360–61; see also FJM, "The Winter Academy," *Nation* 91 (22 December 1910): 613–15.

64. FJM, "Some American Realists," *Art and Decoration* 7 (November 1916): 14.

65. FJM, "The Pennsylvania Academy," *Nation* 90 (3 February 1910): 122.

66. FJM, "The Present State of Art," 584–87. Later critics would not name Matisse a postimpressionist, as Mather apparently meant to here.

67. FJM, "The Post-Impressionists," *Nation* 94 (20 June 1912): 623.

68. FJM, "The Newest Tendencies in Art," *Independent* 74 (6 March 1913): 504.

69. FJM, "Art," *Nation* 90 (28 April 1910): 444.

70. FJM, "The Post-Impressionists," 622; and FJM, "The Present State of Art," 587.

71. FJM, "Paul Cézanne," *Nation* 102 (13 January 1916): 58–59.

72. FJM, "The Pennsylvania Academy," *Nation* 90 (3 February 1910): 123.

73. FJM, "Drawings by Henri Matisse," *Nation* 90 (17 March 1910): 272–73.

74. FJM, "The Present State of Art," 587.

75. FJM to Cox, 15 January 1912, Cox papers.

76. FJM, "Old and New Art," *Nation* 96 (6 March 1913): 241.

77. FJM, *Modern Painting*, 358–59.

78. FJM, "Art Seeks a 'Bridge' to the Public," 19.

79. FJM, "Old Art and New," *Nation* 96 (6 March 1913): 240–43, the quote appears on p. 242; and Milton W. Brown, *The Story of the Armory Show* (New York: New York Graphic Society, 1963), esp. 217–302, which has a catalogue of the works.

80. FJM, "The Armory Exhibition—II," *Nation* 96 (13 March 1913): 267–68.

81. FJM, "The Academy Exhibition," *Nation* 96 (27 March 1913): 317–18.

82. FJM, "The Newest Tendencies in Art," 512.

83. Both quotations are from FJM, "The New Painting and the Musical Fallacy," *Nation* 99 (12 November 1914): 588; this essay includes a review of Wassily Kandinsky's *The Art of Spiritual Harmony* (Boston: Houghton-Mifflin, 1914).

84. FJM, "The Forum Exhibition," *Nation* 102 (23 March 1916): 340; see also Milton W. Brown, *American Painting from the Armory Show to the Depression* (Princeton, N.J.: Princeton University Press, 1955), 65–67.

85. FJM, "Culture vs. Kultur," *New York Times,* 8 November 1914, sec. 3, p. 2.

86. *New York Times,* 9 October 1914, p. 9.

87. *New York Times,* 12 January 1915, sec. 8, p. 6; and FJM, "Nietzsche in Action," *Unpopular Review* 3 (January 1915): 32–42.

88. *New York Times,* 15 June 1915, p. 12.

89. FJM, "Italy in the War," *Unpopular Review* 4 (July 1915): 17–26.

90. FJM, "From German Soldiers' Diaries," *New York Times,* 6 March 1915, pt. 10, p. 6; several critics refuted the veracity of this material in the *New York Times* of 19 March 1915.

91. FJM, "War Posters," *Weekly Review* 1 (17 May 1919): 20.

92. Arthur H. Dakin, *Paul Elmer More* (Princeton, N.J.: Princeton University Press, 1960), 165.

93. FJM, "Rear-rank Reflections," *Unpopular Review* 5 (January 1916): 15–25; see also FJM, "The Continental Army," *Unpopular Review* 5 (April–June 1916): 223–34.

94. FJM to More, 14 December [1917?], More papers; see also Richard Hofstadter and Walter Metzger, *Development of Academic Freedom in the United States* (New York: Columbia University Press, 1955), 502.

95. FJM to More, 10 April 1918, More papers.

96. FJM, "Aims in College Education," *Unpartizan Review* 14 (October 1920): 271–87.

97. The quotation is from FJM, "Peace at Any Reasonable Price," *New Republic* 5 (18 December 1915): 172–73; his comments on restoration of art works are in *New York Times,* 13 March 1917.

98. FJM, "Not a Separate War If We Take Up Arms," *New York Times,* 11 March 1917, pt. 7, p. 4.

99. FJM, "Ethics and Politics of the Treaty Wrangle," *Weekly Review* 1 (15 November 1919): 581.

100. FJM to Oswald Garrison Villard, 22 November 1938, Oswald Garrison Villard papers, Houghton Library, Harvard University. Villard, an opponent of entering the war in 1917, said later: "You were pretty bitter for one moved only by the crusading spirit. Perhaps as you say I have not been understanding enough, but I still marvel that one as deep as you could not see where entering the war would lead us. Of course, a victorious Germany would have been a curse upon us all—but we have something much worse now" (Villard to FJM, 5 May 1939, Mather papers).

101. FJM, "Herman Melville," *Saturday Review of Literature* 5 (27 April 1929): 945–46.

102. FJM, "Herman Melville," [*Weekly*] *Review* 1 (9 August 1919): 176–78.

103. FJM, "Herman Melville, II," [*Weekly*] *Review* 1 (16 August 1919): 301.

104. FJM, "Herman Melville," *Saturday Review,* 945–56. This article, a review of

Lewis Mumford's *Herman Melville* (Boston: Houghton, Mifflin, 1929), summarizes Mather's views on Melville and suggests the great themes that were to dominate the coming wave of Melville scholarship.

105. "In Buying Great Drawings Prof. Mather Also Got Great Names," *Art Digest* 5 (15 December 1930).

106. FJM, "Wanted, A School for Art Collectors," *Nation* 75 (27 November 1902): 416–17; and FJM, "Our Art Market," *Nation* 86 (14 May 1908): 439.

107. FJM, "Art," *Nation* 91 (25 December 1910): 590.

108. FJM, "University Study of Art in America," *Scribner's Magazine* 53 (April 1913): 529; see also FJM, "Drift of the World's Art toward America," *World's Work* 45 (December 1922): 198–205.

109. FJM, "Great Masters in American Galleries," *World's Work* 20 (May 1910), 12937. This is a review of August Jaccaci and John La Farge, *Concerning Noteworthy Paintings in American Private Collections* (New York: Jaccaci, 1909). See also FJM, "The Art Collector: His Forte and Foibles," *Nation* 88 (13 May 1909): 494–97.

110. FJM, "Rivera's American Murals," *Saturday Review of Literature* 10 (19 May 1934): 699.

111. FJM to E. L. Burlingame, 7 July 1907, Scribner's Collection, Princeton University Library.

112. FJM, "Two Theories of Museum Policy," *Nation* 80 (16 February 1905): 128–29.

113. FJM, "Circulating Museums," *Nation* 80 (16 February 1905): 128–29.

114. FJM, "Small Art Museums," *Nation* 80 (2 February 1905): 87–88.

115. FJM, "A Museum Programme," *Nation* 82 (1 March 1906): 171–72.

116. FJM, "Smaller and Better Museums," *Atlantic Monthly* 144 (December 1929): 768–73.

117. FJM, "Atmosphere versus Art," *Atlantic Monthly* 146 (August 1930): 174.

118. Ibid., 173.

119. FJM, "The College Art Museum," *Parnassus* 6 (April 1934): 18–20.

120. FJM, "Irving Babbitt," *Harvard Graduates' Magazine* 41 (December 1933): 65–84.

121. FJM, "A 'Laokoon' for the Times," *Nation* 90 (9 June 1910): 580–81.

122. FJM to More, 10 April 1918, More papers.

123. Dakin, *Paul Elmer More,* 112.

124. FJM, "Humanism: Attitude or Credo?" *Atlantic* 145 (June 1930): 741–48.

125. FJM to More, 27 February 1930, More papers.

126. FJM, "The Babbittiad," *New Republic* 63 (25 June 1930): 158.

127. FJM, "Irving Babbitt," 80.

128. FJM, "The Plight of Our Arts," in *Humanism and America,* ed. Norman Foerster (New York: Farrar and Rinehart), 117–18. Mather brilliantly stated this sociological view in "Art Seeks a 'Bridge' to the Public," *New York Times Magazine,* 23 September 1934, pp. 10–11, 19. See also FJM, *Modern Painting,* 59–60, 93–94.

129. FJM, "The Plight of Our Arts," 114. See also FJM, "Humanism and Esthetics," *Creative Arts* 7 (July 1930): 9–11.

130. FJM to More, 21 March 1909, More papers.

131. FJM, "The Babbittiad," 156.

132. FJM, *Modern Painting,* vii–viii.

133. FJM, "Humanism: Attitude or Credo?", 742–43.

134. Van Wyck Brooks, *From the Shadow of the Mountain: My Post-meridian Years* (New York: Dutton, 1961), 103.

135. FJM, "Glimpses of Russia," *Atlantic* 148 (October 1931): 471–78.

136. FJM, "Notes on Russian Art and Drama," *Saturday Review of Literature* 8 (12 September 1931): 122.

137. Ibid.

138. FJM, "The Plight of Our Art," 122; see also FJM, "Painting Seeks a 'Bridge' to the Public," 10.

139. FJM, "Humanism and Esthetics," 9; see also FJM, *Modern Painting,* 380.

140. FJM, "The Plight of Our Art," 126; see also FJM, *Concerning Beauty,* 105.

141. FJM, "Art Seeks a 'Bridge' to the Public," 19.

142. FJM, *Concerning Beauty,* 117 n. 2, apropos Sheldon Cheney, *Expressionism in Art* (New York: Liveright, 1934).

143. Mather spoke of his survey of Italian painting in FJM to More, 22 November [1908?], More papers; in his preface he said that it was a guidebook he had wanted when a traveler there (FJM, *History of Italian Painting,* v). He outlined this survey, and what become *Estimates in Art, Series II,* and *Modern Painting,* in W. C. Brownell to FJM, 14 January 1921; FJM to Brownell, 9 December 1921; Brownell to FJM, 10 December 1921; and an undated memo, all Scribner Archive. This represented a long period of steady work even though he was not writing much current criticism.

144. Dakin, *Paul Elmore More,* 365.

145. FJM to More, 9 October 1935, More papers.

146. The quotation is from 28 September 1939, Berenson Archive; see also FJM to Berenson, 9 December 1941, Mather papers.

147. See the obituaries of him in *New York Herald Tribune,* 12 November 1953, p. 24; and *New York Times,* 12 November 1953, p. 31

148. FJM to RC, October [?] 1941, Cortissoz papers.

Selected Bibliography

MANUSCRIPTS

Kenyon Cox

The chief repository of Cox's papers is the Avery Architectural and Fine Arts Library at Columbia University. His letters to various correspondents are in numerous collections, as the notes have shown. The papers of his son, Allyn Cox, at the Archives of American Art in Washington, D.C., contain information on the family. Cox himself was an excellent letter writer and discussed friends, family, and work, though there are many gaps in what has survived. His student letters, which offer an interesting glimpse of the maturing man and of the art life of his Paris years, are in H. Wayne Morgan, ed., *An American Art Student in Paris: The Letters of Kenyon Cox, 1877–1882* (Kent, Ohio: Kent State University Press, 1986). Cox wrote in an easy though learned style and produced a wide variety of comment in the public press. His reviews and notes on art matters for the *Nation* are especially interesting. His longer pieces were collected in several books: *Old Masters and New* (1905); *Painters and Sculptors* (1907); *The Classic Point of View* (1911), one of the unsung masterpieces of art criticism; *Artist and Public* (1914); and *Concerning Painting* (1917).

Royal Cortissoz

The Beinecke Rare Book and Manuscript Library at Yale University is the principal repository of Cortissoz's papers. The collection is substantial but does not deal much with his personal life, which is difficult to reconstruct. He corresponded with a wide variety of people, and his letters appear in numerous collections, as shown in the notes. He was an excellent letter writer and, like Cox, was candid in private as well as in public. He left a large collection of scrapbooks of newspaper columns to the Frick Art Reference Library, noting that they represented "practically my life's work" (RC to Ethelwyn Manning, 10 January 1942, in Katherine M. Knox, *The Story of the Frick Art Reference Library* [New York: The Library, 1979], 67–68). Cortissoz wrote an enormous amount of art journalism for the *New York Tribune* and its successor, the *Herald Tribune,* and for a great many magazines. His weekly newspaper reviews were a kind of correspondence with the art public and remain delightful to read. His longer pieces were collected in *Art and Common Sense* (1913); *American Artists* (1923); *Personalities in Art* (1925); and *The Painter's Craft* (1930). His biography, *John La Farge* (1911), testifies to his deep feelings for this friend and also contains a good deal of critical speculation on art. His *Life of Whitelaw Reid* (1921) depicts something of the journalistic life of his youth.

Frank Jewett Mather, Jr.

Mather's papers are in the Princeton University Library. The collection is uneven and does not contain much on his personal life. His letters to friends, as noted, were candid and often amusing, reflecting a genial and realistic personality. He too wrote a great deal of art journalism before the First World War. His longer pieces were collected in *Estimates in Art* (1923) and *Estimates in Art, Series II* (1931). His *Modern Painting* (1927) is very well written and remains worth reading for its thoughtful insights into the nature of change in the arts and on the role of the arts in society. It contains many moving and penetrating passages that testify to Mather's deep love of art. *Concerning Beauty* (1935) was his only foray into formal esthetics and is rewarding chiefly for his focus on the interchange between the art work and the connoisseur and for his ideas on how art shapes and controls life. His two textbooks, *A History of Italian Painting* (1923) and *Western European Painting of the Renaissance* (1940), are written with his usual engaging style and must have been attractive introductions for many college students of his day.

BOOKS

Ackerman, James S., and Williams, Rhys. *Art and Archeology.* Englewood Cliffs, N.J.: Prentice-Hall, 1963.

Amico, Leonard N. *The Mural Paintings of Edwin H. Blashfield, 1848–1936.* Williamstown, Mass.: Sterling and Francine Clark Art Institute, exh. cat., 1978.

Brooklyn Museum. *The American Renaissance, 1876–1917.* New York: Brooklyn Museum, exh. cat., 1979.

Brown, Milton W. *The Story of the Armory Show.* New York: New York Graphic Society, 1963.

Clark, Eliot. *History of the National Academy of Design, 1825–1954.* New York: Columbia University Press, 1954.

Clignet, Remi. *The Structure of Artistic Revolutions*. Philadelphia: University of Pennsylvania Press, 1985.

Davidson, Abraham A. *Early American Modernist Painting, 1910–1935*. New York: Harper and Row, 1981.

Falkenheim, Jacqueline V. *Roger Fry and the Beginnings of Formalist Art Criticism*. Ann Arbor: UMI Research Press, 1980.

Gerdts, William H. *American Impressionism*. New York: Abbeville, 1984.

———. *The Great American Nude: A History in Art*. New York: Praeger, 1974.

Hirschl and Adler Galleries. *Art of the American Renaissance*. New York: Hirschl and Adler, 1985.

Hoeveler, J. David, Jr. *The New Humanism: A Critique of Modern America, 1900–1940*. Charlottesville: University of Virginia Press, 1977.

Holly, Michael Ann. *Panofsky and the Foundations of Art History*. Ithaca, N.Y.: Cornell University Press, 1984.

Huntington, David C. *The Quest For Unity: American Art between World's Fairs, 1876–1893*. Detroit: Detroit Institute of Art, exh. cat. 1983.

Karl, Frederick R. *Modern and Modernism: The Sovereignty of the Artist, 1885–1925*. New York: Atheneum, 1985.

Kirk, Russell. *The Conservative Mind from Burke to Santayana*. Chicago: Henry Regnery, 1952.

Lears, T. J. Jackson. *No Place of Grace: Antimodernism and the Transformation of American Culture, 1880–1920*. New York: Pantheon, 1981.

May, Henry F. *The End of American Innocence*. New York: Knopf, 1959.

Munro, Thomas. *Evolution in the Arts and Other Theories of Cultural History*. Cleveland: Cleveland Museum of Art, 1963.

Murray, Richard. *Art for Architecture: Washington, D.C., 1895–1925*. Washington: National Collection of Fine Arts, 1965.

Nochlin, Linda. *Realism*. New York: Penguin, 1971.

Novak, Barbara. *American Painting of the Nineteenth Century*. 2d ed. New York: Harper and Row, 1979.

———. *Nature and Culture: American Landscape Painting, 1825–75*. New York: Oxford, 1980.

Olson, Arlene R. *Art Critics and the Avant-Garde: New York, 1900–1913*. Ann Arbor: UMI Press, 1980.

Pokinski, Deborah Frances. *The Development of the American Modern Style*. Ann Arbor: UMI Research Press, 1984.

Quick, Michael. *American Expatriate Painters of the Late Nineteenth Century*. Dayton, Ohio: Dayton Art Institute, exh. cat., 1976.

Roeder, George H., Jr. *Forum of Uncertainty: Confrontations with Modern Painting in Twentieth-Century America*. Ann Arbor: UMI Research Press, 1980.

Rosenblum, Robert, and Janson, H. W. *Nineteenth-Century Art.* New York: Abrams, 1984.

Roth, Leland M., *McKim, Mead and White, Architects.* New York: Harper and Row, 1983.

Sanford, Cynthia H. *Heroes in the Fight for Beauty: The Muralists of the Hudson County Court House.* Jersey City, N.J.: Jersey City Museum, exh. cat., 1986.

Underwood, Sandra Lee, *Charles H. Caffin: A Voice for Modernism, 1897–1918.* Ann Arbor: UMI Research Press, 1983.

Weinberg, H. Barbara. *The American Pupils of Jean-Léon Gérôme.* Fort Worth, Tex.: Amon Carter Museum, 1985.

Weisberg, Gabriel. *The Realist Tradition: French Painting and Drawing, 1830–1900.* Bloomington: Indiana University Press, 1980.

Williams, Raymond. *Culture and Society, 1780–1950.* Rev. ed. New York: Columbia University Press, 1983.

Wilson, Richard Guy. *McKim, Mead and White, Architects.* New York: Rizzoli, 1983.

ARTICLES

Ackerman, James S. "Toward a New Social Theory of Art." *New Literary Criticism* 4 (Winter 1973): 315–30.

Aldrich, Virgil C. "Art and the Human Form." *Journal of Aesthetics and Art Criticism* 29 (Spring 1971): 295–302.

Alpers, Svetlana. "Is Art History?" *Daedulus* 106 (Summer 1977): 1–13.

Bradbury, Malcolm. "The Nonhomemade World: European and American Modernism." *American Quarterly* 39 (Spring 1987): 27–38.

Dissanayake, Ellen. "Art as a Human Behavior: Toward an Ethological View of Art." *Journal of Aesthetics and Art Criticism* 38 (Summer 1980): 397–406.

Fink, Lois Marie. "The Innovation of Tradition in Late Nineteenth-Century American Art." *American Art Journal* 10 (November 1978): 63–71.

_____. "Nineteenth-Century Evolutionary Art." *American Art Review* 4 (January 1978: 74–81, 105–9.

Fried, Michael. "Modern Painting and Formal Criticism." *American Scholar* 33 (Autumn 1964): 642–48.

McLaughlin, Thomas M. "Clive Bell's Aesthetic: Tradition and Significant Form." *Journal of Aesthetics and Art Criticism* 35 (Summer 1977): 433–43.

Roeder, George H., Jr. "What Have Modernists Looked At? Experiential Roots of Twentieth-Century American Painting." *American Quarterly* 39 (Spring 1987): 56–83.

Singal, Daniel Joseph. "Towards a Definition of American Modernism." *American Quarterly* 39 (Spring 1987): 7–26.

Taylor, David G. "The Aesthetic Theories of Roger Fry Reconsidered." *Journal of Aesthetics and Art Criticism* 36 (Fall 1977): 63–72.

Weinberg, H. Barbara. "American Impressionism in Cosmopolitan Context." *Arts Magazine* 55 (November 1980): 160–65.

————. "The Lure of Paris: Late Nineteenth-Century American Painters and Their French Training." In *A New World: Masterpieces of American Painting, 1760–1910,* Boston: Museum of Fine Arts, exh. cat., 1983. 16–32.

————. "Nineteenth-Century American Painters at the Ecole des Beaux-Arts." *American Art Journal* 13 (Autumn 1981): 66–84.

————. "Renaissance and Renascenes in American Art." *Arts Magazine* 54 (November 1979): 172–76.

Zucker, Wolfgang. "The Artist as Rebel." *Journal of Aesthetics and Art Criticism* 27 (Summer 1969): 389–97.

DISSERTATIONS

Abrams, Ann Uhry. "Catalyst for Change: American Art and Revolution, 1900–1915." Ph.D. diss., Emory University, 1975.

Amburgy, Patricia Marie. "Art and Social Ethics," Ph.D. diss., University of Illinois, 1985.

Baker, Marilyn Clair. "The Art Theory and Criticism of Willard Huntington Wright." Ph.D. diss., University of Wisconsin, 1975.

Darnall, Margarette Jean. "From the Chicago Fair to Walter Gropius: Changing Ideals in American Architecture." Ph.D. diss., Cornell University, 1975.

Docherty, Linda Jones. "A Search for Identity: American Art Criticism and the Concept of the 'Native School,' 1876–1893." Ph.D. diss., University of North Carolina, 1985.

Fahlman, Betsy Lee. "Guy Pène de Bois: Painter, Critic, Teacher." Ph.D. diss., University of Delaware, 1981.

Feldman, William Steven. "The Life and Work of Jules Bastien-Lepage (1848–1884)." Ph.D. diss., New York University, 1973.

Fink, Lois Marie. "The Role of France in American Art, 1850–1900." Ph.D. diss., University of Chicago, 1970.

Harris, Martha Johnson. "Clive Bell's Formalism in Historical Perspective." Ph.D. diss., University of Georgia, 1985.

Hey, Kenneth Robert. "Five Artists and the Chicago Modernist Movement, 1909–1928." Ph.D. diss., Emory University, 1973.

Hobbs, Susan. "John La Farge and the Genteel Tradition in American Art: 1875–1910." Ph.D. diss., Cornell University, 1974.

Marlais, Michael Andrew. "Anti-Naturalism, Idealism and Symbolism in French Art Criticism, 1880–1895." Ph.D. diss., University of Michigan, 1985.

Mecklenburg, Virginia. "American Aesthetic Theory, 1908–1917: Issues in Conservative and Avant-Garde Thought." Ph.D. diss., University of Maryland, 1983.

Petruck, Peninah. "American Art Criticism, 1910–1939." Ph.D. diss., New York University, 1979.

Platt, Susan Noyes. "Responses to Modern Art in New York in the 1920s." Ph.D. diss., University of Texas at Austin, 1981.

Risatti, Howard Anthony. "American Critical Reaction to European Modernism, 1908–1917." Ph.D. diss., University of Illinois, 1978.

Wright, Glenn Sherman. "The Humanist Controversy in American Literature, 1900–1932." Ph.D. diss., Pennsylvania State University, 1956.

Young, Charles Raiford, "Toward an Art Criticism from the Standpoint of Humanistic Anthropology." Ph.D. diss., University of Georgia, 1983.

Index

Academic approach, 18, 19, 42–43
Académie Julian, 20
Adams, Henry, 65
Allegory in art, 44, 49, 58, 60; and mural painting, 31–32, 33, 35–36, 37
American art: in Armory Show (1913), 130–31; collected by Mather, 137; the Eight, 123–24; in Forum Exhibition (1916), 132–33; impressionist, 75; in National Academy of Design exhibition (1913), 131; New Deal, 87; praised by Cortissoz, 69–70, 84, 86–87; praised by Cox, 46, 50; praised by Mather, 119, 123–24; Whistler's work, 53–54, 122–23. *See also* Mural painting
American Gothic (Wood), 87
American Radiator Building (New York City), 93
American School of Classical Studies, 112
Architectural criticism of Cortissoz: of Beaux-Arts style, 91; City Beautiful plans in, 89; of classicism, 89–90, 91; of International Style, 95–97; Italy in, 88–89; of McKim, Mead and White, 90–91; New York City in, 87–88, 90–95; of skyscraper design, 92–95
Architectural criticism of Cox, 46
Armory Show (1913), 101, 127, 128; American art in, 130–31; reviewed by

Cortissoz, 77–79, 82; reviewed by Cox, 54–55; reviewed by Mather, 129–31
Arnold, Matthew, 3, 66–67, 108
Art: academic approach to, 18, 19, 42–43; collecting of, 137–38; Cox's definition of painting, 43–44; English, 75–76; figure painting, 25–27; in museums, 137–40; and New Humanism, 144–45; in New York City, 23–24; Oriental, 118; and post–Civil War society, 1–2; primitive, 53; romanticism and, 2, 132, 142; Russian, 146–47; Spanish, 76, 121. *See also* Allegory in art; American art; French art; German art; Impressionism; Italian art; Modernism; Traditionalism
Art criticism: attack on academic approach, 42–43; authority of, 113–14; contextual analysis in, 40–41; evolution of, 40; of Matthew Arnold, 66–67. *See also* Cortissoz, Royal; Cox, Kenyon; Mather, Frank Jewett, Jr.
Art Institute of Chicago, 52
"Artist and Public" (Cox), 57
Arts, The (Cox), 32–33, 34
Art Students League, 24, 42, 58

Babbitt, Irving, 114–15, 142–43, 144, 146